ANNUALS

ANNUALS

Ted Marston, Editor

Principal Photography by

Andrew Lawson

HEARST BOOKS

New York

It is the policy of William Morrow and Company, Inc., and its imprints and
affiliates, recognizing the importance of preserving what has been written, to
print the books we publish on acid-free paper, and we exert our best efforts
to that end.

Library of Congress Cataloging-in-Publication Data

Ted Marston
    Annuals / compiled from the Good Housekeeping illustrated encyclopedia
  of gardening: completely rev. by Ted Marston; photography by Andrew Lawson.
  —1st U.S. ed.
      p.   cm. — (Hearst garden guides)
  Includes index.
  ISBN 0-688-10041-4
  1. Annuals(Plants) 2. Annuals (Plants) — United States.
I. Marston, Ted. II. Series.
SB422.A573 1993
635.9'312—dc20   92-23758

Printed in Singapore
First U.S. Edition
1 2 3 4 5 6 7 8 9 10

Produced by Smallwood & Stewart, Inc.
New York City

Editor: Charles A. de Kay
Horticultural Consultant: Ruth Lively
Designer: Michelle Wiener
Managing Editor: Robin Haywood

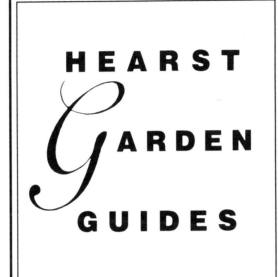

HEARST

GARDEN

GUIDES

CONTENTS

chapter

3

ANNUALS FROM SEED 23

chapter

4

ENCYCLOPEDIA OF ANNUALS 33

1

PLANT NOMENCLATURE AND STRUCTURE

Some of the most beautiful flowers for the garden appear on annual plants, which complete their life cycle in a single year, producing only one season of color. The best of these single-season plants for the garden have been collected here.

This volume of the *Hearst Garden Guides* presents a selection of the annuals and other single-season plants best suited for home landscape and garden use. The Encyclopedia of Annuals (chapter 4) features the most commonly available species and cultivars, as well as other interesting and unusual varieties. The plants were chosen for their beauty, popularity and availability. From *Abelmoschus moschatus* to *Zinnia linearis*, each entry includes key facts and opinions about a given species, and outlines the planting, cultivation and care required for success in the garden.

In addition, the encyclopedia contains plants that are used as annuals for seasonal color, irrespective of their botanic classification. Some of the best-loved plants that are used as annuals are actually tender perennials, meaning they cannot withstand frost. For example, species of *Petunia*, which come from Central and South America, and *Impatiens*, which come from Asia and Africa, live on year after year in their warm native habitats; but in climates where frosts occur, these plants must be treated as annuals. Other select tender and short-lived perennials include such favorites as *Bellis perennis* (English daisy) and *Centaurea cineraria* (dusty miller). Finally, a few vines widely grown for their ornamental annual color, such as *Cobaea scandens* (cup-and-saucer vine) and *Ipomoea* species (morning glory), can also be found in the encyclopedia. In northern areas some tender bulbs, such as *Begonia* × *tuberhybrida* (tuberous begonias), and species of *Canna* and *Dahlia*, are often grown for a single season of flowers (to survive the winter they must be lifted and stored in a frost-free location—for some, this is a prohibitive amount of work); but as bulbous plants they are fully covered in the *Hearst Garden Guides* volume *Bulbs*.

Foliage plants can be as important as flowers to good garden design. Many plants, including some that flower like *Coleus* species, are grown primarily for their foliage (which is used in combination with flowering plants for color contrasts). The encyclopedia includes some of the most important of these annual foliage plants.

THE CLASSIFICATION OF PLANTS

Over the ages, people have classified plants in various ways. The ancient Roman writer Pliny the Elder (A.D. 23–79) used size and form as his criteria, setting up three major groupings: trees, shrubs and herbs. In the Middle Ages, plants were classified according to whether they were medicinal, edible or poisonous. Later the great eighteenth-century Swedish botanist Carolus Linnaeus (1707–1778) used the number of stamens in plants as his basis for classification.

Such arbitrary systems are considered artificial today. While most gardeners continue to classify plants much as Pliny did, modern taxonomists have moved to a so-called natural system of classification in which plants are grouped according to their generic and evolutionary relationships. Under this system, related species of plants make up a genus. Related genera make up a family. Related families make up an order. Related orders make up a class. Related classes make up a subdivision (or subphylum). Related subdivisions make up a division (or phylum). Related divisions make up the plant kingdom.

(Most gardeners do not need to know all this. Generally, only botanists and taxonomists are concerned with classifications higher than family. Home gardeners should only concern themselves with a plant's genus and species—and at times a plant's family, because plants in the same family might share habits of growth, cultural requirements or disease problems. Readers who want to skip the following technical discussion can turn directly to the text on genus, which begins on page 11.)

Starting at the top of the hierarchy, the living world is divided into two kingdoms, the plant kingdom and the animal kingdom. The plant kingdom is broken into two divisions (or phylla): one phyllum is the Bryophyta, which is made up of plants lacking vascular tissues, such as mosses and liverworts; and the other is Tracheophyta, which contains plants with vascular tissues. (Vascular tissues transport water, nutrients and minerals throughout the plant.) The vast majority of plants growing in gardens are tracheophytes.

Subdivision (or subphyllum) Pteropsida, within the Tracheophyta, contains plants that reproduce from seeds, as well as ferns, which reproduce from spores. There are three classes in the subdivision: Angiospermae, which contains the true flowering plants; Filicineae, which contains the ferns; and Gymnospermae, which includes the cone-bearing plants and relatives.

The Angiospermae are, in turn, broken down into the subclasses Dicotyledoneae and Mono-cotyledoneae, commonly called dicots and monocots. The monocot embryos bear one cotyledon (the first leaflike structure to appear after sprouting); the dicot embryos bear two. As the plants grow, the true leaves of monocots are alternate and have parallel veins; dicot leaves are net-veined. (Interestingly, except for annual grasses, which are not covered in this volume, there are few annuals that are monocots.) These subclasses are divided into orders; each order contains one or more families. Each family contains one or more genera, and each genus contains one or more species.

The following outline of the positions of globe amaranth and Johnny-jump-up illustrate this method of classifying plants:

Globe amaranth	Johnny-jump-up
Kingdom *Plantae*	Kingdom *Plantae*
Division *Tracheophyta*	Division *Tracheophyta*
Subdivision *Pteropsida*	Subdivision *Pteropsida*
Class *Angiospermae*	Class *Angiospermae*
Subclass *Dicotyledoneae*	Subclass *Dicotyledoneae*
Order *Chenopodiales*	Order *Violales*
Family *Amaranthaceae*	Family *Violaceae*
Genus *Gomphrena*	Genus *Viola*
Species *globosa*	Species *tricolor*

Note that, in both examples, the names on the same line (except at the genus and species level) have the same endings. Generally, division names end in -phyta; subdivision names in -opsida; class names in -ae; order names in -ales; and family names in -aceae. This helps to identify the classification level at issue.

NOMENCLATURE

Most familiar garden plants have a common name (or names) and a scientific name. Gardeners generally prefer to use common names because they are in English, and so are easier to remember and pronounce. Unfortunately, using only common names often leads to confusion. First of all, many plants have not one but several common names. For example, *Cuphea ignea* is known variously as cigar flower, firecracker plant and Mexican cigar plant. Frequently, two or more totally different plants share the same or similar common names. The name "African daisy," for instance, is widely used; it appears three times in this book alone—for *Arctotis stoechadifolia, Dimorphotheca sinuata* and *Lonas annua*. And who would imagine that the Swan River daisy and the Swan River everlasting were not related? Occasionally, closely related plants have such different common names that their relationship is obscured. Indian cress, canary

creeper and flame flower, for instance, are all closely related members of the genus *Tropaeolum*, the nasturtium group.

Because these problems made it difficult for people to communicate precisely about plants, two hundred years ago botanists adopted a binomial system devised by Linnaeus, which identifies each plant more accurately by using two names—the genus followed by the species.

Both the generic and specific names are for the most part derived from Latin or Greek rendered into Latin. Both names are italicized or underlined when written, and the first (generic) name is always capitalized. Thus, the scientific name of the gillyflower is *Matthiola incana* (which may be abbreviated *M. incana* once the generic name has been spelled out in reasonably close context).

If a species of plant includes varieties or cultivars (defined below), that name is added directly after the specific name—in Latin for varieties and in a Latinized form of a modern language (such as English) for cultivars. Thus, the naturally occurring variety of the gillyflower is known as *M. incana* variety *annua*.

Genus

The word "genus" (the plural is genera) applies to a quite closely related and definable group of plants which includes one or more species. In the classifications in the plant kingdom, a genus lies between a family and a species. The genus name is the first half of the horticultural name of a species. The ever-popular sunflower, for instance, is a member of the genus *Helianthus*. The genus is a member of the Daisy or Composite Family, which bears the horticultural name *Compositae*.

The genus *Helianthus* consists of coarse annuals and perennials with many species that vary greatly in their size and in habit. Each of the different species of the genus shares certain characteristics with the rest of the group: all *Helianthus* species have alternate leaves, and, except for a few varieties, yellow flowers with central disks of brown, gold or dark purple; they twist to follow the sun. Other than the common sunflower, *Helianthus annuus*, the genus includes such annual species as the silver-leaf sunflower, *H. argophyllus*, and the cucumber-leaf sunflower, *H. debilis*, plus the perennial species, the swamp sunflower, *H. angustifolius*, which is commonly found growing wild in bogs.

Species

A species is a particular plant within a genus. Each species within a given genus will be different, but, as noted above, all will share at least one characteristic. In the classification of plants, a species (the word is both singular and plural) lies between a genus and a subspecies or variety. (The abbreviation for singular species is sp.; for plural, spp.)

A genus may contain anywhere from one to over a thousand species. In turn, a species may (but does not always) encompass a number of varieties. Species, in contrast with most varieties, cultivars and hybrids, may reproduce themselves from seeds and may often be interbred; interbreeding among different species of the same genus occasionally takes place in the wild.

To the gardener, species are significant because they are the individual types of plants. When ordering a plant from a nursery, for example, it is essential to use both the species and genus names. Having determined a favorite flower to be a sunflower, or a member of the *Helianthus* genus, it is necessary to identify the particular species wanted. For instance, the cucumber-leaf sunflower (*H. debilis*), an annual with 3-inch flowers, makes a sturdy, temporary bush, 3 to 4 feet tall. If the mail-order form states only *Helianthus* or "sunflower," the nursery is likely to send the common sunflower (*H. annuus*), which forms a single vertical

flower stalk that grows to 12 feet.

According to the accepted binomial system of plant nomenclature, the species name follows the name of the genus. In *Helianthus debilis*, for example, *Helianthus* is the genus name, *debilis* the specific name. The varietal name, which might be, for example, 'Liliput', would be the third name.

The specific name is often descriptive, denoting some featured characteristic of the plant. *Lathyrus odoratus* (sweet pea), has a specific name that refers to its lovely fragrance, while *Lobularia maritima* (sweet alyssum) was named for its preference for coastal sites. Other specific names are derived from names of geographic regions or, in many cases, the name of the person who discovered the species.

Subspecies

While the genus and species cover the majority of plants, there are times when one plant is almost identical to a given species. If such a plant is consistently different in some minor aspect—perhaps the leaves are longer, but the flowers are identical—it merits a subspecies classification rather than its own species name. (In botanical terminology the word "subspecies" is abbreviated as subsp. or ssp.) For example, the popular lupine, *Lupinus hartwegii*, a native of Mexico, produces spikes of blue flowers with the center petal in rose-pink, while *L. hartwegii* subsp. *cruickshankii* has blue flowers marked with gold, bronze and white.

Variety

The lowest or final classification of plants found in nature is the variety. Not all species have natural varieties, but most species have several. Strictly speaking, the word "variety" is used to identify only *naturally* occurring variants of identified species. A variety retains the basic character of the species, but has one or more distinctive characteristics of its own. Varieties usually exist in populations rather than as isolated, individual plants.

For example, the *grandiflora* variety of *Lavatera trimestris* (the rose mallow) has the largest flowers while the *alba* variety has beautiful white flowers. The varietal name of the plant is the third or last one given in plant nomenclature; "*Lavatera trimestris alba*," for example. Sometimes, for clarity, the varietal name is written as "*Lavatera trimestris* var. *alba*." If the the genus name has been spelled out in close context—such as in a catalog where a number of mallows are listed on a page—the name of the genus is abbreviated so that this might read "*L. trimestris alba*."

Varieties that are propagated in cultivation and named are considered cultivars; varieties developed by cross-breeding parents of different species are classed as hybrids. In the commercial world the name "variety" is frequently used to mean cultivars or man-made hybrids. These plants, however, are not, strictly speaking, varieties and should be treated differently (see sections on cultivars and hybrids, below).

Cultivar

A cultivar (short for *culti*vated *vari*ety) or a hybrid (when the plant results from the deliberate crossing of two specific plants) is a new plant selected in cultivation through a breeding program, propagated and named.

Cultivars are noted by the abbreviation "cv." or by single quotation marks, are always capitalized and never appear in italics. *Lavatera trimestris* 'Loveliness', for instance, is much shorter than the species, growing only to 3 to 4 feet and producing deep rose flowers. The award-winning *L. trimestris* cv. Mont Blanc is even shorter, topping out at 2 feet, and bears pure white flowers.

Hybrid

A hybrid is a plant resulting from the crossing of two specific plants. The process of hybridization is unusual in nature; most hybrids are developed as the result of human actions, either accidental or purposeful. An example is the commonly available monkey flower, *Mimulus* × *hybridus*, a hybrid of some importance to the garden.

Hybrids are noted with a multiplication sign or "×." The symbol precedes the genus when the genus itself is a hybrid. It is written between the generic and specific names if the species is a hybrid. Cultivars *can* be (but are not always) selected from hybrids.

Series

A series comprises a group of cultivars that are standard in all elements except one—almost always color. When plant breeders first develop a new cultivar from seed, the plants usually flower in a mix of colors. The first seeds offered to the public are often called "mixed," meaning that their color cannot be predicted. For instance, note the recommended double-flowered hollyhock *Alcea* 'Powderpuff Mixed' or the China aster *Callistephus* 'Perfection Mixed' in the Encyclopedia of Annuals (chapter 4). At the same time that the plant is being established in the trade, an intricate breeding process of propagating and selecting is taking place. Eventually these plants will be divided by color. In a few years there may well be an *Alcea* 'Pink Powderpuff' and a *Callistephus* 'White Perfection'.

A common example is *Antirrhinum majus*, or the garden snapdragon, which comprises many different kinds of snapdragons. There are the Rocket series, the Liberty series, the Floral Carpet series and so forth, each offering a range of colors. These series of snapdragons are identified by a capitalized first letter: "the Rocket snapdragons." Sometimes a specific pure-line color and form of a plant is selected and given a special name; for example, one of the snapdragons, a white variety, is offered as the 'Rocket White' snapdragon or *Antirrhinum majus* 'Rocket White'. Note the single quotes and capi-

PARTS OF A FLOWER

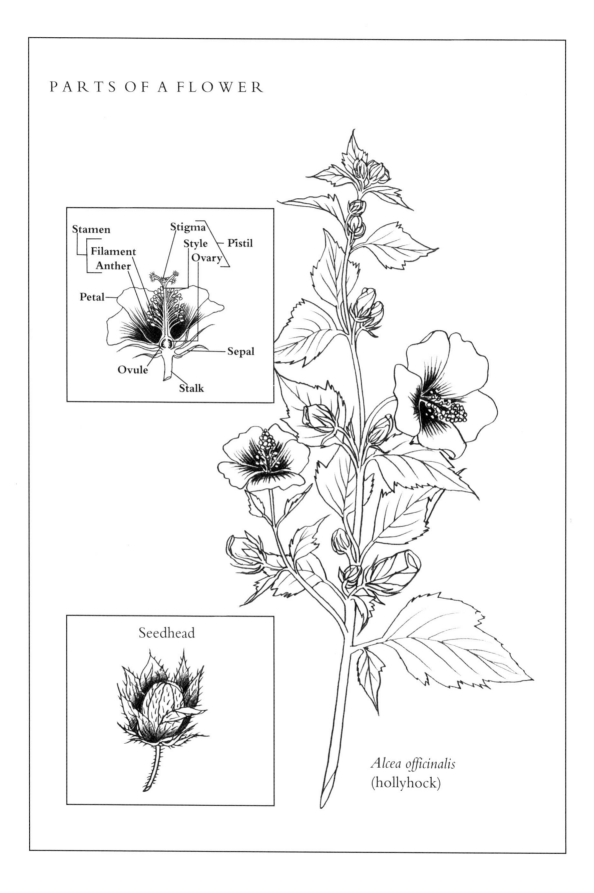

Stamen
Filament
Anther
Petal
Stigma
Style
Ovary
Pistil
Sepal
Ovule
Stalk

Seedhead

Alcea officinalis
(hollyhock)

talized first letters. This tells us that 'Rocket White' snapdragon is a cultivar—that is, a kind of snapdragon selected in cultivation.

FLOWER FORMS

The word "flower" is the popular term for the combination of structures that comprise the reproductive organs of complex plants. The concept usually includes color and a definite organization (or form). Without flowers, plants could not produce seed with which to reproduce their kind.

The variety of colors, shapes and sizes of flowers is almost bewildering. In color, only a true black is missing. As to shape and form, while the majority of flowers are symmetrical, many, such as cockscomb (*Celosia argentea* var. *cristata*), are highly asymmetrical. In size, flowers range from the microscopic to diameters of almost a foot. Some flowers are borne singly on the plant stems, others in clusters (see "Inflorescence," page 17).

The point at which the flower is connected to the stem is the receptacle. Next are the sepals, which collectively make up the calyx. These are the outermost, petal-like structures, which are usually green, that enclose and protect the flower bud before it opens.

Inside the sepals are the petals, which collectively form the corolla. (The petals and sepals together make up the perianth. In cases where the sepals and petals cannot be distinguished from one another, as for example in lilies, they are known as tepals.) Some flowers have only a few petals; others have hundreds. Usually the petals are separate, but they can be united in a single tube or cup, such as in flowers of *Ipomoea* species (morning glories).

The reproductive organs of the flower are surrounded by the petals. The male organs are the stamens (collectively called the Androecium), which produce pollen. The female organs are the seed-bearing carpels (collectively known as the pistil or Gynoecium);

SOLITARY FLOWER FORMS

Simple Flower

Tube Flower

Composite Flower

INFLORESCENCES

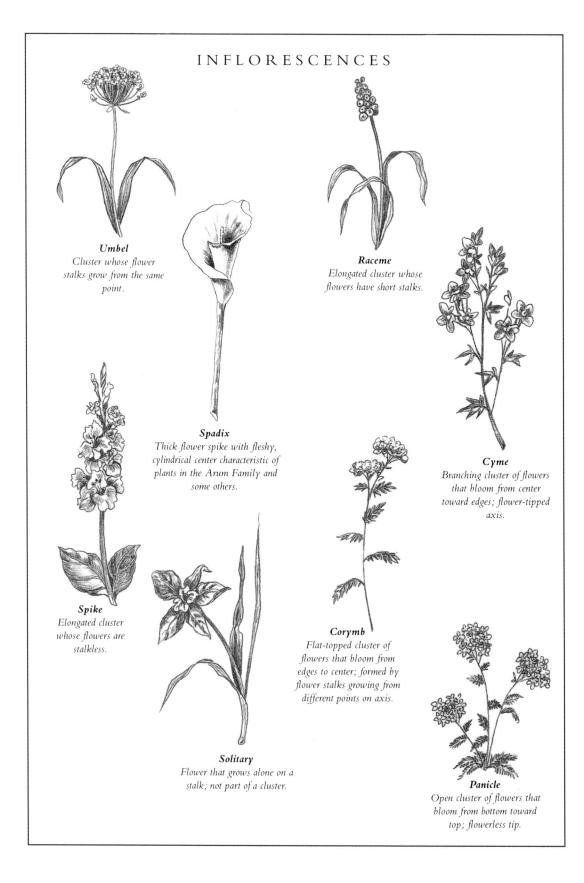

Umbel
Cluster whose flower stalks grow from the same point.

Raceme
Elongated cluster whose flowers have short stalks.

Spadix
Thick flower spike with fleshy, cylindrical center characteristic of plants in the Arum Family and some others.

Cyme
Branching cluster of flowers that bloom from center toward edges; flower-tipped axis.

Spike
Elongated cluster whose flowers are stalkless.

Corymb
Flat-topped cluster of flowers that bloom from edges to center; formed by flower stalks growing from different points on axis.

Solitary
Flower that grows alone on a stalk; not part of a cluster.

Panicle
Open cluster of flowers that bloom from bottom toward top; flowerless tip.

which collect pollen and protect the ovules.

Each stamen consists of a filament (usually a short, slender stalk) bearing at the apex a single, enlarged anther from which pollen is emitted.

Pistils may have three parts: the swollen ovary in which seeds are formed, above this the slender style, and at the end of the style the stigma—often rough or sticky—on which the pollen falls or is deposited to produce fertilization. The pollen germinates on the stigma, grows down the style and fertilizes the ovary, producing seed.

Flowers are often categorized as perfect or imperfect. Perfect flowers have both stamens and pistils and are thus capable of self-fertilization if pollen ripens and the stigma becomes receptive to it at the same time. Imperfect flowers may have either stamens (these are called staminate flowers) or pistils (pistillate flowers). When the staminate (male) and pistillate (female) flowers are borne on separate plants the plants are said to be dioecious. Monoecious plants, on the other hand, have either perfect flowers or both staminate and pistillate flowers.

Inflorescence

Most plants produce just one flower head—a single flower at the end of the flower stalk—and are called solitary flowers. The most common shapes that solitary flowers take are shown in the illustration "Solitary Flower Forms," page 15.

Many flowers, however, are borne in clusters; the shape of the flower head, based on where the flower cluster is branched, varies with the type of plant. The flowers of *Digitalis purpurea* (foxgloves), for instance, form flower spikes, while *Antirrhinum majus* (common snapdragon) blooms in a spike-like form called a raceme and the ever popular *Dianthus barbatus* (sweet William) flowers as flat-topped cymes. The most important flower-cluster arrangements are shown in the "Inflorescence" illustration on the facing page.

chapter

2

FLOWERS FOR A SEASON

An annual plant completes its life cycle—from germination to seed formation—within a single year. Following the formation of seeds, the plant, exhausted of energy reserves, dies. Some annual plants complete their life cycle in a remarkably short time; desert species, for instance, stimulated by a brief rainy season, germinate, flower and make seed in a few weeks. However, horticulturists have managed, through selection and breeding, to extend the blooming period of flowering annuals, as well as the useful period of annual vegetable crops.

Not every plant grown for a single season of color is truly an annual. Biennials, such as most hollyhocks (*Alcea rosea*), Canterbury bells (*Campanula medium*), honesty (*Lunaria annua*) and numerous border plants, offer only one flowering season, but enjoy a two-year lifespan and so are not considered annuals. (For more on these kinds of plants, see "Biennials," on the opposite page.) A number of tender perennial plants are used as annuals in, among other places, display beddings, containers and window boxes. Species of fuchsias (*Fuchsia*), impatiens (*Impatiens*), lantanas (*Lantana*) and geraniums (*Pelargonium*), as well as wax begonias (*Begonia semperflorens*), vinca or Madagascar

periwinkle (*Catharanthus roseus*), marguerites (*Chrysanthemum frutescens*) and more, all live for several years in their frost-free native habitats. But as they bloom quickly from seed or from cuttings and are grown as single-season plants, they are grouped with the annuals and used to brighten the seasonal garden until laid low by frost.

Some plants that grow from bulbs, corms and tubers have also come to be used as annuals. By their very nature, bulbous plants are not single-season growers, for the "bulb" is a modified stem, enlarged to store food for coming seasons. But many of the inexpensive, frost-sensitive sorts that make a grand show are regularly treated as annuals. Dollar-conscious gardeners dig and store these over winter; however, it is a great savings in time and trouble to let the winter take them and buy more the next spring. For information about bulbous plants, see the *Hearst Garden Guides* volume entitled *Bulbs.*

THE SELECTION OF ANNUALS

The list of annuals is so long it can be intimidating. The beginning gardener is likely to wander into a garden center or pick up a seed catalog and, completely overwhelmed by the great range of

BIENNIALS: TWO-SEASON CYCLE

A biennial plant, in nature, makes vegetative growth (usually a leafy rosette) the first season after seed germinates, and then blooms, sets seed and dies the following year. But gardeners have learned to manipulate these plants, altering their natural calendar. For example, quick-blooming biennials are often seeded in the greenhouse or cold frame in late winter so the plants flower during the following summer. Or, in locations with severe winter weather, biennials are sown in late summer in cold frames, where they are somewhat protected as they overwinter. Then these small plants are set out early the following spring to make more growth and blossom.

Most biennials grow on year after year in ideal environmental conditions, but can be troublesome elsewhere. For example, biennials grow well consistently in Zone 6 maritime gardens. With the tempering effect of the sea and a generally mild year-round condition, foxgloves (*Digitalis purpurea*), Canterbury bells (*Campanula medium*), honesty (*Lunaria annua*) and other desirable biennials self-seed freely. But these same species, in harsher climates or in the central part of the country, away from the modifying effect of the ocean, often succumb to cold during the winter, and volunteer (self-sown) plants are virtually unknown.

Many of the finest border plants are biennials. In addition to those already mentioned, favorite ornamental biennials include English daisies (*Bellis perennis*), wallflowers (*Cheiranthus cheiri*), sweet William (*Dianthus barbatus*), most hollyhocks (*Alcea* spp.), sweet rockets (*Hesperis* spp.), and some forget-me-nots (*Myosotis* spp.) and mulleins (*Verbascum* spp.).

You will notice that indefinite word "some." Often, with garden varieties (cultivars), exposure—the severity of winter and the intensity of summer—determines classification. For example, some fairly tender annuals shed seed early—during summer—in the mild Pacific Northwest. The resulting late summer seedlings overwinter as rosettes and bloom the following spring, and are thus considered biennials.

Also, some perennials—especially those grown in cool, oceanic climates or mild mountainous environments—can at times be considered biennials; these plants make vegetative growth the first year when grown in the garden, and strain themselves so much blooming in a foreign environment the following season that they die after having flowered. The hybridized English daisies, Iceland poppies (*Papaver nudicaule*) and many strains of pansies and violas (*Viola* spp.) fall into this category.

possibilities, select a number of varieties quite unsuited to his or her locale.

To avoid this kind of confusion, use the encyclopedia (chapter 4) as a guide to selecting plants. If questions arise, call or visit the local parks department and see what it uses. Or, other ways to make plant selection easier might include: tak-

ing home-garden tours in your area, making notes of which annuals recur garden after garden; get a list of recommended plants from the local County Extension Agent's office or ask its affiliated Master Gardeners, who are usually present at many public locations during the spring. Good garden centers also have knowledgable horticulturists on staff, and many feature display plantings that can be useful in evaluating different species when making a purchase. Finally, conduct a low-cost experiment by taking a chance on two or three plants you have never heard of or that nobody mentioned. With luck, you may enjoy a patch of unusual and lovely flowers. See the section entitled "Regional Gardening" (chapter 4, p. 161).

When you think of planting annuals, think of planting for a season of color. With the majority of annuals this season of color is summer, as most annuals thrive during the summer months or complete their life cycles from early spring to fall. Some species, however, notably native "weeds" such as chickweed, shepherd's purse, annual bluegrass (*Poa annua*, the small, tuft–forming grass that plagues greenskeepers)

and some ornamental plants, germinate during cool fall weather, grow intermittently over winter, and flower sometime after January.

With good plant selection or judicious replanting, annuals can be used in most places to provide color from early spring through late fall. Hardy annuals stand frost; you may enjoy an early burst of color from bachelor's buttons (*Centaurea cyanus*), rocket larkspur (*Consolida ambigua*), Shirley poppies (*Papaver rhoeas*) and other hardy annuals if you sow seed in the fall (or buy already started plants in late winter). Similarly, you can plant such cool growers as pansies, ornamental kale and cabbage (*Brassica oleracea* varieties) to extend your period of color into the late fall or later, depending on the mildness of the weather.

ALL-AMERICA SELECTIONS AND FLEUROSELECT

Frequently, catalog descriptions mention that a particular flower or vegetable has been awarded a medal by All–America Selections or by FleuroSelect. These two programs, the one in North America and the other in Europe, are a bit like the Olympics of the horticultural world. And like Olympic athletes, plants that are AAS and FleuroSelect winners can be expected to perform well.

The All–America Selections are chosen by commercial plant breeders to promote new cultivars of flowers and vegetables grown from seed. The selection procedure begins when the originator of a new cultivar sends seeds to an All–America Selections agent, who is financed by various seed producers' organizations. The seed is then forwarded to some 56 trial locations.

At these growing locations, which are either on the grounds of major seed producers

or at universities, new varieties of vegetables, flowers and bedding plants are tried separately, and final All–America Selections made. Judging is based on a comprehensive set of criteria, and judges include the country's outstanding breeders.

Undoubtedly there is benefit to the amateur grower from this program. As seeds are labeled under numbers (rather than identified as to source), and are grown in widely varying environmental conditions, a plant that does well enough across the country to win the All–America Selection award should be a superior cultivar; gardeners who use these plants are not likely to be disappointed.

A similar program is run in Europe, with judging at 20 different trial sites, under the name FleuroSelect.

STRUCTURE OF ANNUAL PLANTS

When considering the development and structure of annuals, as a precursor to garden design, a helpful place to begin is with the roots. Annual plants do not generally have strong root systems, as the roots only develop during their one year of growth. Small, fibrous roots extend outward from the stem to absorb water and nutrients. Annual roots do not go deep into the soil, making them easy to move during their life cycle.

Before planting, study the natural habitat of the plants. Select a site with growing conditions that most closely approximate those where the plant grows naturally, and prepare the soil accordingly. When an annual is planted in the wrong site (even though the soil is deeply worked), the plant will do poorly. For instance, plants from the forest floor, such as violas, are unlikely to thrive in full sun, whereas species from dry, open areas, which need strong direct sun for most of the day, such as California poppies (*Eschscholzia californica*), should not be planted in the shade.

The stems of annuals usually arise straight up from the roots. Sturdy, well-spaced stems produce better masses of larger, longer-lasting flowers than do spindly, overcrowded stems; so on older clumps, clip out all weak stems at the base when the leafy shoots are half developed.

Annuals and biennials bloom in many ways rocket larkspur (*Consolida ambigua*), foxgloves (*Digitalis purpurea*) and lupines (*Lupinus* spp.) produce flowers on a strong vertical stem. Others, such as annual phloxes (*Phlox drummondii*), bloom with flowers in close-set panicles or clusters. Still others, such as *Gypsophila elegans* (baby's–breath), bear flowers in loose clusters, or in very open sprays. For more information on flower shapes and reproduction, refer to the section entitled "Flower Forms" on page 15.

Seed formation saps the strength of the plant, and results in the reduction or cessation of the current flowering. To prevent seed formation, remove flower heads as soon as blooms fade. Most annuals benefit from this "deadheading," although with a few flowers, such as impatiens, it is unnecessary, for the flowers fall as they expire. With most flowers, however, the only times not to do it are when the seed heads are required for dried arrangements, or when you want biennials to self-sow.

DESIGNING WITH ANNUAL FLOWERS

Even with the current surge of interest in year-round annual gardening, the greatest use of annual flowers is still in summer plantings. Annuals' summertime popularity started during the eighteenth century, when the aristocracy wanted something brighter than colored stones in their scrollwork-hedged gardens. By Victorian days, public parks were filled with extremely complicated geometric flower beds. Highly trained gardeners made endless lists of plants: by height, hue and month of bloom; by foliage color; by opening and closing times for nocturnal and diurnal flowers; and by compatability with various growing conditions. Annual vines, tender perennials used as annuals, and bulbs, corms and tubers that were treated as annuals all went into these lists.

Today, many municipalities still maintain lavish display gardens filled with color, reminiscent of Victorian parks. While they are very useful for getting ideas for plant combinations and flower colors, most of the interest in annuals has shifted to home gardens.

Annuals fit into today's gardens in many ways. Drifts of colorful flowers brighten doorways and terraces. Window boxes and hanging baskets overflow with them. They look fine and grow well in various sorts of planters and containers. Annuals are essential for apartment dwellers, who depend on them almost entirely for color when gardening on a balcony or roof. They are inter-

planted with perennials or placed in mixed borders to extend flower color through the season.
Annuals in containers are even used for bright
splashes of color at short-term events like festivals
or parties.

One of the best reasons to grow annuals is to
have plenty of flowers to cut for arrangements or
bouquets. China asters (*Callistephus chinensis*),
cosmos (*Cosmos* spp.), rocket larkspur (*Consolida
ambigua*), sunflowers (*Helianthus annuus*), sweet
peas (*Lathyrus odoratus*), bachelor's buttons
(*Centaurea cyanus*), snapdragons (*Antirrhinum majus*
and cultivars) and zinnias (*Zinnia* spp.) are just a
few of the many annuals and biennials that make
wonderful cut flowers. A handful of seed packets
will yield flowers for dozens of arrangements, and
cost no more than a couple of ready-made bouquets from the supermarket.

Gardeners today use great numbers of annuals
because they are so adaptable; there is at least one
to fill every gardening need. Annual flowers tolerate a wide range of soil conditions; properly
handled, they bloom week after week and they
do not require the degree of year-round care and
attention necessary for longer-lived species.
There are annuals for growing in full sun, for part
sun and for shade. While most annual flowers
grow best in well-drained soil, a few prefer damp
places. Because most have fairly modest root systems, annuals may be closely planted for a solid
display of color, and so are quite suitable for window and porch boxes and for growing in pots.
Hobby greenhouse enthusiasts rely heavily on
annuals for winter color, often planting dusty
miller (*Cenaurea cineraria*), some greenhouse
primroses *(Primula* spp.), and butterfly flower
(*Schizanthus pinnatus*).

Finally, their low cost is another factor in
annuals' popularity; grown from seed, a colorful
selection of annuals will barely make a dent in
the gardener's pocketbook.

SOURCES FOR ANNUALS

To supply today's large demand, huge quanities of
plants are produced by greenhouses for sale
through garden centers, nurseries, mass market
outlets, and even supermarkets, primarily in the
spring. Although most experts agree that plants
do better when planted green—that is, not yet in
flower—annuals are typically sold heavy with
bloom, ready to provide instant color in the garden. Only a few years ago, most annuals were
sold in flats, which could be separated into cell-
packs containing two to six plants. But recently,
there has been a general switch to larger containers holding more developed plants, with 4-inch
or larger pots taking an increasing amount of
sales, a trend influenced heavily by landscapers
who plant around office buildings and in shop-
ping malls.

Variety is limited at mass market outlets,
which tend to stock only the most popular plants
for short periods in the spring or fall. Selection is
better in garden centers and nurseries, and most
cities have at least a few garden centers or nurseries that offer a substantial choice.

Although most annuals are purchased already
started, gardeners can choose from a much
broader selection by buying seeds through mail-
order catalogs. When ordering seeds, a discriminating gardener can pick from heirloom varieties,
choose less popular but beautiful kinds, and select
taller varieties not favored by plant producers.
(Many of these less popular plants deserve wider
garden use.) In addition, the color selection is
often greater than with started plants, where
sometimes only a mixture is offered.

chapter

3
ANNUALS FROM
SEED

The conditions required for germination and the planting methods vary somewhat with different kinds of seeds and the region in which they are started, but some general rules apply to all. For instance, seeds should generally be started in a container with drainage holes, in a sterile starting medium, and given plenty of direct sunlight or strong fluorescent light.

Luckily, the germination of most annuals is a straightforward affair. The seeds of some plants, such as morning glories (*Ipomoea* spp.), sweet peas (*Lathyrus odoratus*) and lupines (*Lupinus* spp.), have a very hard seed coat and will benefit from soaking in warm water overnight. (Plant the seeds right away; do not let them dry out. Those that have not swelled after soaking can be notched with a file to allow water to enter.) Any such special treatment needed will be detailed on the seed packet.

STARTING SEEDS INDOORS

Many annuals can be sown directly in the garden where they are to bloom. Some gardeners, however, like to start seedlings early, indoors, to get a head start on the season. Seeds of annuals usually germinate quickly, and given basic care, the seedlings tolerate a wide range of conditions.

Pots for Germinating Seeds

Shallow clay pots (bulb pans), plastic pots, peat pots, plastic flats, compressed paper plant trays, or almost any other shallow container with drainage holes that will hold the germinating medium can be used to start seeds. Seed-starting flats are available with several rows so that a number of varieties can be started in a small space. Otherwise, make sure to use a separate pot or container for each variety, labeled to show the plant name and date sown. It is surprisingly difficult to tell young seedlings apart, especially before they have formed their first true leaves.

Soil Mixes

Years ago, gardeners who wanted a soil mix for germinating seeds indoors, or a potting soil for growing plants, had to make it themselves. Some still prefer this method, but most gardeners buy a commercially available soil mix and use it as is, or amend it to give it the specific properties they want.

When starting plants from seed, it is safest to use a sterile soilless mix in order to give tiny seedlings a disease- and weed-free environment. Later, when the time comes to transplant healthy, stout young plantlets into individual pots, there is an advantage to adding some soil to the mix—the positive microbial action that occurs.

Soil is more than a medium to support plants. It also provides nutrients, which dissolve in water, and are absorbed by plant roots. During photosynthesis, for instance, some of these nutrients are utilized to provide the plant's growth.

Commercial Mixes. Commercial soil mixes typically include a combination of ingredients that provides moisture-holding capacity but still retains a significant amount of tiny air spaces so roots do not rot. The constituents most widely used are sphagnum (as opposed to sedge) peat moss, perlite and vermiculite; the gardener supplies the nutrients by fertilizing the seedlings as they grow. The peat is used to retain moisture, while vermiculite and perlite help provide drainage. Sometimes sharp sand is added to enhance drainage further still, and its addition also makes it easier to separate seedlings at transplanting time.

There has also been a lot of fine-tuning of seed-starting mixes. Cornell University has developed a set of peat-lite mixes; a typical peat-lite mix begins as one half peat and one half vermiculite, then 10 pounds of dolomitic limestone, 4 pounds of ammonium nitrate, and $2^1/2$ pounds of superphosphate are added per cubic yard of mix. The Cornell mix is the basis for most commercial soil mixes. A University of California mix for seed germinating contains three quarters peat moss and one quarter sand. (Sand should not be beach sand, which does not

have enough texture.) Vermiculite or shredded sphagnum moss can be used alone, but neither provides any nutrients.)

To check if a commercial potting soil can be used straight from the bag, look for a coarse texture that springs back when you squeeze a handful. If it remains in a tight lump, add up to one third perlite or vermiculite and mix it thoroughly. You can also add compost or well-composted manure to the mix, but be sure you sterilize it to kill any disease organisms and weed seeds and sift it to remove large pieces before adding to the mix. Up to one third sand can also be added as an alternative. Growers of alpine plants, which need very sharp drainage, will frequently add #2 chicken or turkey grit, up to one third in volume.

Garden Soil. Never use unadulterated garden soil as a germinating mix or potting soil. Almost without exception, the soil will be filled with disease organisms injurious to young seedlings, as well as weed seeds that will germinate and compete with the desirable seedlings. If you do use garden soil as part of a soil mix, sterilize it to kill disease organisms and weed seeds before using it in the mix. This can be done by heating it in the oven (be prepared for the heady odor) until an internal temperature of 180°F (check by inserting a soil thermometer) has been maintained for 30 minutes.

While garden soils do provide nutrients, they do not have enough structure to support the root growth, and often turn into a solid mass devoid of air spaces. Garden loam must be mixed with peat or vermiculite, at least one half of the volume, to hold structure.

Fertilizing Seed-starting Mixes
Check to see whether the commercial seed-starting mix you are buying contains starter fer-

tilizer. If it does, do not fertilize seedlings for the first two weeks after germination, then apply a water-soluble fertilizer mixed at one quarter the recommended rate on the package every time you water. If the mix does not contain fertilizer, start feeding as above after germination.

Preparing Pots

Fill pots to within a $1/2$ inch of the rim with the mix; the medium should be moist but not soggy and only slightly compacted. If necessary, wet the mix thoroughly—but not soaking wet—and allow it to drain before sowing the seed. Most garden centers also stock seed-starting soil mixes that are treated with a wetting agent to aid water penetration and that have a light charge of starter fertilizer to feed new seedlings gently.

Recently, special water-holding polymers, which look like grains of sugar, have become available to home gardeners. There are a number of brands, widely distributed in garden centers. When water is added to the polymers, they absorb it, swelling to many times their volume, then release the water slowly. They are very useful in soil mixes for hanging baskets, window boxes and other container plantings. They allow the gardener to space out the time between waterings substantially, easing management considerably. Make sure that the polymer crystals are mixed thoroughly throughout the soil mix, and refrain from using more than the recommended rate. Otherwise, unsightly blobs of liquid jelly will surface in the container.

Sowing Seeds

The rule of thumb is to sow seeds at a depth of two to three times their diameter, but even with big bean seeds no one can be accurate about this, and no one need be. Sow large seeds, spaced evenly, by pushing them into the soil with your finger or with a dibble (in lieu of a dibble, a pen-

cil works well). Or, treat them like most smaller seeds, which should be spread evenly across the soil surface, then covered with a light layer of soil mix or vermiculite. Do not cover tiny seeds, like those of petunias and begonias; instead, spread them on the soil surface and press in lightly. Also, take care not to cover seeds that need light to germinate, such as those of impatiens, and follow directions on seed packets.

Sow the seeds in pots or flats, or in Jiffy-7s (small discs of compressed peat, which, when moistened, swell to form individual pots) or other peat pots, which are especially handy for large-seeded varieties. When using Jiffy-7s or similar peat pots to start vining ornamentals such as morning glory or cypress vine (*Ipomoea* spp.), poke two seeds each into every container. The seedlings grow in these and the whole thing, container and all, goes into the garden.

When the seeds are in place, mist carefully (water tiny seeds with a syringe) to make sure there is firm contact between the seed and the medium. Or you can water from the bottom: set the container in a tray of tepid water for two or three hours (water droplets should glisten on the surface of the germinating mix), then stretch a piece of clear plastic over the face of the container and secure it with a rubber band, to retain moisture (and cut down your watering job). Place in dim light, at moderate room temperature.

Most annual seeds germinate best at 65° to 70°F, and most warm season annuals germinate best at 70° to 75°F, but there is some variation (again, the seed packet will tell). Gentle bottom heat at these temperatures will enhance germination. Simple ways of providing bottom heat include placing the seed container on top of a refrigerator or water heater, or on the reflector of a fluorescent light unit; garden centers also sell heating pads, which can be set to provide even bottom heat.

When germination of the seeds has started, remove the plastic covering over the plant containers. (Carefully lift it off, so that the water, which has condensed on the underside of the glass or plastic top, does not drip onto the planting; this will help to prevent disease.) If the seeds have been planted too close together, thin out the little plants immediately. Do this with tweezers to avoid harming the plants left behind. Then give the seedlings dim light for a day, followed by bright light—a south-facing window, fluorescent light or greenhouse daylight.

Transplanting

As soon as the seedlings have developed their first set of true leaves (after the cotylons, or the first leaves), transplant them into individual cells in flats or into individual pots. For this step, use a soil mix that combines moisture-retention with air spaces, such as provided by many commercial soil mixes, for strong root growth. Space plants at least 2 inches apart in pots for strong specimens with better root systems. If space is at a premium and you have enough time on hand, transplant into individual cells, then transplant again, later, to larger sizes. (Note that a cold frame goes a long way to eliminating these space constraints; see the opposite page for more about cold frames.)

Lift the seedlings carefully with a pointed stick or a dull knife. Make a hole with your finger in the transplanting soil; drop the roots into it; firm up the soil. Water the soil of the transplanted plants well, using a starter solution to stimulate growth and help the seedlings survive the transplanting.

The critical factor at this time is adequate light to prevent the small seedlings from stretching. Best of all is a hobby greenhouse where uniform light comes from all sides. Fluorescent light units are also very satisfactory, and can be as simple as two tubes (one cool white and one warm white to best mimic natural sunlight) covered by a reflector; place the plants 4 to 6 inches from the light tubes.

When it is time to move young plants outdoors, let them grow accustomed to outside conditions gradually. This process is known as hardening off. Harden off plants by moving them outside in their pots during the daytime, then indoors at night, for several days before planting. At the beginning of the process, set plants in filtered sun, and gradually increase the intensity of sun until plants are exposed to the kind of light they will require in the garden.

Transplanting to the garden is a shock to the root system, so keep plants lightly shaded for a few days. If the weather is cold, provide protection, especially at night. Individual plants can be protected under upturned flowerpots, or milk or soft drink containers whose bottoms have been cut out; beds of transplants can be sheltered under lengths of cheesecloth or muslin, tied to stakes. Some varieties, such as pansies, petunias and snapdragons, will tolerate considerably more cold than very tender plants such as impatiens. Tender varieties should not be planted outdoors until all danger of frost is past, and both the ground and air temperatures are warm. When the plants are in the ground and growth resumes, apply half-strength liquid fertilizer.

SOWING IN THE GARDEN

You can sow many annual seeds where the plants are to grow. Plant them in any well-pulverized soil at the time specified on the seed packet. If the soil is heavy, the seeds should be somewhat closer to the surface than if the soil is light and sandy; or, even better, lighten the soil with peat worked to a spade's depth.

In the garden, work up the soil in a well-drained bed; dress prior to turning with $1/4$ cup of 5-10-5 fertilizer and 2 cups of dehydrated manure per square yard (this is a general rule of thumb, and may be modified to meet local conditions), then spade deeply. (Never work chemical fertilizer into the soil around seedlings, as this may burn them. Apply the fertilizer before planting seeds or seedlings and mix it well into the soil.) Rake down the soil, working it to crumble the clods and to develop a reasonably well-settled, even surface.

When ready to sow seeds, scratch out roughly rectangular, trapezoidal or triangular "patches" with a hoe handle for each sort of seed. Then, with a fine-pointed cultivating tool or with a small hoe, mark out shallow drills, or furrows. At the front of the bed the drills ought to run at acute angles to the face of the bed. Drills in a given patch should be parallel to each other, but not parallel to those in adjacent patches. A garden strictly for cut flowers, however, should usually consist of evenly spaced rows for easy access when harvesting the flowers.

Whatever the garden design, make the drills roughly 6 inches apart, closer for very fine sorts such as Dahlberg daisy (*Dyssodia tenuiloba*) or 'Twinkle' phlox (*Phlox drummondii* 'Twinkle'), and much farther apart for large kinds such as the Mexican sunflower (*Tithonia rotundifolia*), castor-bean (*Ricinis communis*) or hollyhock (*Alcea rosea*). Sow seed generously in the drills and plan to thin later; the excess plants may be discarded or transplanted. For large seeds, however, space them as well as you can. There is no sense in being wasteful or in giving yourself extra work when the young plants need thinning. Cover all seeds two to three times their diameter with finely crumbled soil, and tamp firmly to make certain of good contact between seed and soil.

You may broadcast the seeds as well as planting them in drills. Rake and level the soil surface carefully, then scatter the seeds and tamp gently with a board. Cover seeds with soil and tamp lightly with a rake.

If the soil is moist, there is no need to water. However, if you do water in the seed, make sure to use a watering can with a gentle rose nozzle, or a sprinkler with a fine mist, in order not to disturb the seed. At spring planting time there is likely to be enough moisture in the ground, but if the soil dries out, water lightly but thoroughly.

As seedlings appear, keep the bed free of weeds. When seedlings reach a well-established size but before they begin to crowd badly, thin seedlings to at least 6 inches apart for smaller plants like violet (*Viola* spp.), 9 inches for midsize plants such as petunia *(Petunia* spp.) and marigold (*Tagetes* spp.), and 1 foot or more for large plants such as sunflower (*Helianthus* spp.).

Plants you have grown yourself or purchased from the garden center may be planted in the same carefully organized, informal manner. Push young annuals with biweekly feedings of balanced, low-nitrogen liquid fertilizer until buds appear, and keep the soil loose and free of weeds. Some annuals, particularly floss flower (*Ageratum houstonianum*), marigold, zinnia, petunia, geranium and snapdragon, require one or two pinchings to make them branch well. Water often enough so the top inch of soil never dries out completely. When buds begin to show color, discontinue fertilizing.

COLD FRAMES

A cold frame is essentially a bottomless, glass-covered box, heated only by the sun, for the propagation, growing and protection of plants. The only difference between a cold frame and a hotbed, which was used during the horse-and -

carriage days, is that a hotbed used manure, providing heat to young plants as it decomposed. Today's gardeners can achieve the same effect by installing thermostatically controlled heating pads or soil cables on the floor of the structure. In days past, most cold frames were designed for planting directly into the soil bed. Now cold frames are primarily used for protecting plants in pots or flats. In very cold climates, this makes the use of heating mats more important, for the plants are not as well protected as if they were growing in the insulating soil.

Uses. In colder climates, the serious gardener will find a cold frame all but essential. In spring, the cold frame allows the gardener to start seeds several weeks ahead of the time they can be planted in the open ground; to harden off seedlings that are started indoors before planting them outside; and to propagate plants (such as hardwood cuttings of woody plants like trees and shrubs) that might be difficult, if not impossible, to grow otherwise. In winter, the cold frame allows the gardener to protect plants that might not survive; to store potted bulbs in winter until they are ready to be brought indoors to flower when wanted; to grow such semihardy bulbs as anemones and bulbous irises without danger; and to maintain an almost winter-long supply of cold-tolerant crops such as lettuce, radishes, chives and parsley.

Construction. A permanent cold frame can be built from the ground up, or bought ready to use as soon as it is placed on prepared ground.

The home-constructed cold frame will be most durable if built of poured concrete, concrete blocks or brick. A less permanent frame can, however, be more easily built of wood. Redwood and cypress, naturally resistant to rot,

are preferred, but any wood will do as long as it is thoroughly treated with wood preservative and painted. While glass is preferred, greenhouse-grade plastic film makes a very acceptable cover material. Some of these films have a life expectancy of several years, and they weigh less than glass.

There is no limit to the overall size of a cold frame, but anything wider than 6 feet (using two 3-by-6-foot sashes) may be difficult to use. Several separate 3-by-6-foot frames are better. Equally good—and easier to manage because of the much lighter sash—is a long frame, 4 feet wide from front to back and covered with as many sashes as you like.

For minimal frost protection, a shelter can simply and easily be made by inserting flexible PVC pipe into larger pieces of pipe driven into the ground, and draped with plastic film weighted with lath tacked to the ends.

Location. A cold frame should be placed to receive the maximum sunlight during fall, winter and spring. This means that the glass should usually slope toward the south. In the classic cold frame, the four sides of the frame are set into the ground to a depth of 12 inches. The front rises 12 inches above the ground; the back 16 inches. In this way, the glass or other covering is tilted to catch the rays of even the lowest winter sun.

To protect the frame as much as possible from cold, screen it on the north side with a hedge, fence or building. If that is not possible, bank the north side with bales of straw. Locating the frame against the south or east side of the house will help to keep it warm in winter.

Management. When sowing seeds directly into the cold frame bed, good drainage is essential. Provide a 4- to 6-inch layer of coarse gravel or crushed rock under the soil. The soil bed itself should be 6 inches deep and composed of screened loam mixed with compost or peat moss. The top of the bed should be level with the ground outside the frame.

Successful use of the cold frame depends on ventilating, protecting and watering it properly. It should not be allowed to become too hot. Most prefabricated cold frames have automatic venting triggered by the temperature level. These automatic vent controls can also be installed on other units. If your cold frame is not automatic, on sunny days in spring and fall, its sash should be propped up at the bottom, 2 or 3 inches, after the sun comes up, and closed just before the sun goes down. In fall, if the frame is used for the protection of hardy plants, provide even more ventilation on sunny days to prevent plants from being forced into unwanted growth. In winter, keep the sash closed except on unusually warm, bright days.

During the cold months, on very cold or cloudy days, keep the glass covered with a burlap or canvas cover stuffed with straw or excelsior, or with wood planks. Such covering is also advisable to prevent loss of heat on very cold or clear spring nights. The covering does not have to be removed every day in winter. Mounding dirt up against the outside of the frame provides further protection. Another way to moderate night temperatures in the cold frame is to set 1-gallon plastic milk jugs filled with water among the plants. Use two jugs for every 3-by-6 feet of area. The water-filled jugs act as solar collectors, heating up during the day, then releasing their warmth at night.

The frame should be watered regularly—about once a week if evaporation is not excessive. Plants in pots or flats will require more frequent watering than those grown in ground beds. Watering is best done in the early morning on sunny days. The rule of thumb is to

never allow plants to go to bed with wet foliage, which in small seedlings encourages damping-off (see page 31), and in larger plants causes a destructive gray mold called botrytis.

GREENHOUSES

A personal greenhouse carries the advantages of a cold frame one step further—the gardener has additional control over temperature as well as more space.

With a greenhouse, the gardener can maintain a continuous supply of blooming plants for the home. Especially welcome in winter are such cool-season annuals as *Schizanthus* spp. and *Centuarea cineraria*. The greenhouse is also an ideal place for germinating seeds and propagating plants for the outdoor garden. But perhaps its biggest advantage is convenience—working surfaces are at a convenient height, and there is room to stand erect and move among the plants. The plants also benefit from greater air volume than in a cold frame, which means that temperatures do not fluctuate so dramatically; and plants in a greenhouse are able to benefit from all usable light, rather than being limited to overhead light.

Styles. There is as much variety in greenhouses as there is in automobiles, ranging from basic models to top-of-the-line structures, custom-designed to complement a home's architecture.

Two types of working greenhouses are commonly available. Lean-to greenhouses attach to a building, with glass or other covering on three sides and the roof. Freestanding structures are open to the world on all sides. Many manufacturers offer greenhouse units, prefabricated in a number of sizes. They are manufactured in aluminum or wood, and are glazed with glass or various grades of plastic film. They can be ordered as do-it-yourself kits, and many companies also have authorized representatives to do the construction. Small, freestanding structures and construction plans are also widely available.

Hobby greenhouses can be totally automated (at substantial extra expense), so that they automatically open and close vents according to temperature, turn on and close down the heating system and run up blinds to shade plants from the burning rays of summer sun. There are even standby generators that switch on automatically to power the heating system in case of a power failure. This feature will save plants from freezing in severely cold weather. All of these automatic functions can, of course, be installed for manual control.

Although a greenhouse offers important options to the gardener, it also represents a serious investment of both money and time. Before taking the plunge, do thorough research of what is available and carefully consider your needs and how your greenhouse will be best used.

CULTIVATION AND PEST CONTROL

Annuals need to be kept free of weed competition. Cultivate frequently, using a scuffle hoe or a rake to loosen the soil. Avoid deep cultivation, as it may injure roots. An alternative to regular cultivation is to apply a 2-inch layer of an organic mulch such as chopped leaves, grass clippings or buckwheat hulls. Keep the mulch a couple of inches away from the annuals' stems though, to prevent disease.

Stake larger plants when they are half-grown. In a mass planting, an easy way to do this is to use brushy, leafless, dry branches. Stems and branches supported throughout by a mesh of twigs are much more secure than those tied to single stakes. Tie individual or large, unbranched plants such as sunflowers to bamboo stakes inserted deep in the soil.

Remove spent blossoms when necessary. Besides the obvious beauty of flowers without spent flower heads, there is a practical reason for removing flowers: to enhance continued flowering. Annuals attempt to produce seed before dying. By removing the spent flowers and thereby preventing seed formation, you encourage continuous flower production. There is no need to wait until flowers are "gone by" to remove them, however. Cutting annual flowers for bouquets also encourages plants to bloom more.

How and when to remove flowers depends on the plant. For example, when most snapdragons have almost finished blooming, clip the flower stalks back just above a leaf. New secondary shoots will probably develop shortly, particularly if the plants get a light feeding. On the other hand, you should nip off zinnia heads, spent petunia blossoms and spent cosmos once or twice each week, so the plants bloom continuously. Shear back sweet alyssum after each flush of flowering, and it will renew itself. Petunias also benefit from a severe, midseason pruning; they bloom again soon on more compact stems. The flowers of some plants, such as impatiens, drop cleanly away and do not need maintenance.

Cultivating Biennials

Biennials may be started in the open garden where they are to grow; or in special seedbeds, cold frames or hotbeds. Biennials can also be started in pots or flats indoors, then moved to a protected spot outdoors for the winter. In cold climates, biennials that are started in the open garden should be mulched with straw or shredded leaves, or transferred to the cold frame.

In the mountains, where July-to-September temperatures seldom exceed 55°F, most biennial flowers should be sown in July. But where summer heat is extreme and constant, it is better to wait until late August or even into September. Then sow the seed in a cold frame that will be closed after cold weather settles in for the winter season.

As with annuals, sow seed of biennials in a pot or flat filled with a good seed-germinating mixture. Most biennials, like annuals, germinate quickly. Thin or transplant all plants when they begin their second set of true leaves. Transplant individually into 3- or 4-inch pots and place in a cold frame for overwintering. In more congenial climates, these young plants, after they have grown on for six weeks, can go directly to the garden, to be set where they are to bloom. In the open garden where the soil freezes, mulch young biennials after the soil is thoroughly chilled, to prevent them from being heaved out of frost-swollen ground and to keep the plants dormant through freak warm spells in late winter and early spring.

Treat biennials that are subject to crown rot with an appropriate chemical (Dexon is specific for this disease) in early spring. Give them a boost with liquid fertilizer; organic choices

---

DAMPING-OFF

Damping-off is a condition caused by any of several different fungi that may attack seedlings, usually at the ground line, soon after emergence. It may also kill the seedlings before they emerge from the ground. (Gaps in the row may be a symptom of damping-off below ground.) Characteristically, the disease causes healthy young seedlings to suddenly wilt and topple over. Complete control is difficult, but the disease can be minimized by one or more of the following measures:

Sterilize the soil. For seed-starting, always use a sterile soilless mix. There is even a mix available (appropriately called No-Damp-Off) that incorporates a fungicide. If garden soil is a constituent of your seeding soil mix, it must be sterilized before mixing. Bake the soil in an oven at 180°F until a thermometer in the soil reaches that temperature. Continue for 30 minutes. (Note that it is not recommended to use more than half garden soil in a mix for seed germination or as a potting soil, because it loses structure and air spaces, which tiny roots need to grow.)

Use a soilless mix. Sow seeds in vermiculite, perlite, combinations of them, or chopped sphagnum moss. These constituents should have no disease organisms in them and seeds thus started are far less likely to damp off than those started in soil. (Scattering one of these materials on top of soil-based seedbeds after sowing may also help.) These media offer the best practical control for sowing in flats or pots.

Treat seeds with protectants before planting. Shake the seeds in an envelope filled with a pinch of one of the numerous fungicides sold for this purpose. Treatment is likely to be most effective for vegetables but will also aid with many flowers.

Drench pots or seed flats with a fungicide solution after sowing. Treat only at the recommended rate.

Follow good cultural practices. Sow seeds thinly. Make sure soil is well-aerated before planting. Avoid overwatering, which can cause excessive humidity in a cold frame or hotbed. Ensure good ventilation and air circulation.

INSECTS AND DISEASES OF BIENNIALS

Most biennials suffer from the same diseases that attack annual flowers. Where winters are severe and where soil is heavy, crown rot takes a great number of biennials in early spring. Fight the disease three ways. First, try to arrange your planting schedule so the plants that go to the open garden in late summer are not too large; very vigorous, large rosettes (described in "Biennials," page 19), such as those on foxgloves, hollyhocks and other biennials, seem most susceptible to crown rot. Second, after the weather and the soil have cooled in late fall, drench the planting with Terrachlor, an excellent chemical for crown-

rot control during cool weather (but note that this chemical puts some plants into stress during warm weather), and apply snail and slug bait around the plants. Third, in early spring, when the first signs of growth show in the centers of the rosettes, treat again, this time with a Dexon solution.

Also watch biennials for chewing and piercing-sucking insects. If present, treat in the same way as annuals.

Tedious? Somewhat. But with this regimen you can produce a full bed of Canterbury bells, when without it you might lose two thirds of the plants before flowering.

include liquid manure, fish-emulsion solution or a seaweed-extract solution, but equally good results come from feeding with synthetic soluble fertilizers. As most biennials bloom rather early in the season, interplant with a crop of late-flowering annuals to come along after the biennials have made their show.

Insect and Disease Control

Most gardeners are concerned with protecting the environment. Healthy garden plants, are less subject to insect and disease problems than those stressed by insufficient nutrients or water or by other problems. So the first step in pest control is to keep plants growing vigorously. It is also good gardening sense to create an environment that encourages lady bugs, birds and other predators that feed on destructive insects.

However, there are times when even these steps are not enough to prevent insect damage. Watch for signs of aphids and other piercing-sucking insects. They cluster on leaves, tender

shoot tips or buds; these parts of the plants will appear crippled and, perhaps, discolored. Other insect pests chew the leaves. When harmful insects are present, spray plants immediately with a garden insecticide, such as insecticidal soap. If your plants are seriously plagued with insects, consider applying a systemic insecticide.

Few diseases, either bacterial or fungal, attack most annuals, but there are some that make their unfortunate mark. Damping-off, a fungus disease, sometimes kills seedlings. For information on control, see page 31. Crown rot of annual plants may be a serious fungus problem where summers are hot and the soil is heavy with clay. Vinca (*Catharanthus roseus*) is very vulnerable to root rot if the soil remains wet and water-logged. The problem can be alleviated by planting this species in well-drained locations. Powdery mildew can be reduced by making sure there is sufficient air movement through the plants and that their foliage remains dry when watering.

4

ENCYCLOPEDIA
OF ANNUALS

The following encyclopedia lists the annuals, biennials and tender perennials, grown for a single-season of bloom, best suited for the garden. It includes the most commonly available species and cultivars and a substantial selection of lesser-known varieties.

Plants are listed by genus under their botanical names (with a pronunciation key). Species of each genus appear for every entry, together with varieties and cultivars. For instance, the various kinds of sunflowers are all listed under their genus, *Helianthus*. Conversely, if you know only the common name of a plant, you can use the Common Name Index (on page 165) to find its correct botanical name. Look up "sunflower" in the index, for example, and it points to the genus entry for *Helianthus*.

Plant Ratings

A rating system in the encyclopedia also singles out the most outstanding landscape plants for the garden. Virtually indispensable genera, such as *Pelargonium* (geraniums), *Petunia, Impatiens* and *Tagetes* (marigolds) are noted with two stars (★★). Unusually outstanding species or varieties, such as *Antirrhinum majus* (common snapdragon), are indicated by a single star (★).

The Encyclopedia Entries

General horticultural information, such as the type of soil and amount of light that plants require, their susceptibility to disease, overall hardiness, planting times, depths and techniques, and appropriate methods of propagation, appears with each genus. General gardening information, such as the valued ornamental aspects of the plants—flowers, form and foliage to name a few—that earn the plants a place in the garden are discussed.

Each species entry contains a detailed botanical description of the plant, which includes average mature height; flower shape, size, color and blooming period; and leaf structure, color, size and texture. Suggestions as to where plants might best be used in the garden or indoors highlight each species' aesthetic strong points. Recent and time-tested subspecies, nursery-introduced series, varieties, hybrids and clones worthy of their own place in the garden are included; their variations from the species are described.

Geographical information, such as the plant's place of origin (which is a key to the conditions under which it thrives in nature) and hardiness zones indicate the ability of biennial species to grow well in a region. (The USDA Plant Hardiness Zone Map is reproduced on pages 162-163.)

UNDERSTANDING
THE ENCYCLOPEDIA ENTRIES

Two stars indicating genus indispensable to the home garden. ——————

Common name for this genus. A cross-referenced entry appears listed in the Common Name Index.

Each entry gives you a —————— detailed description of the genus, including average height; flower shape, size, color and blooming period; and leaf structure and size. In-depth cultivation information, including zone ranges for biennials, light and soil requirements and propagation techniques, are covered.

Genus. A plant group of related species.

★★ **Antirrhinum** (an-tihr-*rye*-num). ——————

SNAPDRAGON.

Figwort Family (*Scrophulariaceae*). ——————
Tender perennials and annuals, chiefly from southern Europe, usually grown as annuals in the U.S. Magnificent range of colors, white through yellow and pink to darkest red, with innumerable color combinations. They vary in height from 6 in. to 3 ft. or more. Snapdragons are excellent for the cutting garden, for the mixed border and for greenhouses, especially when grown in greenhouse beds or benches rather than pots. The small varieties are much used for display beds and for border edging. The tallest or giant varieties may need staking.

Pronunciation key. Accent on italicized syllable.

Botanical name of the plant family.

Sow seeds indoors in January for blooms in May. Pinch back early for bushiness. Set them outdoors when weather is warm, in rich, well-dug soil that has plenty of humus and added lime. Keep flowers cut back to encourage growth and blooming of side shoots.

Stands for *Digitalis purpurea,* a biennial species belonging to the *Digitalis* genus.

Single star indicates species of outstanding merit.

★ **D. purpurea** (pur-*pew*-ree-uh).

COMMON FOXGLOVE.

Spikes of white, pink, rose or purple florets, usually with dark spots, on stems that are 3 to 6 ft. high. Handsome in large drifts in the late spring border, in front of shrubs and in the naturalized garden. Can be treated as a biennial; once established it often self-sows. Zone 3. ——————

Indicates this biennial will survive cold weather generally prevailing as far north as Zone 3. The USDA Zone Map is reprinted on pages 162-163.

Abelmoschus (ab-el-*mosk*-us).

Mallow Family (*Malvaceae*).

A genus of six to twenty species (depending on the botanical authority cited) of annuals, biennials and perennials originally native to southern and southeastern Asia. Okra (*Abelmoschus esculentus*) is widely grown for the edible young seed pods that form immediately after bloom.

A. moschatus (mo-*shaw*-tus).

(Syn. *Hibiscus moschatus.*) A species that grows to 15 in. tall with a spread to 30 in. Flowers are 2^1/$_2$ to 4 in. in diameter. Grows and flowers best in hot, humid summers in full sun. Since it takes approximately 100 days from sowing until bloom, plant indoors in February or March. 'Mischief' has cherry-red flowers with white centers. 'Mischief Pink' bears salmon-colored flowers with white centers. Relatively new to most gardeners, these hibiscus-like flowers each last only a day but are produced continuously until frost.

Abutilon (uh-*bute*-ih-lon).

Flowering Maple.

Mallow Family (*Malvaceae*).

More than 100 species in this genus are found throughout tropical regions of the world, but most cultivated kinds originated in South America. These plants reach 5 ft. in height where they winter over, 3 ft. tall elsewhere, and they grow well in full sun and average soil. In cold climates, they have been widely used as indoor plants, and more recently, as plants for seasonal display outdoors. Most *Abutilon* are not frost-tolerant, but *A. megapoticum* will tolerate temperatures as low as 20°F. In frost-free locations or those nearly so, many kinds are used in perennial plantings. The different species may be grown from seed, but mutations or selections must be grown from softwood cuttings.

Abelmoschus moschatus 'Mischief'

A. hybridum (*high*-brih-dum).

Derived from several species or even mutations, they have lobed, toothed leaves, some with variegation. They are frequently utilized in outdoor container plantings. *A. hybridum savitzii* (suh-*vit*-zee-eye) is a compact form growing to 3 ft., with gray-green leaves margined in white. The taller *A. hybridum* 'Souvenir De Bonn' has leaves with white borders and salmon-colored flowers veined in red.

A. megapoticum (meg-a-*pot*-i-come).

The most popular of the annual flowering maple varieties, including *variegatum* (ver-ee-a-*gaw*-tum), are variants of this species. They have long, narrow, toothed leaves, with the leaves blotched yellow in the variegated form. The flowers are lemon-yellow.

Abutilon

Abutilon striatum thompsonii
FLOWERING MAPLE

A. striatum thompsonii (stry-*a*-tum thomp-*son*-e-i).

A variant of a shrubby species from Guatemala, with mottled yellow leaves up to 6 in. long and almost 6 in. wide. Flowers are orange, veined in red. Propagate from cuttings; culture according to details in genus entry.

Acroclinium. See *Helipterum*.

Ageratum (aj-er-*ray*-tum).
Composite Family (*Compositae*).
These tender annuals, native to tropical America, range in size from 6 in. to 2 ft. The small blue flowers (occasionally pink or white) are each only $^{1}/_{2}$ in. across, but they are clustered in attractive, fluffy heads and bloom all summer and fall until frost. Much hybridization of these plants has produced many dwarf and compact varieties, as well as a wider color

Ageratum houstonianum 'Adriatic'
FLOSS FLOWER

Agrostemma githago
CORN COCKLE

range. The dwarf varieties are excellent for edgings. For early bloom in the garden, start seeds indoors in March and plant out in ordinary garden soil in either full sun or partial shade. These versatile small plants also grow well as pot specimens in the home or cool greenhouse. For use indoors, either dig up plants in the fall (they should be cut back first) or sow seeds in September, using a seed-starting soil mix. If you want to preserve an attractive color, take stem cuttings, which root easily. (Young wood is ideal when the stem snaps cleanly when bent.) Propagate by cuttings or seeds.

★**A. houstonianum** (hoost-oh-nee-*ay*-num).
FLOSS FLOWER.
Clusters of feathery florets in blue, pink, lavender or white form the flower heads of this Mexican native. Bloom period extends through summer and fall to frost. Leaves are opposite and ovate to triangular in shape, with rounded teeth around the margin. Heights range from 4 to 12 in. and the growth habit is in mounds. This plant is very susceptible to frost, so start seed indoors or in a cold frame and move outside after all danger of frost has passed. Plant in full sun in well-drained, rich, moist soil. Keep the soil moist, for if it is allowed to dry out, the plant will grow and flower poorly. As with most annuals, "deadheading," or cutting off dead flowers, encourages new flowers to form.

The plant makes an attractive edging or filler in an annual or perennial border or can be used to edge shrub beds. The texture of this flower combines well with many other annuals. Some good cultivars are the early-blooming 'Adriatic', 8 in. tall with blue flowers; 'Blue Blazer', 12 to 14 in. tall with blue flowers; 'Blue Danube', 6 in. tall with blue flowers; 'Hawaii Blue', 8 to 12 in. tall with blue flowers; 'Hawaii Royal', 6 in. tall with deep lavender-blue flowers; and 'Hawaii White', 6 in. tall with white flowers.

Agrostemma (ag-row-*stem*-a).
CORN COCKLE.
Pink Family (*Caryophyllaceae*).
An annual (biennial in the South) from Europe, now naturalized in the eastern U.S. This has small, linear leaves sparsely produced along 3-ft.-high, occasionally branched stems. Stems and leaves are densely matted with short, silver-white down. Five-petaled blossoms, 1 to 2 in. across, are brilliant fuchsia with a few tiny black dots radiating in each petal from the center of the flower. This blooms all summer and deserves a spot in the sunny border. Propagate by seed sown in place, in late fall or early spring.

A. githago (gith-*ah*-go).
This is the only species in cultivation. Sow seed in place where plants are to bloom in April or May. Thin plants to 8 in. About 3 ft. tall and blooms May, June and July. The pod contains poisonous purple-black seeds. A good selection is 'Milas', with plum-pink blossoms that fade to white centers.

Alcea (al-*see*-uh).
HOLLYHOCK.
Mallow Family (*Malvaceae*).
Native to Europe and Asia. Favorites in old gardens, equally effective in new, hollyhocks give architectural dignity to the simplest planting, with their height, 3 to 8 ft., and the size of their sturdy spikes of bloom, $1/3$ to $1/2$ overall plant height. White, yellow and red flowers in every shade and blend may be single or double. Likes full sun and rich, well-drained garden soil, well turned to a spade's depth. In some areas, hollyhocks are much disfigured by rust on

Alcea

Alcea rosea
GARDEN HOLLYHOCK

Alternanthera ficoidea rosea-nana
COPPERLEAF

Alcea rosea 'Powderpuff Pink'
GARDEN HOLLYHOCK

Amaranthus caudatus
LOVE-LIES-BLEEDING

the leaves, but even with rust they are still satisfactory and hardy. (Rust can be minimized by plenty of spacing between plants, which improves air circulation.) Hollyhocks are effective at the back of borders, as a foundation planting and in clumps in the wild garden. Propagate by seeds or root division. Sow in place when soil is warm—May in most places. Zone 4.

★**A. rosea** (*roh*-zee-uh).
GARDEN HOLLYHOCK.
This biennial, 5 to 8 ft. tall, is a stately plant, with flowers in white, many shades of pink to garnet and pale to dark yellow. The leaves are basically round with slight lobes. Some varieties have frilled or double flowers, many with white centers. All are handsome. Though strictly biennials, the plants self-sow and may be treated as perennials, although they will not come true to their parents. Sow seeds in where plants are to grow and thin to 12 in. apart, in full sun and an average, moist soil. 'Powderpuff Mixed' provides a wide range of colors with double flowers. 'Majorette' produces semidouble and laced flowers on 3-ft. stems. 'Summer Carnival', with double blooms, will flower as an annual if sown sufficiently early—January—indoors, to be planted out later.

Alternanthera (all-ter-*nan*-ther-ah).
COPPERLEAF.
Amaranth Family (*Amaranthaceae*).
A genus with nearly 200 species native to the tropics and subtropics. Mostly tender herbaceous perennials. The flowers lack any special ornamental appeal; the plants are grown for foliage. There are numerous color variations which make dramatic plantings in the garden. Quickly and easily propagated by cuttings.

A. ficoidea (fee-coy-*dee*-uh).
A bushy species with long, pointed leaves often splashed with color. Variants include *A. ficoidea bettzickiana* (bett-zeek-*ee*-an-uh), which has olive-green to red leaves; *A. ficoidea rosea-nana* (roh-*zee*-uh *nay*-nuh), with rosy-pink leaves; *A. ficoidea amoena* (ah-moe-*ee*-nuh), which has leaves splashed and veined with red; *A. ficoidea aurea-nana* (or-*ray*-uh *nay*-nuh), with yellow leaves; *A. ficoidea brilliantissima* (brih-lee-an-tee-see-muh), which bears leaves of brilliant red. One of the most attractive is *A. ficoidea versicolor* (verse-*see*-cuh-lor), whose leaves of dark green or red have veins of purplish-pink and are edged with pink and white.

Amaranthus (am-ar-*ranth*-us).
AMARANTH.
Amaranth Family (*Amaranthaceae*).
A large genus of coarse, weedy annuals native to many parts of the world. Pigweed is a member of this family. There are a few species, however, that deserve a place in the garden. Alternate leaves, sometimes riotously colored in cultivated forms. Showy clusters of small flowers bloom in summer. Outdoors, full sun and a relatively poor but cultivated soil are needed to maintain the variegated colors of the leaves.

A. caudatus (kaw-*day*-tus).
LOVE-LIES-BLEEDING.
TASSEL FLOWER.
Grows 3 to 5 ft. high, with white, pink or red flowers and colored leaves. Transplants easily when small. A showy plant for the border. The long, slender, drooping spikes of bloom are excellent for cutting, to use fresh or dried. *A. caudatus* 'Love Lies Bleeding' bears pendant spikes of bright red; in *A. caudatus* 'Viridis' they are of rich green. *A. caudatus* 'Green Thumb'

bears erect spikes of bright green; *A. caudatus* 'Pigmy Torch' has upright maroon-colored spikes.

A. hybridus (*high*-brih-dus).
PRINCE'S-FEATHER.
This is a common weed of the tropics, but it is often grown elsewhere as an annual in the attractive variety *erythrostachys* (air-reth-roh-stack-is). This plant grows about 4 to 5 ft. high and bears upright spikes of crimson flowers.

A. tricolor (*trye*-kol-or).
JOSEPH'S-COAT.
A native of China and India, this is a dramatic foliage plant. The greenish leaves are spotted with patches of red, violet and yellow. Growing 1 to 4 ft. high, it is assertive but sometimes useful at the back of borders and in formal beds. Seedsmen offer cultivars of this under such names as 'Illumination', 'Joseph's Coat' and others.

Anagallis (ann-ah-*gal*-lis).
Primrose Family (*Primulaceae*).
Twenty-eight species of plants found worldwide, but most numerous in Africa and western Europe. They include annuals, biennials and herbaceous perennials. They are easy to grow in any ordinary garden soil and are useful for edging flower beds.

A. linifolia. See *A. monellii.*

A. monellii (moh-nell-*ee*-eye).
PIMPERNEL.
(Syn. *A. linifolia.*) A half-hardy perennial that is usually treated as an annual. Because it forms a low-growing ground cover, it is best used as an edging for beds. Sow seeds outdoors early in the spring, directly in the ground. It starts

blooming in early summer and continues until frost. Blue flowers are star-shaped and borne in great profusion. Good selections include 'Gentian Blue', which grows 6 to 9 in. tall and spreads to 20 in. and 'Pacific Blue', with bluish-purple petals surrounding an orange-red center.

Anchusa (an-*koo*-sa).
BUGLOSS.
ALKANET.
Borage Family (*Boraginaceae*).
A genus of approximately fifty species, widely distributed in Europe, western Asia, northern Africa and South Africa. Some are annuals, some biennials and some perennials. Sow seeds in early spring directly in the ground, then thin plants to 9 in. apart. Alternatively, sow indoors but transplant individually into peat pots before the taproot forms, then transplant into the garden, pot and all.

A. capensis (cuh-*pen*-sis).
A biennial often grown as an annual. Plants grow from 9 to 20 in. tall, and have narrow, hairy leaves to 3 in. in length. Flowers of blue, pink or white are ¼ in. in diameter, borne in profusion. In mild winter areas, it is often grown as a biennial; seed in the summer for bloom the following spring. For use as an annual, start early indoors and plant out as soon as soil dries for bloom before hot weather. Best adapted for cool seasons or cool climates, it does not stand hot, humid summers well. 'Blue Angel' grows to 9 in. and bears ultramarine-blue flowers. 'Blue Bird' is taller, up to 18 in., with indigo-blue flowers. 'Dawn', growing to 20 in., is a mix of blue, pink and white flowers.

Anagallis monellii 'Pacific Blue'
PIMPERNEL

Angelica archangelica
HOLY GHOST

Angelica (an-*jell*-ik-uh).

Carrot Family (*Umbelliferae*).

Tall, handsome, perennial or biennial herbs with large, decorative, light green leaves and large clusters (umbels) of small white or greenish flowers on hollow stems. Both seeds and stems are used for flavoring, the stems often candied for decorating pastry. Propagate by seeds sown when fresh, sometimes by division.

A. archangelica (ark-an-*jell*-ik-uh).
HOLY GHOST.

A native of Europe and Asia, this species is a sturdy biennial, 4 to 6 ft. high, with large, divided leaves at the base of the plant. This plant has stalks, or ribbed stems, that are similar in appearance to celery; it also has a similar fragrance. It creates a bold effect in the back of borders or in the herb garden, where it is most often grown. Moist, well-drained soil, light shade. The large heads of small flowers bloom in July. Perennial if flowers are removed before they go to seed. Zone 5.

Antirrhinum (an-tihr-*rye*-num).

SNAPDRAGON.

Figwort Family (*Scrophulariaceae*).

Tender perennials and annuals, chiefly from southern Europe, usually grown as annuals in the U.S. Leaves are long and narrow, to 2 in. Magnificent range of flower colors, white through yellow and pink to darkest red, with innumerable color combinations. Plants vary in height from 6 in. to 3 ft. or more. Heat-resistant strains and rust-proof varieties, which were developed after a disastrous spread of rust, have brought a new popularity in recent years. Generally, flats purchased from nurseries or professional greenhouses are the surest way of securing healthy plants.

Antirrhinum

Antirrhinum majus 'Dwarf Bedding Mixed'
Snapdragon

Snapdragons are excellent for the cutting garden, for the mixed border and for greenhouses, especially when grown in greenhouse beds or benches rather than pots. The small varieties are much used for display beds and for border edging. The tallest or giant varieties may need staking. Fair in the house for winter flowering, if garden plants are dug up, potted and cut back.

Sow seeds indoors in January for blooms in May. The seedlings are very susceptible to damping-off, so they must be transplanted as soon as possible into individual cells or pots. Pinch back early for bushiness. Set them outdoors when weather is warm, in rich, well-dug soil that has plenty of humus and added lime. In mild climates, snapdragons may live over winter. Modern cultivars include tetraploids, open-faced forms, F1 and F2 hybrids and improved selections of older strains. Keep flowers cut

Antirrhinum majus 'Floral Carpet Mixed'
Snapdragon

back to encourage growth and blooming of side shoots.

A. majus (*may*-jus).

This perennial species from the Mediterranean region is the precursor of all the fine hybrids developed for outdoor and greenhouse culture: Dwarf—6 to 9 in.; the Dwarf Bedding, Floral Carpet and Royal Carpet series are good examples and 'Little Darling', a rust-resistant cultivar flowers very early; Intermediates—12 to 24 in., Sonnet series; Giants—2 to 4 ft., include the Rocket and open-faced Madam Butterfly series. Recently developed tetraploid varieties are available in a brilliant range of colors.

Arctotis (ark-*toh*-tiss).

Composite Family (*Compositae*).

Decorative, tender annuals from South Africa, with velvety-gray, alternate leaves and daisylike flowers in beautiful tones of blue, orange and yellow. They are exceptionally fine for cut flowers, lasting a week, but since they close at night, use them only for daytime arrangements. They grow best in full sun and well-drained garden loam, well turned to a spade's depth. Propagate by seeds.

A. breviscapa (breh-vih-*scape*-uh).

AFRICAN DAISY.

A stemless annual whose flowers are 2 in. across on hairy scapes that are shorter than the leaves. Petals are orange–yellow above and copper–colored underneath, with a dark brown bee. The variety *aurantiaca* has yellow–orange petals surrounding a purple disk.

A. grandis. See *A. stoechadifolia*.

Antirrhinum majus 'Little Darling'
SNAPDRAGON

Antirrhinum majus 'Royal Carpet'
SNAPDRAGON

Arctotis

A. stoechadifolia (steek-ad-if-*foh*-lee-uh). African Daisy.

Often listed in catalogs as *A. grandis*. A bushy plant, 2 to 3 ft., with large, toothed leaves and marguerite-like blossoms, white with lavender-blue reverse, 2 1/2 to 3 in. across, blooming from July to frost. Sow seeds indoors in March for early bloom. Sow seeds outdoors about 1/4 in. deep in May or as soon as the ground is warm. The blooming season will be prolonged if fading blossoms are kept picked off. Useful in mixed borders and in the cutting garden. Often self-sows. Also good for cool-greenhouse culture. The variety *grandis* is larger and more worthwhile for cultivating under glass as a pot plant. Other seldom-encountered but desirable species available from foreign seed specialists are *A. acaulis,* carmine-orange to buff; and *A. laevis,* brownish-orange suffused red.

Argemone (are-*je*-mo-ne).
Prickly Poppy.
Poppy Family (*Papaveraceae*).
Ten species of plants from the New World, of which all but one are annual or biennial. The leaves are prickly, an easy way to distinguish them from poppies (*Papaver*).

A. grandiflora (grand-i-*flor*-a).
This annual blooms from early to late summer with white silky flowers up to 4 in. in diameter. Leaves are green with white veins and are prickly.

Argyranthemum frutescens.
See *Chrysanthemum frutescens.*

Asparagus (uh-*spare*-uh-gus).
Lily Family (*Liliaceae*).
A genus of about 300 species, including the edible vegetable. There are many ornamental varieties, many grown primarily indoors, but some of these are often used outdoors seasonally, especially as filler plants combined with flowering plants in containers. They are easily grown from freshly harvested seed in any good soil mix. Water thoroughly when the soil surface dries; large, fleshy roots absorb large quantities of water and serve as a buffer between waterings.

A. densiflorus (den-si-*flor*-us).
The species is not a significant garden plant, but the cultivar 'Sprengeri', commonly called emerald fern or trailing asparagus, is the most widely used ornamental asparagus. It is a rambling evergreen with many short branches up to 2 ft. long. *A. densiflorus* 'Myers' is a variant with erect foxtail-like branches.

Begonia (beg-*goh*-nee-uh).
Begonia Family (*Begoniaceae*).
An extremely large and diverse genus of herbaceous (usually) perennials from tropical America, though several Asiatic species of note are also grown. Some species produce tuberlike corms, others remain fibrous-rooted. Some develop a heavy rhizome, others send up tough, vertical canes that become almost woody with age. Though most commercial strains of begonias are grown for their flowers, numerous species and breeder-produced (or hybridizer-produced) strains develop showy, colorful leaves, often with a metallic sheen.

The Begonia family is rich in beauty for every gardener. There are thousands of different kinds from which to choose. There are miniatures no bigger than a teacup, and towering bushes or treelike plants, which are used primarily in greenhouses or conservatories. Then there are intermediate sizes for pots, boxes, tubs and baskets of every size and shape. Begonias

Arctotis breviscapa var. *aurantiaca*
AFRICAN DAISY

Begonia semperflorens 'Prelude Rose'
WAX BEGONIA

Asparagus densiflorus 'Myers'
ORNAMENTAL ASPARAGUS

Begonia semperflorens 'Varsity White'
WAX BEGONIA

Begonia

Bellis perennis
ENGLISH DAISY

Borago officinalis
COMMON BORAGE

can be had in flower all year in every color except blue. Except for the large, tall-growing types, begonias are outstanding plants for a fluorescent-lighted garden.

The begonias suggested here have been selected on the basis of a long flowering season and all-around good performance outdoors.

As a matter of horticultural convenience, not at all based on natural relationships, begonias can be divided into three categories: tuberous-rooted, fibrous-rooted and kinds with notably ornamental foliage. Tuberous–rooted begonias (*Begonia × tuberhybrida*), while often treated as annuals, are found in the *Hearst Garden Guides* volume *Bulbs.*

★**B.** 'Richmondensis'.
A seedling from the progeny of an interspecific cross between *B. semperflorens* and *B. fuchsioides* is this lovely mounding plant with glossy, serrated, triangular-shaped leaves. It blooms profusely all

summer long with buds of cherry-red, opening to a clear pink. Superb as a hanging basket plant in full sun in cooler climates, it enjoys partial shade elsewhere. Propagate by cuttings.

B. semperflorens (sem-per-*floh*-renz).
FIBROUS-ROOTED BEGONIAS.
WAX BEGONIAS.
The common wax begonias have fine, brown, fibrous root systems, which send up cupped, roundish leaves set on crisp, fleshy stems with an endless number of flowers. In fact, *semperflorens* means ever-blooming. Some varieties have very dark green, almost chocolate colored foliage, which contrasts dramatically with the blossoms. Plants form shapely mounds up to 12 in. tall and 12 in. wide by summer's end, and bloom continuously until cut down by frost. Indoors, they will bloom continuously but less vigorously unless in very bright light. Best growth and bloom comes

from seedlings; otherwise take cuttings of stems with branches. Choose from named cultivars with single, semidouble or fully double flowers. Some wax begonias are grouped together and called "calla-lily" because leaves may be almost or completely white, cupped and resembling a calla. Suggested semperflorens cultivars include 'Pink Avalanche' and 'White Avalanche', both with an open habit and large blossoms, ideal for containers. 'Pink Charm' is another good cultivar; good series are Prelude, Varsity, and Olympia. The Cocktail series includes 'Rum', 'Whiskey', 'Gin', 'Vodka' and 'Brandy'; they are distinguished by dark leaves that contrast with the flowers.

Sunlight and biweekly feedings of fertilizer keep wax begonias in bloom indoors. Pot in a mixture of equal parts soil, sand and peat moss. Allow this to approach dryness between waterings. When plants begin to be too large and have long, weak branches, use a sharp knife to cut out all old branches right at the soil line. Leave only healthy new shoots showing around the base of the plant. They will soon form a well-rounded specimen covered with bloom.

Start seeds in milled sphagnum or any lean, pasteurized germinating medium. Transplant seedlings into the soil mixture given above for either mature *B. semperflorens* plants or for the tuberous-rooted kinds. Outdoors, wax begonias perform well in light conditions from partial shade to full sun if planted in deep, rich soil and never allowed to suffer from drought. These, too, are superior pot plants for winter use. They tolerate cool room temperatures; water sufficiently to keep moist, and give bright light.

Bellis (*bell*-is).
Composite Family (*Compositae*).
Annuals and perennials native to Europe and the Mediterranean region. The most familiar species is the English daisy—a perennial, usually grown as a biennial, with decorative foliage and perky, colorful flowers—which is generally considered to be the true daisy of tradition. Fine for edgings and for massing in beds with poet's narcissus or tulips. Also pretty in the rock garden. Easy propagation by seeds sown in late summer for the species and by division in the fall for the improved varieties. Full sun, ample water and rich soil are required for good results, but extreme summer heat must be avoided or the plant usually dies.

B. perennis (per-*ren*-niss).
English Daisy.
A native wild flower of England, it blooms abundantly in spring and often repeats, though not so heavily, in fall. Decorative, crisp, large, basal leaves, above which rise pink or white, or white-, red-, or pink-edged, double, daisylike blooms, $1^1/2$ in. across, on sturdy stems 4 to 5 in. tall. 'Goliath' produces flowers up to 6 in. in diameter. In most of the U.S. it is best treated as a biennial and is well worth the trouble of bringing along each year. Zone 6.

Borago (boh-*ray*-go).
Borage.
Borage Family (*Boraginaceae*).
Rough-stemmed, coarse herbs of the Mediterranean region. Grayish-green, bristly foliage and star-shaped blue flowers. Very attractive to honeybees. Useful in flower and herb gardens. Also effective in hilly ground or in sloping rock gardens. Easily grown in ordinary garden soil and full sun. Propagate by seeds sown in spring.

B. officinalis (off-iss-in-*nay*-liss).
Common Borage.
A universal favorite since the time of the ancient Greeks, who used the young leaves in

Borago

cooling drinks for their medicinal and supposedly soothing qualities. It attracts bees to the garden. A hardy annual to 3 ft. tall, with oblong woolly leaves and clusters of 3/4-in. blue flowers, sometimes purple or white, blooming from midsummer to frost. The small, tender leaves have a cucumber-like flavor and are delicious in salads, iced drinks and for pickling. Pick them before the bloom begins. The flowers last well when cut. In late summer, mature plants cut back to a few inches from the ground will send up fresh new growth for fall bloom. The plants self-sow readily and are propagated from seed. They do not transplant.

Brachycome (brak-*kik*-om-ee).

Composite Family (*Compositae*).

A genus of Australian herbs containing one popular, tender annual with feathery, alternate leaves. This easily grown plant, flowering six weeks after planting, has small, daisylike blossoms. Blooms all summer.

B. iberidifolia (eye-ber-*id*-if-foh-lee-uh).

SWAN RIVER DAISY.

An easily grown annual, 8 to 18 in. high. Seeds can be sown indoors or out. The plant is very free-flowering, with individual flowers 1 in. across. The blue, white or rose blossoms, with yellow centers, are abundant enough to fill in bare spaces in the garden, and the plant makes a good addition to container plantings. Sow seeds 1/4 in. deep in garden loam, in full sun. It is an excellent plant for massing in borders and for edging. It is also widely available as a started plant. The Splendor series is available in white, blue (actually a lavender-blue) and purple, while pink and rose colors will be found in seed mixtures.

Brassica (*brass*-ik-uh).

Mustard Family (*Cruciferae*).

A large genus of annuals, biennials and perennials containing spices, the mustards and many vegetables, as well as several weeds. They are erect, branching plants with toothed leaves and yellow or yellowish-white flowers in spring. Most of the perennials are hardy as far north as Zone 4. These plants are subject to an assortment of wormy pests, and it is good garden practice to avoid planting a brassica species where another plant of the same genus was grown the previous year.

B. oleracea (oh-lair-*ay*-see-ay).

Acephala Group (a-seh-*fay*-lah).

CABBAGE.

ORNAMENTAL CABBAGE.

A true biennial, ornamental cabbage is usually grown as an annual and has been gaining popularity in recent years. *Acephala* means headless, and these plants do resemble cabbages that have not formed a head. The leaves are variable with each cultivar but generally they are thick and glaucous, held in loose rosettes and can be colored toward the center (again depending on cultivar) in shades of white, cream, pink and red to purple. The edges of the leaves can be smooth, curled or fringed. Sizes range from 10 to 15 in. tall and 15 to 24 in. wide. These are best grown in the fall when the cool weather brings the color to its peak and keeps the warm weather insect pests away. In warmer weather, the plant produces its unattractive flower stalk, which ruins the show. 'Dynasty', with colored midrib and veins and ruffled leaves, is the most popular ornamental cabbage.

Brachycome iberidifolia
SWAN RIVER DAISY

Brassica oleracea Acephala Group
ORNAMENTAL CABBAGE

Capitata Group (cap-i-*tot*-ah).
KALE.
ORNAMENTAL KALE.
FLOWERING KALE.
Like ornamental cabbage, ornamental kale is usually grown as an annual and has been enjoying incresing popularity. Also, like ornamental cabbage, ornamental kale can be used in the spring garden; but it is more often seen in the fall, when its rich colors complement chrysanthemum and aster displays. To time it right, start the seed inside at 70°F in February through March for spring display or June through July for fall use. In six to eight weeks the plants will be ready to set out where they are to be grown. Plant in full sun in moist, well-drained soil and give plenty of water. If planted in the fall, the plants will survive until a heavy frost or good freeze occurs. They have remained an appealing garden accent as late as Christmas in many parts of the country.

The color, form and intriguing texture lend a creative show when the plant is used in a bedding planting or container. Some good cultivars of ornamental kale are: 'Nagoya', 12 in. tall with curled and fringed leaves; 'Peacock', 15 in. tall with deeply cut and fringed leaves; and 'Chidori', coloring up better under warmer temperatures with fringed leaves and ruffled edges.

★★**Browallia** (broh-*wall*-lee-uh).
Nightshade Family (*Solanaceae*).
Bushy, branched annuals, 1 to 2 ft. high, from tropical America. The small lavender-blue tubular flowers bloom abundantly all summer. It is an effective plant in borders, the cutting garden, window boxes, hanging baskets, indoors as a pot plant and in the cool greenhouse. For early bloom outdoors, start seeds indoors in February and plant outside when ground has warmed. For

Browallia

Browallia speciosa 'Marine Bells'

Calceolaria herbeohybrida
SLIPPERWORT

bushy plants, pinch them back when they are about 5 in. tall. They like full sun indoors, dappled sun outside and garden soil enriched with humus and well dug to a spade's depth. For winter bloom in the greenhouse, sow seeds in mid-summer and pot seedlings in a standard soil mix.

★**B. speciosa** (spee-see-*oh*-suh).
This species grows 2 ft. tall and is fine for summer flowering in the garden or for the greenhouse. The flowers are blue or white. With plenty of light it is an especially good houseplant in the winter. Dig sturdy specimens in fall, well ahead of frost, and cut them back. The cultivar 'Major' is an excellent plant also for use in hanging baskets, either in the house or on a porch or terrace in summer. 'Blue Troll' is a very compact variety, growing up to l0 in. The Bell series is larger (up to l5 in.), with a more open habit. 'Silver Bells' is white; 'Marine Bells' is deep

indigo blue; and 'Blue Bells' is a mid-blue. A mixture named 'Jingle Bells' contains these colors plus intermediate shades of blue and lavender.

Bupleurum (bu-*ploor*-um).

Carrot Family (*Umbelliferae*).

Nearly 150 species of shrubs, herbaceous perennials and annuals are all from the Old World, chiefly around the Mediterranean. An unusual feature is that all leaves have parallel veins. They are useful at seaside sites growing well in poor soil and exposed sites in full sun. They bloom from midsummer to fall. Sow seed where plants are to grow and thin seedlings to 8 in. apart.

B. rotundifolium (roh-tun-dee-*foh*-lee-um).

THOROUGH WAX.

THROW WAX.

The upper leaves surround the stem, which appears to grow through them. The leaves are bright green, with individual yellow flowers arranged above the green calyxes like a euphorbia. It will grow well in full sun or light shade. The flowers last well after cutting. 'Green Gold' is one selection. No special care is required except occasional light pruning to keep it shapely. Propagate by seed or from cuttings.

Calceolaria (kal-see-oh-*lay*-ree-uh).

POCKETBOOK PLANT.

SLIPPERWORT.

Snapdragon Family (*Scrophulariaceae*).

There are both herbaceous and shrubby plants in this group of South American natives, most of them coming from the area that extends from Mexico to Chile. They are prized for their brilliant pouchlike blossoms and are grown in greenhouses and as annuals. Colors range from yellow through orange to red, brown and purple, often spotted.

The annuals grow easily from seed sown in the greenhouse in February and set out in the garden in late May. Seed is very fine and should be sown on top of finely milled sphagnum moss or seed-starting mix. Water with great care to avoid disturbing the fine seed, but do not allow to dry out until the seeds have germinated. In the greenhouse, these plants are often infested with red-spider mites and whiteflies.

C. herbeohybrida (herb-e-o-*high*-brih-duh).

This herbaceous plant is used as an annual and is derived from a number of species. It has flowers up to 1 in. long in pure lemon-yellow carried in bright clusters. It blooms throughout the summer and does particularly well in cool summer locations. For outdoor plants, sow seed in February. Two selections are 'Sunshine' and 'Lemon Drops'. A selection with flowers of many colors is 'Little Sweeties Mixed'.

Calendula (kal-*lend*-yew-luh).

Composite Family (*Compositae*).

These are the "marigolds" of Shakespeare and the ancient herbals, now called pot marigold to distinguish from the later-introduced *Tagetes*. Annuals and perennials native to the Mediterranean region. The most popular species, described below, is a favorite garden annual, long grown as an herb for its petals, used to flavor and color puddings and cakes. It is excellent in the border for constant bloom all summer where the weather is cool and in the herb garden for a brilliant spot of color. On the West Coast and along the Gulf Coast it flowers in winter and early spring. It is hardy enough to withstand light frosts and grows readily from seeds planted early in spring in ordinary garden soil, but does poorly where summers are hot. It needs full sun. It makes an attractive plant for a cool greenhouse (45° to 55°F). Grow in a commercial potting

Calendula

mix, kept evenly moist. Use a fertilizer low in nitrogen every two or three weeks.

★**C. officinalis** (off-iss-in-*nay*-liss).

POT MARIGOLD.

Grows 1 to 2 ft. high, with alternate, blue-green leaves, 3 in. long, on sturdy stalks. Dark orange flowers up to 4 in. Sow seeds in July for October to January bloom; sow in October for bloom in February through the summer; sow in January for bloom starting in May. There are named hybrids in many shades, from palest yellow to darkest orange. Two favorite series are Bon Bon and Fiesta Gitana, and Calendula 'Touch of Red' is recommended for its combination of yellow petals surrounding a dark red bee. Blossoms are long-lasting when cut. *Calendula officinalis* yields petals that in dried form were once used as a potherb to flavor puddings, cakes, salads and meat dishes. Bread pudding can be flavored with two tablespoons of fresh-plucked petals, and one tablespoonful makes a nice addition to cream cheese dips.

Callistephus (kal-*liss*-tef-us).

CHINA ASTER.

Composite Family (*Compositae*).

The only species, which is not a true aster (*Aster*), is a popular annual from Asia, in a great range of colors, styles and sizes. The varying shades of the flowers, from white through pink and red to violet-blue and purple, combined with its long blooming season and lasting qualities when cut, make it a universal favorite. For early bloom, start seeds indoors at the beginning of March and plant out as soon as possible. Outdoors, when the ground has warmed, sow seeds in well-drained garden loam dug to a spade's depth and enriched with humus and fertilizer as well as lime. Full sun is necessary. Very appealing in borders of annuals, to fill in bare

spots in perennial borders and in the cutting garden. To prevent disease build-up, avoid planting in successive years in the same soil. Keep the ground clean of weeds and the plants well watered and sprayed against pests.

★**C. chinensis** (chin-*nen*-siss).

Grows 1 to 2^1/$_2$ ft. tall, with alternate leaves. The blossoms vary from showy, flat-rayed types with golden-yellow centers to every form of double, stiff or fluffy, with flat or quilled petals (with tubular rays), and in almost all shades. There is also much variety in the growing habit, from upright through branching and spreading forms. Many named varieties are offered in catalogs. Often blooms from summer to frost, but is a standout among annuals for its late-summer flowers. The more they are cut, the more they will bloom. 'Perfection Mixed' plants grow to 2 ft. with 4 in. fully double

Calendula officinalis 'Touch of Red'
POT MARIGOLD

Calendula officinalis 'Bon Bon Mixed'
POT MARIGOLD

Callistephus chinensis
CHINA ASTER

flowers, while the different colored flowers of 'Super Giants Mixture' grow to 2¹/2 ft. with 5-in. double spidery flowers.

★★Campanula (kam-*pan*-yew-luh).

BELLFLOWER.

Bellflower Family (*Campanulaceae*).

A large genus of annuals, biennials and perennials, native mostly to Europe and Asia, and all but indispensable to gardeners everywhere.

While the bellflowers are an enormously varied group, differing even more in plant size and growth characteristics than in color, the quality of airy and dancing grace is perhaps the most prized of their garden attributes. The flowers of almost all species seem to catch and spill the sunlight, and the leaves of many, particularly the lower-growing species, have a casual but tidy look. To be sure, there is a great difference in every aspect between, say, *C. isophylla*

on the one hand, and the statuesque *C. pyramidalis* on the other. But in all there is a family resemblance—especially in the clarity of the flower colors. (One other characteristic, the graceful, bell-shaped flower, occurs in all the species.) Few flowers can be so well represented in gardens of every kind.

Bellflowers have many uses, but are especially prized in borders and rock gardens, depending on the species. Almost all bellflowers are blue or white, but there are a few pinks in an enormous range of subtle shadings. Well-drained garden soil, full sun, or, with some species, filtered shade and adequate moisture are needed. It may be necessary to add lime to the soil. Propagate by seeds or division.

C. isophylla (eye-saw-*fill*-a).

A species used primarily for containers and hanging baskets, since it forms a trailing mound

Campanula isophylla
BELLFLOWER

Campanula medium
CANTERBURY BELLS

completely covered with a profusion of bell-shaped flowers from midsummer until frost. Formerly grown only from cuttings; seed is now available for 'Stella Blue' and 'Stella White'. Sow seed in January for bloom from June on. (It is sensitive to day length and develops buds only when days are longer than nights.)

★**C. medium** (*mee*-dee-um).
CANTERBURY BELLS.
A biennial, 2 to 4 ft. tall, with white, pink or blue blossoms. It makes a fine show in late May and June when planted in masses in rich soil. Propagate by seeds sown in spring for bloom the following year. The cultivated variety 'Medium Double Mixed' is double-blossomed and cup-and-saucer-shaped, with flowers of pink, white and blue. 'Canterbury Musical Bells Mixed' is a selection of singles. Zones 4 to 5.

Capsicum (*kap*-sik-um).
RED PEPPER.
Nightshade Family (*Solanaceae*).
Woody plants of tropical America, grown in the North as tender, bushy annuals, primarily for their edible fruit. If seed is planted early, fruit will be produced in a single season. All the common garden peppers, hot or mild to the taste, are derived from *C. annuum.* Powdered black or white pepper comes from *Piper nigrum,* a tropical vine. Treat as an annual north of Zone 10.

C. annuum (*an*-you-um).
ORNAMENTAL PEPPER.
This ornamental is grown for its showy fruits, which appear in summer and last up to frost. The plants grow to be 10- to 20-in. mounds and when mature are covered with fruits that vary in color from white, yellow, orange, red and purple to black. The color range of the fruit represents different degrees of ripeness, and therefore, there are usually several different colors present on each plant at a given time. The leaves are dark green and form a rich backdrop to the fruit color. Plant the seed indoors six to eight weeks prior to the transplanting date but do not cover the seed with soil. The very tender seedlings should not be planted outside until all frost danger is over. Plant in full sun in rich, moist soil that is high in organic matter, and provide plenty of water. With enough moisture, this is one annual that can tolerate the hot summer sun and the stress that accompanies it.

Use as a bedding or border plant. They can be brought indoors or started indoors in containers, and the red-fruited varieties are attractive and unusual decorations at Christmas, especially when grouped with poinsettias. Some good cultivars are: 'Fiesta', 10-in. plants with 2-in. fruits that turn from cream to yellow to orange to red; 'Aurora', purple fruit; 'Candlelight', orange-red fruit; 'Fips', 7-in. conical red and yellow fruit; and 'Holiday Flame', yellow to fiery red. Other varieties of this species are the common garden or bell pepper and chili peppers.

Catharanthus (cath-ah-*ran*-thus).
MADAGASCAR PERIWINKLE.
ROSE PERIWINKLE.
VINCA.
Dogbane Family (*Apocynaceae*).
A genus of five species, all native to Madagascar. In addition to garden use, cancer chemotherapy agents are derived from plants in this genus. Because of their tropical origin, they all thrive in hot weather, languishing in the garden during protracted cool spells. They grow in full sun in ordinary garden soil, but it must be well drained to prevent root diseases.

Catharanthus

★**C. roseus** (*rose*-ee-us).

(Syn. *Vinca rosea*.) The only species grown as a garden ornamental in North America. The leaves are opposite, oblong, 1 to 2 in. long and a glossy green. It grows to a height of 3 to 18 in. tall. The flowers are 1 1/2 in. wide and cover the plant all season long, right up to frost. Flower colors may be pink, white or mauve; new colors are introduced every year. The hottest sun on the hottest summer day does not adversely affect this plant. Plant it in full sun to partial shade in moist, well-drained soil. Use this flower in mass plantings, in the annual border or in containers. Leaf texture, profuse flowering and plant form make this a traditional favorite not to be over-looked. Some good cultivars can be found among: the Carpet series, 3- to 4-in.-tall plants that creep across the ground or trail from containers in pink, rose, red and white; the Little series, 10-in. compact plants with white, white with red eye, pink with rose eye and pink flowers; the cultivar 'Parasol', with its short white flowers and bright red center; and the Pretty series, 15- to 18-in.-tall plants with large white or pink flowers.

★★Celosia (sel-*oh*-see-uh).

Amaranth Family (*Amaranthaceae*).

Tender annuals from the tropics, grown principally for their flamboyant flower clusters, which take many forms. The showy blooms, in tones of red, yellow, green, purple and white, are often dried for winter decoration. Use in the cutting garden and in borders with shrubbery or other annuals. In cool sections of the country start seeds indoors in March; set out in May, when all danger of even light frost is past. Sow outdoors in warm regions. Light, rich soil, sun and plenty of moisture are needed. The blossoms dry readily and keep their color if hung upside down in a warm, dry area for a week.

★**C. argentea** (ar-*jen*-tee-uh).

COCKSCOMB

PLUMED CELOSIA

The species is known primarily for its attractive variety, *cristata* (kriss-*tay*-tuh), which is divided into two forms: *plumosa,* with brushlike plumes, and *cockscomb,* with fasciated blooms, which resemble brains. The *cockscomb* kinds are often grown as curiosities, while the *plumosa* types are considered quite beautiful and are widely grown. The plants grows 1 to 2 1/2 ft. high, with alternate leaves, 9 to 12 in. long, often variegated, and flowers of velvety texture in brilliant red, purple and yellow shades. The flowers bloom all summer until frost and are effective in arrangements, both fresh and dried. Dwarf forms are available of both the plumed and crested types, and in yellow or red shades. 'Jewel Box Mixed', with brightly colored, crested blooms in blood-red, gold, yellow, pink and salmon, 5 in. across, is the crested type most often grown, while 'Treasure Chest Mixed' offers a similar appeal. Favorite *plumosa* hybrids include 'Apricot Brandy', which is grown for its early, bright red plumes, which are compact (20 in. tall), making them prized for cutting; the Century series, 24 in. tall and 18 in. wide; and the Fairy Fountains series, which grow to 12 in.

★★Centaurea (sen-*taw*-ree-uh).

Composite Family (*Compositae*).

Annuals and perennials mostly from Europe and Asia. Easy to grow, pleasant in the garden, in a buttonhole or in a bouquet. Fluffy flower heads in shades of blue, pink, maroon, yellow and white bloom during the summer. Plants vary considerably in size, from 1 to 4 ft. Sow annuals where they are to stand, in well-drained light garden soil dug to a spade's depth. Thin the plants to stand 6 to 12 in. apart; they make a better show if left close enough to lend one

Catharanthus 'Parasol'

MADIGASCAR PERIWINKLE

Celosia aregentea var. *plumosa* 'Apricot Brandy'

PLUMED CELOSIA

Celosia argentea var. *cristata* 'Treasure Chest Mixed'

COCKSCOMB

Centaurea

Celosia argentea var. *plumosa* 'Century Mixed'
PLUMED CELOSIA

another some support. All grow best in full sun. Useful in borders, edgings and the cutting garden. Propagate by seeds or root division. These plants often self-sow in warm regions.

★**C. cineraria** (sin-er-*ray*-ree-uh).
DUSTY MILLER.
A perennial and one of the large group of gray-leaved plants that can add pleasant tonal variety to gardens. It thrives on coastal dunes and prefers a sandy, well-drained soil. Its large flower heads, rose-colored or lavender, are almost never produced. The plants are slow to reach full size (1 to 1^1/$_2$ ft.) and so should be started indoors in cooler sections. Watch out for damping-off of seedlings. Useful as a bedding or edging plant or in clumps to show the cool grayness of the leaves. Zone 5.

Centaurea cyanus
BACHELOR'S-BUTTON

Cheiranthus cheiri
WALLFLOWER

★**C. cyanus** (sye-*ay*-nus).

BACHELOR'S BUTTON.

CORNFLOWER.

Deservedly the favorite buttonhole flower of all. No cutting garden is complete without this fine annual. Grayish leaves and crisp double blooms, 1 in. across, of blue, purple, pink or white. Grows to 3 ft., dwarf forms to 12 in. Sow outdoors where plants are to stand; broadcast seed in the fall or as soon as the ground is warm in spring, or start indoors. The plant may also self-sow, which gives bloom the following summer. Favorite blues are 'Blue Diadem', 30 in., and 'Jubilee Gem', 15 in. 'Frosty Mixed' bears flowers with pastel or white contrasts at petal tips. 'Snowman' is white and 'Polka Dot' is a mix that includes white, blue and crimson.

C. maritima. See *Senecio cineraria*.

★**C. moschata** (mos-*kay*-tuh).

SWEET SULTAN.

A boon to sunny borders needing quick, bright color. This sturdy, branching annual, 1 to 2 ft. high, has fragrant flowers, to 2 in. across, in a wide range of colors, including yellow, blue, pink, purple and white. Feathery, bright green leaves give plants a fresh appearance. *C. × imperialis* (im-peer-ee-*ay*-liss) is purported to be a hybrid of this species and grows almost twice as tall with pink, purple or white flowers. Sow seeds indoors or outside when the ground is warm. 'The Bride' is a white selection. Other seed offers are mixtures of all colors.

Cheiranthus (kye-*ranth*-us).

Mustard Family (*Cruciferae*).

A small group of perennials from southern Europe and Asia. The most common species, the familiar wallflower, has long been a favorite in English gardens for its glowing shades of brown and yellow, and for its fragrance. A wide variety of separate colors are available in orange, red, deep red, yellow and orange. Grow as a biennial, sowing seeds in fall or spring and renewing each year for bloom the following season. For propagating especially fine colors, make cuttings of young wood in spring. These plants need full sun, a relatively cool climate, moist atmosphere and rich, well-dug soil. Very successful in the Pacific Northwest. In cold regions, carry plants over in a frost-free cold-frame. The diamondback moth caterpillar and potato flea beetle may attack *Cheiranthus*. Zones 6 to 7.

C. cheiri (*kye*-rye).

WALLFLOWER.

Grows 1 to 2 ft., with narrow, opposite leaves, 2 in. long, and small fragrant florets in attractive heads of bloom in every tone from yellow through orange to brown and intermediate mixed shades. Blooms from April through mid-June. This species is much hybridized. Unsurpassed for spring borders and rock gardens in cool, moist climates.

Chrysanthemum (kri-*san*-the-mum).

Daisy Family (*Compositae*).

A genus of 200 species of annuals, herbaceous perennials and subshrubs. They are mostly natives of the Old World. While chrysanthemums are most often recognized as the colorful perennials which bloom in the fall, or as florist's flowers, many other kinds are used in the garden. Botanists have just broken up this well-known genus, placing plants under a variety of new names. As it will be some time before these plants are generally recognized by their new classifications, however, they have been retained under their old names here.

Chrysanthemum

Chrysanthemum frutescens
MARGUERITE

Chrysanthemum parthenium
FEVERFEW

Chrysanthemum paludosum

C. frutescens (froo-*tess*-sens).

MARGUERITE.

PARIS DAISY.

(Renamed *Argyranthemum frutescens*.) A tender perennial that is often used for summer garden plantings. The daisylike flowers are available in both yellow and white cultivars, and there are both single and double varieties. Plants are shrubby with long, narrow, finely divided leaves and a profusion of flowers all summer.

C. multicaule (mul-ti-*call*-ee).

An annual species that grows from 6 to 12 in. tall, bearing an abundance of yellow daisylike flowers up to $2^{1}/_{2}$ in. in diameter. One recommended selection is 'Yellow Buttons'.

C. paludosum (pal-yew-*dose*-um).

A dwarf annual species with lax stems growing 6 in. tall during the summer. The plants are smothered in white flowers with yellow centers. One seed selection is 'White Buttons'.

C. parthenium (par-*theen*-ee-um).

FALSE CHAMOMILE.

FEVERFEW.

(Syn. *Matricaria capensis,* now renamed *Tanacetum parthenium*.) A delightful short-lived perennial, 2 to 3 ft. tall and as wide, native to Europe and Asia. This herbaceous plant is bushy and much used in perennial borders. White flowers with yellow centers, $^{3}/_{4}$ in. across, bloom from June through frost, especially if spent flowers are deadheaded. Excellent for cut flowers. Propagate by seeds or by cutting: sow seeds indoors ten to twelve weeks before planting outdoors, or take cuttings from stock plants at about the same time. The cultivar 'Alba' has single white flowers, and 'Aureum' has yellow foliage that turns green at flowering time. 'Snowball' has double white flowers. 'Santana' is lemon-yellow. Zone 4.

Clarkia (*klark*-ee-uh).

GODETIA.

Evening Primrose Family (*Onagraceae*).

Named for Captain Clark of the Lewis and Clark expedition, these plants have historical interest as well as much delicate charm. Hardy and showy annuals native to Oregon and California, they are easily grown, flowering in three months from seeds, with white, pink or rose-colored blooms. They thrive in full sun or partial shade, but will not survive in hot climates. Small seedlings should be transplanted into 3- or 4-in. pots before the taproot develops for easier transplanting into the garden. Alternatively, seeds can be sown, when ground is warm, where plants are to stand. They need well-dug, porous soil. Plant fairly thickly to make a good display. Useful in annual borders and the cutting garden.

C. amoena (uh-*mee*-nuh).

FAREWELL-TO-SPRING.

In the wild, an erect or lax-stemmed plant from 1 to 3 ft. tall, with satiny, broad-petaled flowers. The most popular varieties, garden plants more compact and upright than the species, were derived from this species. Flowers are rose, white, pink, lavender and salmon, often with contrasting markings or picotee edges. A popular selection is 'Grace'.

C. concinna (kahn-*sin*-nuh).

SATIN FLOWER.

Low growing, 8 in. to 1 ft. high, with large white, pink or red flowers, 3 to 5 in. across, blooming from June to October. When grown in substantial groups in the border, they make a bold show of color, the masses of bloom nearly hiding the foliage. Sow seeds outdoors in April. There are many improved varieties for garden use—some dwarf forms, others taller and some

Clarkia

doubles. 'Dutchess of Albany' has slightly frilled white flowers; 'Firelight' is crimson; and 'Sybil Sherwood' is in lavender-pink shades with a white edging.

C. elegans (*ell*-eg-anz).

This much-hybridized species, growing 2 to 3 ft. high, provides masses of color in the annual border. The handsome flower spires of white, rose or purple have individual florets, single or double, up to $2^1/2$ in. across. Seeds germinate readily, and the season of showy bloom will start about twelve weeks from planting. The flowers tend to diminish in hot summers. 'Royal Bouquet' is a selection with double flowers.

Cleome (klee-*oh*-mee).

Caper Family (*Caparaceae*).

The most commonly grown species is a tall, striking annual, commanding attention in any border. Native to the subtropics, it is easily grown and enjoys a long season of bloom. Full sun and light, slightly sandy soil. For early bloom, seeds can be started indoors, but this plant does better if planted outdoors when the ground has warmed up. Self-sows freely in the garden.

★**C. hasslerana** (hass-ler-*an*-ah).
CLEOME.
SPIDER PLANT.
(Syn. *C. spinosa*.) This is a good tall plant to give an annual bed some height or to fill in the back of the perennial border. It generally reaches 3 to 4 ft. tall and benefits from staking, but will stand fairly well on its own in most locations. The leaves are palmately compound with five to seven leaflets. The flowers are held on long pedicels and are spaced around the stems of the plant. The spiderlike openness and grace of the flowers and seed capsule make this an exotic textural addition. As the flowers die and fall off, the seed capsules remain at the end of the long pedicels, giving a "whiskery" look. Botanically, the flowers are characterized as indeterminate racemes, which means that flowers continue to appear as the stem grows taller and taller. It will continue to flower until frost. These are vigorous and free self-seeders— to avoid buying seeds or plants ever again, just transplant the errant seedlings! With this method of propagation, be aware that some plants will have to be culled out if the flowers are to be limited to all pink or all white. If plants are not culled out, the colors can be anything from white or pink to rose or violet.

Plant the seed outside directly into the flower bed, after all frost danger is past. Thin the seedlings to 3 to 4 ft. apart. Plant in full sun to part shade in rich, moist, well-drained soil, although it will do well in many soils. Give a thorough watering regularly. Use this plant as a background to the annual bed, in a mass planting or as a one-season shrub. The blooms last well as cut flowers. Some good cultivars are 'Cherry Queen', cherry-rose flowers; 'Helen Campbell', white flowers; 'Pink Queen', pink flowers; 'Rose Queen', rose-pink flowers.

C. spinosa. See *C. hasslerana*.

Cobaea (co-*bay*-a).

Phlox Family (*Polemoniaceae*).

A genus of American plants of the tropics and subtropics. There are perhaps eighteen species. The name honors a Jesuit naturalist, Father Bernardo Cobo.

Clarkia amoena 'Grace'
FAREWELL-TO-SPRING

Clarkia elegans

Cleome hasslerana
SPIDER PLANT

Cobaea

C. scandens (*scan*-dens).

CUP-AND-SAUCER VINE.

CATHEDRAL BELLS.

This species, from Mexico, is the only one commonly cultivated. Although a perennial in frost-free locations, it is most often grown as an annual in the U.S. This vine will attain 25 ft. if growing conditions are favorable. The calyx is the "saucer" and the greenish-purple to violet corolla is the "cup." Very prominent, they can measure up to 3 in. long and 2 in. wide. There is also a white flowering form. Plant seeds 1 in. deep outdoors when the ground and air temperatures are warm. Train to grow over a fence, trellis or other support.

★★Coleus (*koh*-lee-us).

FOLIAGE PLANT.

Mint Family (*Labiatae*).

A group of popular bedding or house plants from tropical Africa and Asia. They are widely grown for their brilliant foliage colors, which include lime, chartreuse and other greens, pink, yellow, purple and burgundy, in very interesting patterns depending on variety. Members of the mint family, they share the most prominent feature of that family, a square stem. The flowers are typical of the mint family, although coleus is not grown for its flowers and flower heads, which often detract from the plant's appearance. The small and inconspicuous, usually bluish flowers should be removed if they appear, to help produce a bushier plant. Pinch off flower buds to encourage branching, otherwise plants are apt to become leggy. Outdoors they are used as border plants and, like *Canna* and *Ageratum*, are often planted in formal beds in public gardens. They require rich garden soil and shade to full sun, except in hot, dry regions, where some shade must be provided or the plants will burn. *Coleus* are sometimes trained to standard (tree) forms. Indoors, use a general soil mixture. Mealybugs may be a pest when these plants are grown indoors.

Coleus can be grown from seeds, and there are many improved, surprisingly consistent strains and named varieties. They can also be propagated from cuttings and the colors and forms of the leaves can thus be exactly duplicated. Tip or stem cuttings, taken any time, root rapidly in sand or a vermiculite-perlite mixture, or in water. Old plants are subject to root gall, so fresh cuttings yearly are desirable.

C. blumei (*bloom*-ee-eye).

Grows 1 to 3 ft. high, with variously colored foliage—sometimes brilliantly handsome, sometimes garish, sometimes drab. The leaves, to 4 in. long, are either red, yellow, purple, white or green. It has small, inconsequential dark blue flowers. One of the best varieties is *verschaffeltii* (ver-shaf-*felt*-ee-eye), with very showy leaves. It is a rich crimson with green frilled edges. Zone 5 if treated as a tender plant to be set out when weather is sure; otherwise Zone 9.

★C. × hybridus (*high*-brih-dus).

COLEUS.

A very easy annual to grow, coleus prefers partial shade, and the bright colors of the leaves can add color to your shade garden. The plants grow from 9 to 48 in. in height and width. Leaves vary from somewhat heart-shaped to long, linear and deeply lobed and are colored in a variety of hues, depending on cultivar. Leaves are opposite and coarsely toothed and sometimes almost fringed on the leaf margins. The coloration can be in concentric zones or just in the leaf margin. The degree of coloration in any leaf can range from complete zones of a solitary color to speckling. The list of possible colors includes white, cream, yellow, chartreuse, green, bronze, purple, red, rose and many different combinations of all these colors. Propagation can be achieved rapidly from stem cuttings. They root very easily in any medium—from water to a soil mixture. Taking successive cuttings and rooting the plants will quickly establish a ready supply of bedding plants.

Coleus makes an effective mass planting or lends an interesting texture and color accent when used as part of a bed of shade annuals. They also do well in pots or tubs or as houseplants and make a popular choice as first plants for children, as they withstand abuse. Some good cultivars have been selected: the Dragon series, cultivars of vigorous, erect habit with leaves that have a fine, yellow-green leaf margin; the Fiji series, featuring fringed leaves; the Rainbow series, with striped and mottled leaves in many colors; the Saber series, a collection of dwarf plants with swordlike leaves; the Wizard series, with leaves of various colors and a distinctive cream or green leaf margin.

Consolida (con-*sah*-lih-dah).

LARKSPUR.

Buttercup Family (*Ranunculaceae*).

A large, handsome and popular genus of annuals, widely scattered from the Mediterranean region to central Asia. The common name derives from the noticeable spur on the florets, which usually occur in showy spikes of bloom. Colors vary from white through every shade of blue and purple and include some pinks and reds. They are easily grown in cool climates that have no extremes of heat or drought.

Larkspur is the name generally applied to the annual, *C. ambigua*, which was once known as *Delphinium ajacis*. Shorter than most perennial and biennial delphiniums, it will bloom early in the season and flower for many weeks if

Coleus × hybridus 'Red Wizard'
COLEUS

Coleus × hybridus 'Saber Mixed'
COLEUS

Consolida

Consolida ambigua
ROCKET LARKSPUR

Cosmos bipinnatus 'Sea Shells'

Coriandrum sativum
CORIANDER

planted the previous fall. Its compact stalks generally do not require staking. Larkspur used to be offered primarily in shades of white, pink and pale blue, but recent horticultural efforts have led to scores of named varieties and improved colors. One of the early improved larkspurs is 'Giant Imperial'.

Where winters are mild and there are extremes of heat or drought, the hardy perennial species of delphinium may not always succeed, but *C. ambigua* fills the delphinium role of backdrop to the shorter plants in the border. It is propagated by seed, and in warm climates may be sown in the fall and simply watered in. Transplant seedlings when very small. Porous, well-drained soil is essential, along with a good supply of soil sweeteners such as ground limestone, bone meal and superphosphate. Ample moisture and full sun are important. A location partially shaded some of the day will also suffice. In colder regions, sow seeds in early spring.

C. ambigua (am-*big*-you-ah).
ANNUAL DELPHINIUM.
ROCKET LARKSPUR.
(Syn. *Delphinium ajacis*.) This is an annual with good spiky form for the sunny garden or cut flower garden. It blooms all summer with spikes of rounded, spurred flowers in pastel shades of blue, pink, white, purple or mauve. The feathery foliage makes an interesting texture in the garden. There are tall varieties growing up to 4 ft. in height and short varieties growing to only 1 ft. Plant in full sun in rich, moist, fertile, well-drained soil. To start from seed, plant indoors six to eight weeks before setting out in early spring, or plant seeds directly in the garden bed, where they will stay, in early spring. Stake the taller varieties. For the best effect, plant in masses at the back of the annual border or in a mixed border of annuals and perennials. These plants rival delphiniums for beauty and form and are much easier to grow. They prefer cool soil, so cover the bed with several inches of mulch to keep the sun off the soil, and water regularly. There are scores of named varieties, including several tetraploides (so called because their chromosomes have been doubled). The Imperial series is 4 ft. tall with double flowers. The Giant Imperial series is also 4 ft. tall, but flower heads are larger than the Imperial series types. Recommended cultivars from this series include 'Blue Spire'; 'Brilliant Rose'; 'Dazzler', a scarlet-shaded cinnabar; 'Los Angeles', a bright salmon; and 'White King'.

Coriandrum (koh-ree-*an*-drum).
Carrot Family (*Umbelliferae*).
Aromatic plants from southern Europe. The only cultivated species, grown for the seeds used in seasoning, is a lacy-leaved annual of graceful habit. Plant seeds in the spring where plants are to stand. If the conditions are just right, they will self-sow. Easily grown in full sun and ordinary garden soil.

C. sativum (sat-*tye*-vum).
CILANTRO.
CORIANDER.
Usually planted in the herb garden. The seeds of this annual have a pleasant fragrance when eaten, and used powdered in baking, give cookies, cakes and pastries a delightful flavor. It is also a constituent of curry powder. The foliage of coriander is sometimes used in salads and sauces. Grows 1 to 3 ft., with finely dissected leaves and tiny white flowers. Plants grow to 18 in. and transplant badly, so sow in place.

Cosmos (*kos*-moze).
Composite Family (*Compositae*).
Showy, late-flowering annuals and perennials from tropical America. The popular annual species are tall, graceful plants, with feathery foliage and attractive, wide-petaled flowers in pale yellow, orange, red, pink, magenta, purple or white, with yellow or pink centers. Grown extensively at the back of borders, where the constant succession of bloom and lasting qualities after cutting make cosmos (*bipinnatus* varieties) very desirable. Full sun and ordinary garden soil, not too rich and a little sandy. They like hot summers. Sow seeds indoors in March or outdoors when ground is warm. Usually sturdy, healthy plants, they may sometimes be attacked by borers and blight.

★**C. bipinnatus** (bye-pin-*nay*-tus).
This is the Sensation-type cosmos commonly grown in gardens. A tall, self-seeding annual, 3

Cosmos

Cosmos bipinnatus 'Sensation'

Cosmos sulphureus 'Sunny Red'

Cuphea ignea
FIRECRACKER PLANT

to 7 ft. high, with feathery, decorative foliage of opposite leaves. Pink, white or crimson flowers. Single, double and double-crested forms are available. Plants sold as 'Sensation Mixed' range in color from white through pink to carmine. 'Sea Shells' has unusual fluted petals. 'Sonata' is a recent introduction, a winner in Fleuroselect garden trials, and more compact, growing only to 24 in.

C. sulphureus (sul-*fur*-ree-us).
YELLOW COSMOS.
A tall plant, 3 to 6 ft. high, whose large, golden-yellow flowers, 3 in. across, have broad petals and dark-tipped centers. This annual produces an effect of windblown grace in the summer border. The Klondike strain includes 'Sunny Gold', with yellow flowers 2 in. across, and 'Sunny Red', a bushy plant with orange-scarlet flowers that bloom all summer.

Crepis (*kreep*-iss).
HAWKWEED.
Composite Family (*Compositae*).
This genus consists of annuals and perennials, some weedy and rank in growth. One that is well worth growing in cultivation is described below. It is a sturdy and decorative annual from Italy and Greece. Easily grown in full sun and well-drained, sandy soil. Propagate when ground has warmed up by seeds sown where plants are wanted.

C. rubra (*roob*-ruh).
This species grows 1 to 2 ft. tall, with abundant heads of pink flowers, 1 in. across, that have pink centers. Blooms in August and September. 'Snowplume' bears feathery white flowers with apricot centers.

Cuphea (*kew*-fee-uh).
Loosestrife Family (*Lythraceae*).
Unusual and interesting plants of tropical America, with brilliant-colored, oddly shaped flowers. Tender perennials grown as annuals, they make striking subjects for warm sections of the country, and some are effective indoors under glass. There is great variation in petal formation in the various species: some have no petals, but a brilliantly colored calyx tube; others have regular flowers of six to twelve petals. Intermediate types show variant arrangements. Easily grown in partial shade and rich soil. Plant seeds outdoors in the spring. Indoors, use a standard soil mix. Cuttings from new shoots are possible in spring.

C. hyssopifolia (hiss-op-i-*foll*-ee-a).
MEXICAN HEATHER.
A compact, tender shrub often used for seasonal color. Narrow leaves up to 1 in. long are densely packed on the stems. Flowers, which come continuously, are white, lilac or violet. Grown from seed or cuttings, plant outdoors after all danger of frost is past and the ground has warmed.

C. ignea (*ig*-nee-ah).
CIGAR FLOWER.
FIRECRACKER PLANT.
MEXICAN CIGAR PLANT.
This Mexican native is actually an evergreen subshrub in its native land. In most parts of the U.S. it is grown as an annual or houseplant because it is not frost-hardy. The leaves are 1 to 2$^{1}/_{2}$ in. long, narrow and dark green. It blooms continuously if given enough light. The 1-in.-long, bright red tubular flowers appear in the leaf axils. They have a dark band and then a white band around the end of the tube. Plant in full sun in well-drained soil. Pinch back after

Cuphea

Cynara cardunculus
Cardoon

Dianthus barbatus
Sweet William

Cynoglossum amabile
Chinese Forget-me-not

flower shoots fade to maintain a bushy habit. Plant size is generally about 12 in. tall and nearly as wide. Start from seed or cuttings in spring. Plant outside after all danger of frost has passed. It will tolerate a wide range of outdoor conditions from hot and dry to humid. Use in the rock garden, in mass plantings or as an edging plant.

Cynara (*sin*-er-uh).
Composite Family (*Compositae*).
The round, many-petaled, edible artichoke and the cardoon are the two species known here; both are grown in vegetable gardens. Cynaras are coarse, herbaceous, thistlelike herbs with large, lobed leaves and terminal heads that turn violet, blue or white. Native to the Mediterranean region and the Canary Islands. In the U.S. it is being planted more frequently as an ornamental for the statuesque plants and vibrant large this-

tles. Some less tender varieties of artichoke are being offered for cooler gardens.

C. cardunculus (card-*unk*-yew-lus).
CARDOON.

This vegetable has a faint licorice flavor and looks like giant celery. Delicious raw or cooked. It is grown as artichokes are, and blanched as is celery, by hilling earth around the thickened leaf stalk. The plants are propagated by seed, generally raised to seedlings in hothouses and planted in the open garden when danger of frost is past. Primarily Zone 9.

C. scolymus (sko-*lee*-mus).
ARTICHOKE.

The artichoke is not known in the wild but was probably developed from the cardoon by ancient agriculturists. It forms an arching plant 3 to 5 ft. high, with deeply cut leaves of an especially handsome gray-green. The artichokes are unopened flower heads. Flowers of a rich blue are larger than those of cardoons. For uniformity of artichokes, grow from cuttings or divisions. 'Green Globe', the most available seed selection, will bring considerable variation in form, particularly of flower heads, with many of them not suitable for eating.

★★Cynoglossum (sin-oh-*gloss*-um).
HOUND'S-TONGUE.
Borage Family (*Boraginaceae*).

A genus of fairly weedy annuals, biennials and perennials, all with the rough, hairy leaves that give the genus its common name. Small, pink, purple or blue flowers, the last containing some very beautiful clear tones. Easily grown in ordinary garden soil well dug to a spade's depth. Full sun or partial shade. Propagate annuals by seed sown in early spring.

★**C. amabile** (am-*mab*-il-ee).
CHINESE FORGET-ME-NOT.

This species, from eastern Asia, grows $1^1/2$ to 2 ft. tall. Though a biennial, it is best grown as an annual. This is one of the few available garden plants with clear and brilliant blue flowers. There is a pink variety that is not as desirable. Blooms all summer until frost and withstands drought, making it very useful for hot, dry sections, as well as in more favored climates. Excellent in annual beds, in borders in front of shrubbery and in the cutting garden. When cut, the stems must be plunged into water immediately or the flowers will collapse. Sow seeds indoors for early bloom; outdoors if wanted from the middle of July to frost. A good seed selection is 'Blue Showers'.

Delphinium ajacis. See *Consolida ambigua*.

★★Dianthus (dye-*an*-thus).
Pink Family (*Caryophyllaceae*).

This genus includes the tall clove-scented florist's carnation, the smaller sweet William and the low-growing, fragrant, little evergreen forms called grass or border pinks. Pinks and sweet William are found in most gardens in the Northern Hemisphere, and are increasingly loved for their textured clumps of handsome foliage and lacy blooms.

Sweet William is somewhat less fragrant and usually taller than the grass pinks. The flowers are larger and have more brilliant coloring. They range from dark scarlet through reds to pinks and whites, and many varieties flash circles and stains of contrasting color. Though most are perennial, sweet Williams are best considered as biennials.

Dianthus

Dianthus chinensis
CHINA PINK

Dianthus chinensis 'Black and White Minstrels'

The carnation is the most imposing of all *Dianthus* and, after the rose, is probably the world's favorite cut flower as well as one of its best greenhouse plants. Some carnations are somewhat hardy when protected through the winter, but most prefer warmer zones and even there may require protection. Parent to the greenhouse carnation is a Eurasian species, *D. caryophyllus*, which grows 1 to 3 ft. tall. Its flowers are few to a stem and colors include pink, rose, purple, red to white and, rarer, yellow.

Greenhouse cultivation of carnations requires a temperature range of from 50°F at night to 60°F during the daytime. To propagate, take cuttings in the midwinter months from shoots growing at the base of the parent plant. Rooted in sand, they will be ready in four to six weeks. In warm climates such as Zone 8, the rooted cuttings may be planted outdoors after all danger of frost is past, 6 in. apart in rows 12 in. apart. Grow in full sun, or in partial afternoon shade to prolong bloom in hot regions.

Extra-large carnation blooms are obtained by pinching off all side shoots during the growth period. Plants will generally begin to bloom about seven weeks after planting and many produce as many as eighteen flowers in the following season.

The smaller *Dianthus*, the pinks and sweet Williams call for light, well-drained soil slightly on the alkaline side. All succeed in full sunshine, though many will also bloom in partial shade. The biennial species are generally propagated by seed.

D. barbatus (bar-*bay*-tus).

Sweet William.

Native to eastern Europe (from the Pyrenees to as far east as China). A biennial, its self-seeding habit perpetuates it much like a perennial. The gardener has the opportunity to select new plants in the border each fall. In more southern areas, plants act as true perennials if the seed heads are cut off, but they must be divided every other year. Sweet Williams prefer a slightly alkaline soil, and frequent liming is necessary.

This old-fashioned garden favorite grows to $1^1/2$ ft. tall and offers single or double blooms in either plain or vibrant multicolors, often in gay stripes. Though it lacks in fragrance, it makes a spectacular display when planted in large groups. Native, it sometimes runs wild in the eastern U.S.

Because most plants are seed-propagated, there is a great deal of variation in the colors. 'Blood Red' is one of the darkest colors and grows to 15 in.; 'Homeland' is another deep red; 'Indian Carpet' is a dwarf that comes in various solid colors and in forms with splotches of red, scarlet and pink; 'Newport Pink' bears deep pink flowers on 1-ft. plants; 'Pink Beauty' covers itself with salmon-pink flowers on 15-in. plants; and 'Scarlet Beauty' has rich scarlet blossoms. 'Wee Willie' is very short, growing only 3 to 6 in. Zones 2 to 3.

D. chinensis (chin-*nen*-siss).

China Pink.

Perennial grown as an annual, 1 to $1^1/2$ ft. high, with white or reddish flowers 1 in. across and slightly fragrant. *D. chinensis heddewigii* (hed-uh-*wig*-ee-eye) is a sturdy plant, blooming all summer long from seed started in April. Frilled and fringed, striped and zoned, the blossoms are gay and attractive in the annual border, the rock garden or the cutting garden. 'Black and White Minstrels' has frilled black petals with white fringe; 'Snowfire' has white petals with red center. The Princess series is available as separate colors in crimson, white, salmon, scarlet and violet. Other popular series are Charms, Telstar and Carpet, all compact growers. New are the very compact Parfait series, and the Rosemarie series. Zone 2.

Digitalis (dig-it-*tay*-liss).

Foxglove.

Figwort Family (*Scrophulariaceae*).

The common foxglove (*D. purpurea*) grows wild in English hedgerows and is one of the most successful border plants in American gardens. Though some species are perennial and will persist for years, most are treated as biennials that will bloom the second year. Nodding showers of bells, usually flecked inside, are produced on tall, graceful racemes and are extremely showy when massed as background clumps in the garden. In recent years striking hybrids and cultivars have been developed, notably the cultivar *D. purpurea* 'Excelsior'.

Foxgloves thrive in any moist location affording a moderately rich soil and either semi-sun or light shade. Both biennials and perennials are easily propagated by root division in early fall. Biennial plantings are easily maintained by an annual August sowing of seeds around the established group. Clumps started the season before can be separated in early spring. For their first season new plants can be treated as an edging for the border and transplanted the following season to the back of the border to bloom.

D. ambigua. See *D. grandiflora.*

Digitalis

★**D. purpurea** (pur-*pew*-ree-uh).

COMMON FOXGLOVE.

One of the very great and almost indispensable border flowers in cooler regions. Spikes of white, pink, rose or purple florets, usually with dark spots, on stems that are 3 to 6 ft. high. Handsome in large drifts in the late spring border, in front of shrubs and in the naturalized garden. Can be treated as a biennial; once established it often self-sows. Does best along our northern coasts.

The variety *gloxiniaeflora* (glox-in-*ee*-aye-flo-ruh) has handsome 4-ft.-tall trusses of gloxinia-like bloom in white, rose, purple and yellow ('The Shirley', in shades of pink, is one example). The variety *monstrosa* (mon-*stroh*-suh) is topped by a single huge campanula-like flower. The cultivar 'Excelsior' makes an ideal backdrop for the perennial border. The flowers of the species tend to face in one direction, but 'Excelsior' carries the blooms all around the spike, at right angles to the stem, effectively displaying the very rich markings. It is a biennial that blooms in June and July and often reseeds itself. 'Foxy', a cultivar, 3 ft. tall at maturity, blooms five months after sowing. It is colorful, prolific and long-blooming. 'Alba' is a pure white, unspotted variety, and 'Apricot' is a soft, buttery hue. The leaves of *D. purpurea* are poisonous; they yield the drug digitalis, a powerful heart stimulant. Zone 3.

Dimorphotheca (dye-mor-foh-*theek*-uh).

CAPE MARIGOLD.

Composite Family (*Compositae*).

(Some plants once considered part of this genus are now listed under *Osteospermum*.) Annuals and perennials from Africa, these are sun-loving plants, lending a festive air to the border. The showy, long-rayed flowers, yellow, orange, white and a few pink or purplish, with yellow and orange centers, bloom in summer. They need a long season for best results. The narrow, toothed leaves are opposite. Easily grown from seeds sown in rich, light, loamy soil if plenty of heat and sunshine are present.

D. aurantiaca. See *D. pluvialis.*

D. pluvialis. (ploo-vee-*al*-is).

(Often mistakenly called *D. aurantiaca*.) Grows 12 to 18 in. high. Tender perennial, usually treated as an annual. This species makes its glossiest, most brilliant showing in bright sunshine, closing on dull days, in shade and at night. Shear off to about 3 in. in late summer and side-dress lightly with fertilizer for lots of fall bloom. The large blooms, to $2^1/2$ in. across, are in shades of palest buff through apricot and yellow to orange, making this a very desirable plant. The named variety 'Glistening White' is a delightfully shiny white. Numerous hybrids have been developed between this species and *D. sinuata*. One of these, the cultivar 'Starshine', bears flowers of white, pink, carmine or rose, all with a yellow eye.

D. sinuata (sin-you-*ay*-tah).

AFRICAN DAISY.

CAPE MARIGOLD.

WINTER CAPE MARIGOLD.

Composite Family (*Compositae*).

This annual takes its common name from South Africa, its place of origin and is actually a tropical perennial there. It reaches 12 to 15 in. tall and is rounded and sprawling in habit. The leaves are 3 in. long, alternate and coarsely toothed. The daisylike flowers come in orange, yellow, salmon, buff or white and open on sunny days, closing at night or when it is overcast. Plant in full sun in light, well-drained soil. They are drought-tolerant but flower best if

Digitalis purpurea
COMMON FOXGLOVE

Digitalis purpurea 'Alba'
COMMON FOXGLOVE

watered regularly. Use as a border or in mass plantings.

Dipsacus (*dip*-suh-kus).

Teasel Family (*Dipsacaceae*).

Biennial herbs to 8 ft. tall, they are heavily naturalized in North America. They have prickly, thistlelike heads. Teasels grow in a wide range of habitats, frequently on heavy clay soils. Give them full sun, and grow from seed sown the year before bloom is desired. Zone 5.

D. fullonum (full-*oh*-num).

TEASEL.

(Includes plants listed until recently as *D. sylvestris*.) This native of Europe is the most important species of the genus, since it was grown commercially for the prickly fruit heads, which were used to raise the nap on woolen cloth. It grows to 6 ft. and has purple flowers.

Dimorphotheca pluvialis

Dipsacus

Dipsacus fullonum

TEASEL

Dorotheanthus bellidiformis

LIVINGSTONE DAISY

Dolichos lablab

HYACINTH-BEAN

Dyssodia tenuiloba

DAHLBERG DAISY

Of little interest in the garden, it is grown primarily for dried arrangements.

D. sylvestris. See *D. fullonum.*

Dolichos *(dol-ik-oss).*
Pea Family (*Leguminosae*).

Twining, annual vines from the tropics, grown with the greatest success in warm regions, but also with occasional success in cooler climates. They are very attractive and well worth trying. Sow seeds where plants are wanted when the ground is warm. Full sun and rich, light loam, well dug to a spade's depth. Useful for covering trellises, porches or fences.

D. lablab *(lab-lab).*
HYACINTH-BEAN.

This is the species usually seen in cultivation. A perennial vine grown as an annual, it makes prolific growth in warm regions, occasionally to 20 ft. or more in a single season. Usually, however, its height is 10 to 15 ft. A decorative plant, with graceful clusters of purple or white flowers, broad, dark green leaves, and large, purplish seed pods. Like the familiar scarlet-runner bean, *Phaseolus coccineus,* which is hardier, it needs wire or some other support.

Dorotheanthus *(dor-o-thee-anth-us).*
Carpetweed Family (*Aizoaceae*).

A genus of ten species separated from *Mesembryanthemum* and often still referred to as such. They have succulent leaves and many-petaled, daisylike flowers.

D. bellidiformis (bell-id-ee-*form*-is).
LIVINGSTONE DAISY.

(Often listed as *Mesembryanthemum bellidiforme*). Horticultural varieties are probably all hybrids between *D. bellidiformis* and *D. gramineus.* All

the flowers are dark-centered but have brilliant petals of bright pink, orange or white, tipped with dark or red margins. The foliage is succulent, made up of fleshy, rough leaves. They grow only 2 to 3 in. high but spread nicely, making them good additions for rockeries or edgings, even in poor, dry soil; they will also thrive in better soil so long as it is well drained. They like full sun and warm, dry conditions. Propagate by seeds started indoors in late winter, ten to twelve weeks before transplanting outside.

Dyssodia *(diss-ode-ee-uh).*
Composite Family (*Compositae*).

A genus of North American annuals, perennials and subshrubs. The name *Dyssodia* is from the Greek *dysodes,* or stinking, apt because of the smell of the crushed foliage of some kinds. They all have small, yellow, daisylike flowers.

D. tenuiloba (ten-you-ih-*loh*-bah).
DAHLBERG DAISY.
GOLDEN-FLEECE.

(Formerly *Thymophylla tenuiloba*). This is a little-used annual with impressive potential for many areas of the garden. The low-growing, fine foliage is attractive and mossy-looking. Sprinkled over this foliage are the small, yellow daisy flowers, approximately 1/2 in. across. They appear all summer and into the fall. The plants grow to about 8 to 10 in. tall, are rounded in habit and are impressive when massed. If planted in the rock garden, they offer bright spots of color all summer. They also do well planted between stepping stones and patio stones, and they make good trailers in hanging baskets or other containers, when combined with other plants of more substance. They are ready reseeders and will return year after year. This can be a nice effect, as nature sometimes seems to have a more artistic eye than we do, but reseeding can also be troublesome in the wrong location. Plant in full sun in sandy, well-drained soil of average fertility. Do not overwater or plant in poorly drained soil, as it will readily rot. It can withstand heat and drought.

Eschscholzia (esh-*sholt*-see-uh).

Poppy Family (*Papaveraceae*).

Native to western North America. Graceful, airy annuals and perennials, the latter treated as annuals in cultivation. Light, sandy, dry soil and full sun. Sow seeds where plants are wanted when ground is warm. Keep seedpods picked off to encourage a long season of bloom.

★**E. californica** (cal-ih-*fore*-nih-cah).

CALIFORNIA POPPY.

Poppy Family (*Papaveraceae*).

This native American annual can be found growing wild across the hills of Southern California. It was brought to Europe and into cultivation in the late 1700s and has since been hybridized extensively to produce double and semidouble flowers and to broaden the color range. The brilliant golden and red colors of this species can really brighten a summer garden or wild garden (one that is allowed to reseed naturally). The poppy flowers are four petaled if single, with $3/4$- to $2^1/2$-in.-long petals, present in summer and fall, in colors ranging from white to yellow, orange, bronze, scarlet, carmine, salmon and rose. The ternately dissected leaves are mostly basal and are blue-green. This plant grows to be 12 to 15 in. high and is rounded in habit. Plant in full sun in well-drained sandy soil, although it is tolerant of poor soils and drought, in spring or in fall (where the winters are mild). Put in the spot where it is to grow, as it does not transplant well. One of the secrets of getting good germi-

nation seems to be frequent watering after planting, as this seems to help the seed overcome its dormancy. California poppies will self-sow, but remember that if they are hybrid plants, the offspring will revert back to one of the parents of the cross. Plant in an annual border, a natural area or in a mass planting for a spectacular effect. Some good cultivars are: 'Ballerina Mixed', fluted blossoms in mixed colors; 'Double Ballerina Mixed' and 'Thai Silk Mixed', sinuous fluted forms and wavy petal edges.

Euphorbia (yew-*forb*-ee-uh).

SPURGE.

Spurge Family (*Euphorbiaceae*).

A large genus of tremendous variety, widely distributed. Included are cactus-like, tropical succulents, weeds, popular annuals and perennials, as well as the striking florist's poinsettia and snow-on-the-mountain. Some of the cactus-like species grow into picturesque specimen plants and may be used for hedges in regions where they are hardy. There are a number of good greenhouse plants. All contain a milky juice, which produces severe dermatitis in some people. Propagate by seeds or cuttings.

E. marginata (mar-jin-*nay*-tuh).

SNOW-ON-THE-MOUNTAIN.

A handsome annual, 10 to 20 in. high, and native to prairies and dry fields of North America. Bright green foliage and showy white bracts all summer make this plant good for the flower garden. Sow seeds where wanted when ground has warmed up and thin to stand 10 in. apart. Self-sows freely, but dislikes transplanting. Likes sandy, well-drained soil and sun. 'Summer Icicle' is a dwarf with green and white foliage.

Eschscholzia californica
CALIFORNIA POPPY

Euphorbia marginata
SNOW-ON-THE-MOUNTAIN

Eustoma (yew-*sto*-muh).

Gentian Family (*Gentianaceae*).

A small genus of North American annuals with gray-green, opposite leaves and white, or, more usually, blue, bell-shaped flowers, much like those of *Campanula*. The only species common in cultivation is a hardy and decorative annual from the Southern Plains states, where it is a persistent weed and is often called "Canada pest." Sow seeds in December for summer bloom. Do not overwater in the seed flat or after transplanting, as it is prone to root rot. Water only when pots approach dryness; plants grow best in well-drained soil and bloom best in full sun. Transplant in the garden after the soil is warm and the weather is settled, when the first true leaves are formed. Grow on at 65° F.

Eustoma grandiflorum
LISIANTHUS

E. grandiflorum (grand-i-*flor*-um).
LISIANTHUS.
PRAIRIE GENTIAN.
This species has gained the widespread attention of hybridizers, who have introduced varieties for use as cut flowers, as florist-potted plants and for bedding out in the garden. They have also broadened the color range to include clear white and a lovely pink as well as the more common blue or blue-violet. Some varieties are also double. 'Blue Lisa' is an award-winning cultivated variety with brilliant blue flowers and a compact habit, growing to 10 in. in the garden. 'Double Eagle Mixed' includes shades of rose and cream as well as bicolors in this double strain.

Evolvulus (e-*volv*-yew-lus).
Morning Glory Family (*Convolvulaceae*).
A genus of 100 species mostly from the Americas. Most are from warm areas and are not tolerant of frost.

E. glomeratus (glom-er-*at*-us).
This species bears quantities of bright blue flowers over a long season—all summer—when grown in good light. A herbaceous plant, prostrate or trailing if grown in containers, that branches frequently, making a dense mound. A selection, 'Blue Haze', is becoming known as a good container plant or hanging basket for the sunny deck or patio. It is normally propagated by cuttings, which root easily.

Felicia (fel-*lish*-ee-uh).
Composite Family (*Compositae*)
Unpretentious but tidy annuals from South Africa. Grown outdoors in warm sections of the U.S. or in a cool greenhouse. The small, daisylike blossoms are usually blue, sometimes white, with yellow centers, and bloom most of the summer. These plants need full sun and a light, loamy soil, well dug to a spade's depth. For early flowering, start seeds indoors in March and plant out when all danger of cold weather has passed. Spring cuttings brought into the greenhouse in the fall will bloom in midwinter. Removing spent flowers will enhance continued bloom. Felicias are also widely planted as constituents of mixed containers for summer bloom.

F. amelloides (am-el-*loy*-deez).
BLUE DAISY.
BLUE FELICIA.
Annual to perennial. A slightly bushy plant, growing 3 ft. high, with blue flowers $1^1/2$. in. across. It should be started indoors. Also grows from cuttings. After bloom (July to October), lift and pot for bloom throughout the winter in the greenhouse or in a cool, sunny window. Zone 7.

F. bergerana (burg-er-*an*-a).
KINGFISHER DAISY.
A species rarely growing more than 8 in. high, it forms a bushy mound covered with sky-blue flowers with yellow centers.

Foeniculum (fee-*nik*-yew-lum).
FENNEL.
Carrot Family (*Umbelliferae*).
A small genus of which only one species is cultivated in this country. It is a graceful, feathery perennial, grown as an annual in herb gardens for its decorative and tangy foliage and in vegetable gardens for its edible stems. Propagate by seeds, sown where plants are to stand, early in May, in full sun and ordinary garden soil, well dug to a spade's depth.

Evolvulus glomeratus

Felicia amelloides
BLUE DAISY

F. vulgare (vul-*gay*-ree).

COMMON FENNEL.

Tall, 4 to 6 ft. high, fennel has a strong anise- or licoricelike flavor and makes a delicious vegetable blanched, raw or in sauces. Another popular use is as an herb for seasoning, made by chopping the tiny leaves and adding them, like parsley, to omelets and fish sauces, tomato dishes and salads. If allowed to flower, plant has a large, round, flattish cluster of greenish-white, tiny florets, similar in appearance to Queen Anne's lace. It is best to plant fennel on the north side of the garden to avoid shading smaller plants. The variety *dulce* (*dul*-see), called sweet fennel, Florence fennel or finocchio, is smaller, 2 ft. high. Its leaves have an enlarged and thickened, bulblike base, used in salads or as a vegetable when blanched. Widely grown in California. Bronze-leaved fennel, planted for its attractive foliage, is *F. vulgare purpurea*.

Foeniculum vulgare
COMMON FENNEL

Fuchsia

Fuchsia 'Perky Pink'

Fuchsia 'Gartenmeister Bohnstedt'
HONEYSUCKLE FUCHSIA

Fuchsia 'VooDoo'

Fuchsia (*few*-shuh).

Evening Primrose Family (*Onagraceae*).

Always colorful and vivid showy shrubs of South America and New Zealand. Simple leaves are opposite, alternate or whorled. The flowers are enormously varied; usually they have a graceful pendulous habit. The fruit is a small berry. Popular plants for the cool greenhouse, fuchsias dress up window boxes and are excellent for hanging baskets and summer bedding, if planted in partial shade. Allow plants to rest in summer. For winter bloom in the home greenhouse, keep bushy by pinching. May be trained in pyramidal and standard form. Plants may be kept for years by resting in winter and cutting back in spring. They need light, rich, but well-drained moist soil. Fertilize lightly every two weeks when making growth. Not unlike orchids, the tender fuchsias fall into the category of fancier's plants and are just difficult enough to grow well to justify specialization. Propagate by seeds in late summer or by cuttings.

Fuchsias are gaining popularity because there is an increasing number of heat-resistant varieties, and because of better cultural techniques. Fuchsias bloom on new wood, so the important thing is to keep vigorous growth coming all through spring and summer.

Every fuchsia specialist has a favorite growing mix. At White Flower Farm, Litchfield, Connecticut, the recommended combination is 70 percent loam, 15 percent leafmold or compost, and 15 percent coarse builder's sand. At Merry Gardens, Camden, Maine, a mixture of equal parts organic matter (leafmold, peat moss or compost), well-rotted manure and sandy loam is used. One commercial grower in California recommends two parts sandy topsoil to one part each of redwood compost and peat moss.

Fuchsias need a soil that is kept moist at all times. Mist the foliage at least twice daily in hot weather. Protect from strong winds. Feed biweekly with a liquid houseplant food. Morning sun, like that on the east or north side of a building, is ideal; very bright reflected light, like that off a roof overhang, is also good.

To overwinter fuchsias, keep them in a cool place (40° to 50°F), and water just enough to keep old wood from drying out. Bring to sun or put in a fluorescent-lighted garden in February. Cut back after leaf buds show. Zone 9.

★**F. hybrida** (*high*-brih-duh).

A loose and really unnecessary designation for the many garden fuchsias of mixed origin, varying in habit, size and color of flowers. A number of species are almost untraceably mixed in the hundreds of available named varieties. Leaves to 4 in. long. Showy single or double

flowers to 3 in. long, with white, pink, lavender or crimson calyx and white, rose, red, blue and purple petals. Handsome shrubs for growing outdoors in California, as well as in summer elsewhere. Fine in baskets or window boxes. The principal pest of all the hybrids is whitefly; use a natural pyrethrum to control.

Popular varieties include: 'Carmelita', with double white flowers; 'Little Beauty', lavender-blue and pink; and 'Tropic', double white to violet-blue flowers. Catalogs of fuchsia growers list varieties recommended for bush, pot, basket, tree and espalier culture.

Favorites for summer color outdoors (even for gardeners not in ideal fuchsia country) include: 'Brigadoon' (purple and red double; basket), 'Display' (pink; upright), 'Pink Galore' (double; always in bloom), 'Swingtime' (white and red double; basket), 'Whitemost' (white with sepals of palest pink; basket or upright) and 'VooDoo' (crimson and purple double; basket or upright).

Small upright fuchsias are ideal for limited space; cultivars useful as houseplants include 'Buttons and Bows', 'Little Beauty', 'Mme. Dacheau' and 'Mrs. Marshall'. The honeysuckle fuchsia, 'Gartenmeister Bohnstedt', with orange blooms and dark foliage, is a vigorous upright, easily cultivated indoors or out. For plants with variegated foliage, try 'Golden Marinka' (red stems, gold-edged green leaves) and 'Sunray' (leaves green, cream, silver and white).

Gaillardia (gay-*lard*-ee-uh).

BLANKET FLOWER.

Composite Family (*Compositae*).

Annuals and perennials, native to North America. Showy, variously colored flowers on sturdy plants with rough, 3- to 6-in. alternate leaves. The florets of the blossoms are indented and are yellow, orange, brownish-red or white, with purple centers. Excellent as cut flowers. The annuals make good cool greenhouse plants, flowering in late winter and spring. Light, porous, not too rich, well-drained soil and full sun are required. A good choice for sunny, dry locations. Will bloom all summer if faded flowers are kept picked. Propagate by seeds. Zone 5.

G. pulchella (pull-*chell*-a).
ANNUAL GAILLARDIA.
Native in the southern U.S. from Virginia to Texas, this species has been hybridized to produce continuously blooming summer flowers of great charm. 'Double Mixed' is a seed strain with flowers of many colors inluding gold, cream, red and many bicolors. 'Red Plume' is a new award-winning variety, with fluffy, very double flowers of vibrant red.

Gazania (gaz-*zay*-nee-uh).
Composite Family (*Compositae*).
Daisylike, tender annuals from South Africa that withstand drought and hot sun very well. Grown for the long stems, 4 to 10 in., and showy flowers that open when there is sun and close when the sun is hidden. Foliage has densely woolly or silvery-white underside. *Gazania* is especially useful as a colorful pot plant in the cool greenhouse. Ordinary garden soil and full sun. Start seeds early in pots, flats or frames, and transplant. Cuttings of basal shoots taken in mid- to late summer can be inserted in a cold frame until rooted and transferred to the greenhouse in flats for the winter.

G. × hybrida.
GAZANIA.
TREASURE FLOWER.
The three species *G. linearis, G. pavonia,* and *G. rigens* are the parents of the many intercrossings that created the hybrids available today. There is a wide variety of flower color available, ranging from cream to yellow, golden-orange, bronze, pink and red, with many combinations. The plants grow to a height of from 6 to 15 in., the habit being a rosette of basal leaves and long flower stems carrying the flowers up above the leaves. These lanceolate leaves are green and smooth above and tomentose below. The flowers are 2- to 3-in. daisy flowers, typical of the composite family. They open during the day and close at night and when the sky is overcast. These flowers will appear all summer and fall until frost. The plants will even stand a light frost.

Sow the seeds indoors in early spring and transplant in late spring after the danger of frost is past. Gazanias prefer full sun and light sandy soil, but will tolerate poor soils and growing conditions. They will not, however, tolerate wet soils or overwatering.

Use in the front of borders and as an edging. Some good cultivars are: 'Chansonette', compact plant with mixed colors; Daybreak series, bronze, yellow or orange early flowers; Mini-star series, a large flower in a variety of colors; 'Morning Star Mix', a mix of colors; 'Starburst Mixture', large flowers in a mix of bright colors; Sundance hybrids, with very large flowers of several colors, including some with striped petals.

G. rigens (*rye*-gens).
GAZANIA.
This half-hardy perennial from South Africa is usually grown as an annual in regions with harsh winters. The leaves are lanceolate, hairy underneath and 3 to 4 in. long. The flowers are 3 in. across on stems 4 to 6 in. long. A typical daisylike composite flower, the ray flowers are yellow with a basal spot. The flowers stay open

Gaillardia pulchella 'Red Plume'
ANNUAL GAILLARDIA

Gazania × *hybrida*
TREASURE FLOWER

only when there is strong light present, closing at night and on overcast days. For those who work in the daytime, expect to see the flower only on weekends!

Plant in full sun in light sandy soil. It will not tolerate wet soils or overwatering but will tolerate poor soil, wind, summer heat and drought. The species is one of the parents of the many hybrids available today, and this name is often used to label the many offspring.

Gerbera (jerb-*er*-uh).
Composite Family (*Compositae*).
From South Africa and the warm parts of Asia. Only one species is in cultivation, a colorful perennial that is a popular greenhouse plant and can also be grown to beautiful effect outdoors. Full sun and rich, porous loam, well dug to a spade's depth. Propagate by seeds sown in pots in January; don't cover seeds as they need light

to germinate. Place pots outdoors when there is no danger of frost. Cuttings should be kept under glass until rooted and then potted. Many varieties are now increased by tissue culture. Seed selections are most widely used for outdoor growing.

G. jamesonii (jaym-*soh*-nee-eye).
BARBERTON DAISY.
TRANSVAAL DAISY.
The bright blooms, 3 to 4 in. across, are now available year round. Shining and polished in appearance, they are very familiar as cut flowers. The leaves form a basal rosette up to 12 in. in diameter, with flowers, on long stems reaching up to 1½ ft. high, ranging in color from orange-red and red through white, pink, rose, burgundy and purple. Can be treated as a perennial from Zone 8 and southward, or usually blooming in late winter. To the north, treat

Gerbera

Gerbera 'Tempo'

Gomphrena globosa 'Pink'
GLOBE AMARANTH

Helianthus annuus 'Russian Giant'
COMMON SUNFLOWER

it as an annual. In all cases, it should be grown on well-drained soil to prevent root rot.

'Fantasia Double Gerbera' is a full double form in rose, pink, scarlet, yellow and shades between. Seed selections include 'Happipot', a compact mixture of many colors; 'Festival', similar but earlier to bloom; and 'Skipper', a very compact form.

Gomphrena (gom-*free*-nuh).
Amaranth Family (*Amaranthaceae*).
A small genus found in widely separated tropical regions in America, Australia, Europe and Asia. The commonly grown species is a popular garden annual, which resembles red clover in appearance, and is grown for its fresh and dried blooms. Sow seeds indoors in late March and set out, 8 to 12 in. apart, in May. Or sow seed where it is to bloom, in April. Full sun and good garden soil, well dug to a spade's depth.

G. globosa (gloh-*boh*-suh).
GLOBE AMARANTH.
A tender annual, 1 to 1^1/2 ft. high, useful for summer and winter decoration, since the blooms dry well. Cut them just before they are at their fullest bloom and hang to dry, upside down in small bunches in a well-ventilated room, until wanted for winter decoration. The Buddy series is available in white or purple. 'Strawberry Fayre', derived from *G. haageana,* is bright red.

Gypsophila (jip-*soff*-il-uh).
BABY'S-BREATH.
Pink Family (*Caryophyllaceae*).
Showy, well-branched, tiny-flowered annuals and perennials, mostly of Europe and Asia. Hardy and easily grown, they are invaluable as fillers in the hardy border and for cut flowers. Distinctive for their feathery, light profusion of pink or white florets, which are graceful indoors or out. Reblooms intermittently through summer. Small, blue-green, opposite leaves. They grow best in full sun and well-drained, slightly sandy loam with added lime, well dug to a spade's depth. For best effect, grow in fairly thick groups. For support, corset the plants by closely surrounding them with small stakes and trussing them with string. Sow seeds in late fall in warm sections, elsewhere in early spring, as soon as the soil can be worked. Hybrids and named varieties are best bought in small sizes. Propagate by seeds or root division. Zones 4 to 5.

G. elegans (*ell*-eg-anz).
Handsome, widely grown annual, 1 to 1^1/2 ft. high, with pink or white flowers and tiny leaves. The variety *grandiflora* (gran-dif-*floh*-ruh) has larger blossoms than the species and makes a fine display in the border. 'Covent Garden', with masses of tiny white flowers, is by far the most widely grown, and 'Red Cloud' is a selection with flowers in various shades of pink.

Helianthus (hee-lee-*anth*-us).
SUNFLOWER.
Composite Family (*Compositae*).
Large, widespread genus, consisting of coarse perennials and annuals, with many species varying greatly in size and habit of growth. All have alternate leaves and, except for a few varieties, yellow flowers with center disks of brown, gold or dark purple. These cheerful and familiar flowers twist to follow the sun and are sturdy and attractive to seed-eating birds. They thrive in full sun or light shade in poor soil, and at least some of the species grow well in drought areas. All should have soil well turned to a spade's depth. Propagate annuals by seed sown in spring where plants are wanted.

Helianthus

H. annuus (*an*-yew-us).

COMMON SUNFLOWER.

Annual, native from Minnesota to the West Coast. Grows to 12 ft. The flower heads are 1 ft. across with brownish-purple centers. Useful at the back of large borders or in the wild garden. Blooms from July to frost. Sow seeds in early spring where plants are wanted, and thin to stand 3 ft. apart. 'Piccolo' grows to 4 ft., with 4-in. yellow flowers centered in black. 'Sunspot' has 8- to 12-in. flowers on plants only 18 to 24 in. tall. 'Russian Giant', selected for size, can be grown for the tallest plants and largest flower heads.

H. argophyllus (ar-goh-fill-us).

SILVER-LEAF SUNFLOWER.

Annual, native to Texas, growing about 6 ft. high, much branched and very showy. The stems and leaves are covered with a soft, gray-ish down, and when dried the leaves are effective in winter arrangements. Yellow blossoms, just 3 in. across, in August and September. Useful in beds of bulbs for color at the back, as background for shorter annuals, in large plantings and the wild garden. Thin plants to at least 1 ft. apart.

H. debilis (*deb*-il-iss).

CUCUMBER-LEAF SUNFLOWER.

A bushy annual, 3 to 4 ft. high, with flowers, only 3 in. across, smaller than on many of the species. Very abundant, golden-yellow blooms are long-lasting when cut. There is a dwarf variety, 'Lilliput', and other named varieties with brownish, pink or purple flowers. This species makes a good temporary hedge and blooms from July to frost.

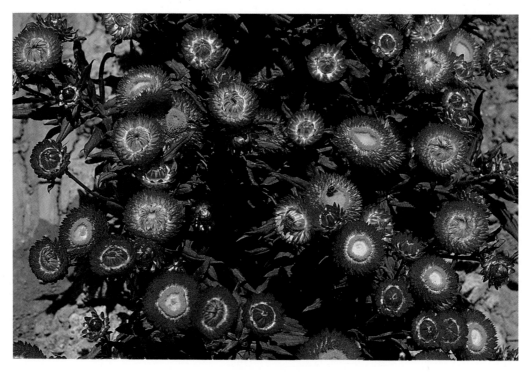

Helichrysum bracteatum 'Hot Bikini'
STRAWFLOWER

Helichrysum (hel-ik-*krye*-sum).

EVERLASTING.

Composite Family (*Compositae*).

Of this large genus of annual and perennial plants, the most familiar species is the strawflower, long a favorite in arrangements of dried material. This species is easy to grow and has no pests. Propagate by seeds.

H. bracteatum (brak-tee-*ay*-tum).

STRAWFLOWER.

This tender annual, $2^1/2$ ft. tall, is a native of Australia. It is easy to grow, effective in the annual border, useful in the cutting garden for fresh flowers and excellent as a dried flower for winter arrangements. The decorative blooms, $2^1/2$ in. across, should be cut for drying before they are fully expanded. Hang bunches in a dry, shady, airy place until crisp. The type is a bright yellow, and there are varieties in shades of pink, red and white. Favorite cultivars include 'Monstrosum' and the bright Bikini series. They all hold their color well when dried. Sow seeds indoors in late March or early April; set out in May to stand 15 in. apart. Full sun and a fairly light soil well dug to a spade's depth.

H. petiolare (pete-ee-o-*lar*-ay).

A rather tender perennial subshrub native to South Africa, it is treated as an annual in areas with freezing winter weather. The stems and foliage are cloaked with feltlike hairs. Rapid-growing, it is widely used in annual and perennial borders for weaving its way through other plants. It is also a splendid addition to mixed containers. The species is gray in color, the selection 'Limelight' is a glowing chartreuse, and a third form is distinguised by variegated leaves. Special selections must be grown from cuttings.

Heliotropium (hee-lee-oh-*troh*-pee-um).

HELIOTROPE.

Borage Family (*Boraginaceae*).

Tender annuals and perennials from the tropics and subtropics. The sweet scent of the species listed makes it indispensable to the gardener who enjoys delicious scents as well as visual beauty. Grown as tender annuals outdoors, these have lavender, purple or white blossoms in showy clusters, effective against its dark green, alternate leaves. In the greenhouse, their rich fragrance is especially appreciated. The most common species in cultivation is *arborescens*.

★H. arborescens (ar-bor-*ress*-senz).

CHERRY PIE.

HELIOTROPE.

Half-hardy shrub from Peru, growing to 1 to 3 ft. in the garden, 4 to 6 ft. as a conservatory plant. Colors range from darkest purple through palest lavender and rose to white. Most varieties are sweetly fragrant, but some of them, with handsome blooms, lack the characteristic delightful scent. Sow seeds indoors in early March and set out in May, 10 to 12 in. apart. Pinch back the plants when they are 4 to 5 in. high to make them bushy, otherwise they will be straggly. They are most effective when massed in sizable groups. Plant in full sun, in a light, rich loam, well dug to a spade's depth. Keep continuously moist; manure water gives best growth and bloom. In bloom all summer. Useful for annual borders, in window boxes, for fragrant cut flowers and in the cool to intermediate greenhouse, though in the latter, plants may be subject to aphids and red-spider mites (they are quite free of insect pests outdoors).

Indoors, use standard soil mix with doubled peat and rotted manure. Sow seeds in June for

Heliotropium

winter bloom. In warm regions, or if a cool greenhouse is available for carrying over plants, heliotrope can be trained to standard form by pruning off side shoots. Plants will reach a good size, 3 to 4 ft., and will last for many years in pots if given fertilizer regularly. 'Marine', a relatively compact variety, has very fragrant flowers of deep purple. An even smaller form is 'Dwarf Marine'. Zone 10.

Helipterum (hee-*lip*-ter-um).

EVERLASTING.

IMMORTELLE.

Composite Family (*Compositae*).

(Sometimes listed in catalogs as *Acroclinium* or *Rhodanthe*.) Familiar small flowers in winter arrangements of dried material, the immortelles, annuals from Africa and Australia, are also effective in borders. Since they bloom in three months from seeds, a sowing in mid-April will give flowers from the middle of July to the middle of September, just at the time when annuals are most wanted. The alternate leaves are usually woolly and whitish. The flowers close at night and often do not open much on dull days. Sow seeds outdoors in late April or when warm weather has come. Can be started indoors, but plants are a little difficult to transplant. Full sun and a dry, well-drained soil, not enriched, give best results. To dry, pick before flowers are fully open and hang in loose bunches upside down in a well-ventilated place.

H. humboldtianum (hum-bolt-ee-*ay*-num).

Grows about 1 ft. high, with small yellow blossoms, which turn a pale green when dried. They hold their color all winter. Thin plants to stand 6 in. apart.

H. manglesii (man-*glee*-see-eye).

SWAN RIVER EVERLASTING.

This is the most familiar species, with greenish, woolly leaves and attractive red, pink or white flowers, 1 to 2 in. across, on stems $1^{1}/_{2}$ ft. high. Thin to stand 6 in. apart.

Hesperis (*hess*-per-iss).

ROCKET.

Mustard Family (*Cruciferae*).

Hardy perennial and biennial herbaceous garden ornamentals with fragrant flowers. These grow easily in ordinary garden soils in full sun, do best in rich, moist beds, and bloom adequately even in poor soil and half-shade.

H. matronalis (mat-roh-*nay*-liss).

SWEET ROCKET.

DAME'S ROCKET.

DAME'S VIOLET.

From a basal rosette of elongate, ovate, hairy leaves, flower stalks rise to 2 to 3 ft. high from May to July. Flowers to 1 in. across are borne in heads that are flat to high-crowned and phloxlike. Blossoms are white, pinkish, mauve or purplish, single or double. Often called biennial, this is a perennial in Zone 5 (-10°F) and southward, but biennial or annual northward. Sow seed in fall or spring, where plants are to bloom. A fine, old-fashioned, fragrant flowering plant, but likely to serve as a reservoir for viruses that debilitate other garden ornamentals. This has become naturalized locally through much of eastern North America. 'Alba' is a white selection. Zone 6.

Hibiscus moschatus.

See *Abelmoschus moschatus*.

Heliotropium arborescens
HELIOTROPE

Humulus japonicus
HOPS

Humulus (*hew*-mew-lus).

HOPS.

Mulberry Family (*Moraceae*).

Annual and perennial vines of the temperate regions of America, Europe and Asia, including the hops vine of commerce, used in brewing beer. *H. japonicus* is the species usually grown for decorative purposes.

H. japonicus (juh-*pon*-i-cus).

(Often called *H. scandens.*) A rampant, fast-growing annual from Asia, climbing by twining stems up to 30 ft. It is useful as a quick-growing cover for rough places, fences or walls. On vertical surfaces, strings or wires are needed to help it climb. The chief ornamental feature is the large, deeply cut, abundant leaves that are sometimes variegated white or yellow. A golden-leaved form 'Aureus' is also much prized. The long, greenish blossoms are plenti-ful but not very pretty. Needs full sun and a moist, rich soil, well dug to a spade's depth. Sow seeds outdoors in mid-April where plants are wanted and thin to stand $1^1/2$ ft. apart. Since it self-sows freely, it may become a weedy pest.

Hunnemannia (hun-em-*man*-ee-uh).

MEXICAN GOLDEN-CUP.

MEXICAN TULIP POPPY.

Poppy Family (*Papaveraceae*).

There is only one species, a showy herb popular in flower gardens. Perennial in its native Mexico, it is always grown in cooler sections as a tender annual and given an early start. In Zone 5, start indoors in mid-March and set out in May to stand 1 ft. apart. In warmer sections, seeds may be sown outdoors in April for a long season of bloom.

Hunnemannia

Hunnemannia fumariifolia 'Sunlite'
MEXICAN GOLDEN-CUP

Impatiens New Guinea hybrids

Iberis umbellata
CANDYTUFT

Impatiens New Guinea hybrids

H. fumariifolia (few-mare-ee-eye-*foh*-lee-uh). Grayish, deeply cut leaves and handsome blossoms, 2 to 3 in. across, bright yellow with many orange stamens, make this plant a good garden subject. Bloom is abundant from early July to frost, on plants 1 to 2 ft. high. Since it reacts badly to the usual transplanting procedures, it must be handled with care. Use plant bands or peat-pulp pots for separate sowings of a few seeds to facilitate transfer outdoors with as little disturbance as possible. Full sun, a sheltered location, ordinary garden loam and well-drained soil, dug to a spade's depth, are needed. Well worth all the care it takes to grow it. Breathtaking in combination with blue delphiniums. Useful in the annual border, on sunny slopes and in the cutting garden. For arrangements, cut before the flower is fully opened. Since *Hunnemannia* often self-sows, it can become a permanent inhabitant of undisturbed garden spots. 'Sunlite' is a selection with 2- to 3-in. glossy yellow blossoms.

Iberis (eye-*beer*-iss).
CANDYTUFT.
Mustard Family (*Cruciferae*).
Annuals and perennials, native to the Mediterranean region. Annual species make a good summer display in the border. Likes full sun and ordinary garden soil, well turned to a spade's depth. Propagate annuals by seeds sown in early spring where plants are wanted.

I. umbellata (um-bel-*lay*-tuh).
A much hybridized annual (often crossed with *I. amara*), 8 to 16 in. high, with fine, large heads of white, pink, rose, red or purple flowers. A standby in the annual border, it makes a fine display and is excellent as a cut flower. Bloom may be prolonged by successive plantings and by picking the flowers to keep them from going to seed. Easy and very showy in the greenhouse or plant room.

★★Impatiens (im-*pay*-shee-enz).
BUSY LIZZIE.
TOUCH-ME-NOT.
PATIENCE PLANT.
SULTANA.
Balsam Family (*Balsaminaceae*).
Annuals and tender perennials from warm sections of Asia, Africa and North America, easily grown from seeds (some from cuttings). Useful for borders, bedding out and as houseplants. They need light, rich, friable soil, well dug to a spade's depth, and sun or light shade. For early bloom, start seeds indoors in early April and set out in May, or sow outdoors in May for later bloom. Indoors, use standard soil mix. Calls for generous watering.

I. balsamina (bal-sam-in-nuh).
GARDEN BALSAM.
Pretty, old-fashioned annual from Asia. Bushy and compact, it grows to a height of $1^1/_2$ to $2^1/_2$ ft., with single or double axillary flowers, which grow close to the stem for 8 to 10 in. at the top of the plant. Colors range from white through yellow, pink, red and purple. The plant thrives in a good rich soil. In the border, plants should stand 15 to 18 in. apart to allow for full development. To make bushy, pinch out the tips when plants are about 4 in. tall. Effective for color and sturdy habit. Does not last well as a cut flower, but massed in the summer border, it is a delight. From plants started indoors, will bloom all summer until frost. 'Dwarf Hybrids' is one selection.

I. holstii. See *I. wallerana*.

I. sultanii. See *I. wallerana*.

IMPATIENS

What makes an ideal annual flower? Impatiens have all the attributes that most experts would name. It blooms prodigiously with sparkling color all summer long. Its color range is wide—a variety of hues and shades encompasses the entire color spectrum except yellow and true blue (although new introductions are narrowing that gap). Impatiens flowers abundantly in the shade, becoming increasingly important as gardens age and woody plants—and the shadows they cast—grow larger. The flowers of impatiens drop away cleanly when spent, and therefore do not require deadheading or other maintenance. Plants are self-branching to form a compact mound, although in extremely hot, humid climates they will stretch taller and have a looser habit. They thrive on low fertility, performing well with no supplemental feeding in most soils. And finally, although impatiens are succulent plants needing abundant water, they will revive from a severe wilt with no apparent damage.

Today's impatiens have traveled a long road from their native African ancestors—tall, narrow plants with small flowers tucked down among the leaves. Reputedly, early trading ships carried impatiens seed quite by accident from Africa to Central and South America, where they grew and naturalized along roadsides. It is primarily in the last twenty years that impatiens have been molded by breeders into the plants we know today.

Seed production of hybrid impatiens is done in greenhouses by hand pollination. When seed capsules are ripe, they explode, scattering the seed widely. To contain the seeds, the production plants are surrounded by mesh tents from which seed is collected.

For garden use, sow seed ten to twelve weeks before the last frost date. Do not cover the seeds, for they need light to germinate. To prevent damping-off, use a sterile soil mix; treating seed flats with a fungicide is also recommended. Keep the seed flats at 75°F; germination will take from ten to twenty days. Transplant seedlings into pots or cells at least 2 in. in diameter so plants can develop without crowding. Space pots and shift plants to larger pots as necessary.

Impatiens and Garden Design

Impatiens is superb in ground beds, but is an ideal container plant, too, either alone or combined with other annuals in patio planters, window boxes or hanging baskets. When planting containers, it is particularly interesting to combine the mounding shape of impatiens with tall spiky plants and trailing plants to create a luxurious look. Because of its tolerance for low light levels, impatiens can provide color for shaded porches or roof overhangs where annuals demanding more sun would languish.

Plants range in size from 6 in. to 16 in. Some of the most popular named varieties from different species include: Accent series, mound-shaped plants, 12 to 15 in. tall, covered with 2-in. blossoms in fifteen colors, including five with star patterns in the flowers. The Super Elfin series comes in sixteen colors including 'Super Elfin Swirl', with picotee (edged in a contrasting color) flowers. Tempo series provides eight different colors with exceptionally large flowers and a mounding habit to l5 in. 'Blitz', a more vigorous variety in scarlet and several other colors, is especially suitable for containers or hanging baskets. Seed-grown doubles include 'Confection' and 'Rosette', each in several colors, while 'Duet' impatiens are doubles with bicolored flowers. (Only about 50 percent of the flowers of seed-grown doubles are the fluffy balls of color that look like miniature roses. The balance of plants bear semidouble or single flowers.) A number of

dwarf varieties, such as 'Tom Thumb Mixed', are useful as long-lasting edging plants. Propagated from cuttings are variegated varieties, with either gold or white markings combined with green.

Choosing New Guinea Impatiens
Of the dozens of varieties, most have been propagated from cuttings, which root quickly and easily in ten to fifteen days in a standard soil mix. Recommended types are primarily named varieties of the Bull series, the Danziger series, the Kienstler series and the Sunshine series from the breeder Mikkelsen. 'Spectra' is a seed mix producing a variety of plants with different flower colors and foliage types. 'Tango' is an award-winning seed-grown variety with large orange flowers, bright green foliage and a vigorous growth habit.

★**I. wallerana** (wall-ur-*ann*-a).
(Sometimes called *I. sultanii* or *I. holstii*.) Tender perennial from Africa, grown as an annual in cultivation. From this background come the plants that are now the most popular summer annual, planted everywhere for dependable and prolific flowering in light shade. It is also useful as a houseplant and for the cool greenhouse.

Stems are succulent. A few unusual varieties are easily rooted from cuttings, but most are propagated from seeds indoors started in February and March. Very frost-sensitive, they

should not be planted outdoors until the weather is thoroughly settled. They will thrive in any soil so long as they are watered abundantly; and except in the most barren soils, their best flowering performance comes without supplemental fertilizer. In most of the country, impatiens do not like sun all day, but keeping root areas continually moist will make them more tolerant to exposed conditions. They are probably the premier annual for partly shady to shady locations, with fewer flowers and more height as light quantity diminishes. In bright light, they are literally covered with flowers until frost strikes. In hot,

Impatiens

humid areas, even the compact varieties that have been introduced recently will grow more vigorously, easily becoming knee-high or more by summer's end. In cooler areas, they will top out at 12 to 15 in. with a 25 percent greater spread.

New Guinea Hybrids.

A joint Longwood Gardens-United States Department of Agriculture expedition to Southeast Asia in 1970 brought back many species of impatiens that have since been interbred to bring a startling new race of plants for the summer garden. Plants are bushy and long; linear leaves may be various shades of green, many overlaid with burgundy or purple, still others with yellow or white markings. Flowers are up to $2^{1}/_{2}$ in. in diameter in a wide variety of hues from pink and rose through crimson and orange to white. Many of them are bicolored with distinct markings or shadings in the petals. Distinctly more sun-tolerant than the impatiens above, in cooler parts of the country they will thrive in full sun, but in warmer areas will definitely benefit from afternoon shade.

Ipomoea (eye-poh-*mee*-uh).

MORNING-GLORY.

Morning-glory Family (*Convolvulaceae*).

A large group of annual and perennial vines, widely distributed in tropical and temperate zones, with representatives as varied as the utilitarian sweet potato and the decorative and familiar common morning-glory. *Ipomoea* differs from *Convolvulus*, another member of the family, in having a stigma instead of two linear stigmas. All have trumpet-shaped flowers.

The fast-growing vines are useful for covering rocky spaces, trellises and fences, and are also effective in the cool, sunny greenhouse or on a sunny windowsill. They grow easily in not too rich a garden soil, well dug to a spade's depth, full sun or light shade and, in the case of most species, ample water. The seeds are slow to germinate; they should be soaked overnight to speed the process.

I. alba (*al*-buh).

MOONFLOWER.

(Syn. *I. aculeatum*.) These night-blooming relatives of the morning-glory perfume the garden as they open. Tender, perennial, twining vines from tropical America, they are usually treated as annuals in all but the warmest regions of the U.S. The seeds are slow to germinate and should be notched or soaked overnight in room temperature water. Seeds started indoors in March, two or three in a 5-in. clay pot, can be set outdoors when all danger of frost is past. Full sun, light, rich, porous soil, a sheltered spot and plenty of water are needed. The closed flowers, if cut late in the day, will open in the evening and are effective for decoration. They also make a pleasant choice for the cool greenhouse, lending shade in the daytime, if trained along the roof. The fragrant, beautiful, large white flowers, reminiscent of morning-glory, are 5 to 6 in. across and as long, and open at dusk. Very abundant in bloom and fast-growing, covering as much as 20 ft. in a few months. The large, heart-shaped leaves make a substantial screen on trellises.

I. × nil (nill).

A tender perennial, it is normally grown as an annual. Many horticultural varieties have been developed from it including some with double flowers, some with frilled or fluted flowers and some with variegated foliage. 'Scarlet O'Hara', a bright red, is one popular variety. 'Early Call Mixed' provides a variety of flower colors, including red, pink, sky-blue, lavender, violet, chocolate and deep blue.

Impatiens 'Rosette Rose'

Impatiens 'Super Elphin'

Ipomoea

Ipomoea purpurea
MORNING GLORY

★**I. purpurea** (pur-*pew*-ree-uh).
MORNING GLORY.
The familiar, hardy annual morning-glory vine. Hairy-stemmed. Reaching 10 ft. in a season, it has large leaves and white, pink, purple or blue flowers, 2 to 3 in. long. Forms include some double flowers. Sow seeds in mid-April where plants are wanted or start indoors in individual pots in March, for transplanting in May.

I. quamoclit (*kwam*-o-clit).
CYPRESS VINE.
Fernlike foliage and red, pink and sometimes white flowers distinguish this climber. 'Relli-Valley Strain' is one selection.

I. tricolor (*try*-kull-or).
A tender perennial, it is usually used as an annual. Vines grow up to 20 ft. in a summer

Iresine herbstii
BLOOD LEAF

Kochia scoparia
SUMMER CYPRESS

season. Variety 'Heavenly Blue' is a beautiful large-flowered plant—a forget-me-not blue, typical of the best horticultural varieties. Some varieties have blooms notched with white.

Iresine (ear-i-*seen*-a).

BLOOD LEAF.

Amaranth Family (*Amaranthaceae*).

A genus of eighty tropical and subtropical species, mostly herbaceous. The cultivated varieties are mostly grown for their colorful foliage. Widely used as indoor plants and for conservatory displays, they are also colorful additions to outdoor plantings for foliage contrasts with flowers. Particularly useful in formal displays, they can often be found in floral clocks and other special plantings.

Normally grown from cuttings that root in ten to fifteen days in a standard soil mix. Plants should be started no later than early March for outdoor planting in May, and grown in 4-in. pots. They should be given enough space, and the tips pinched to develop compact, bushy plants. Plant outside only after the soil and air temperatures are warm, in any well-drained soil. Give compact plants full sun; taller, rangier plants need partial to full shade.

I. herbstii (*herb*-stee-eye).

A native of South America, leaves are nearly rounded with a notch at the ends. Typically the leaves are purplish-red or green with yellowish midribs and veins. *I. herbstii aureo-reticulata* has bright green leaves with yellow midribs and veins and red leaf stalks and stems.

I. lindenii (lynn-*den*-ee-eye).

Another native of South America, its leaves are narrow and sharp-pointed. Normally, they are very dark red. *I. lindenii formosa* has green leaves with yellow ribs and veining with leaf stalks and stems that are red.

Kochia (*koh*-kee-uh).

Goosefoot Family (*Chenopodiaceae*).

Only one species of this sizable genus of plants from Europe and Asia is in general cultivation. It is a tender annual useful for temporary hedges. In cool regions, start seeds indoors in late March and set out when the ground is thoroughly warmed. In warmer areas, sow seeds in outdoors in April where plants are desired. Plant in light soil, well dug to a spade's depth, and in full sun. Kochia self-sows in warm climates, and if untended can spread and become a nuisance.

K. scoparia (skop-*pay*-ree-uh).

BELVEDERE.

BURNING BUSH.

SUMMER CYPRESS.

The variety *K. scoparia trichophylla* (trik-oh-*fill*-uh) is the form most commonly grown. It reaches a height of 2 to 4 ft. and grows to a bushy, compact oval shape. The narrow 2-in. leaves are pale green all summer and turn a purplish-red with the coming of frosty nights. The flowers are minute and inconspicuous. Useful for a solid accent when grown in groups in the large border, and occasionally used as a pot plant in the cool greenhouse.

Lamium (*lay*-mee-um).

Mint Family (*Labiatae*).

DEAD NETTLE.

Somewhat weedy herbs of European origin. Leaves are opposite, the stem square. The plant thrives in partial shade, and is easily propagated by division in spring, or by seeds.

L. maculatum (mack-yew-*lay*-tum).
SPOTTED DEAD NETTLE.
Cultivars of this perennial species are most often used as ground covers but are sometimes a constituent of containers with flowering plants for seasonal interest. 'White Nancy' has silvery-white leaves with a narrow margin of green, and white flowers borne in June. 'Beacon Silver' is similar but its flowers are pink.

Lantana (lan-*tah*-nuh).
Verbena Family (*Verbenaceae*).
Tender, perennial shrubs from the tropics and subtropics, with pretty clusters of small, tubular flowers, hairy stems and crinkled opposite leaves. Grown outdoors as a hardy plant only from Zone 9 south. In these conditions, it can become invasive, and gardeners should be aware of this propensity. However, it is familiar in florists' displays, as a houseplant, a greenhouse plant and as a summer bedding plant.

Indoors, use a standard soil mix. If a graceful tree form is desired, the plant will need to be trained by pinching. At the base of each leaf on the main stem are dormant growth buds or eyes. Some will naturally develop into lateral or side branches, but the dormant buds will grow sooner than they would otherwise when the top of the main stem is removed. Then if the tips of these side growths are pinched, even more shoots will develop.

To obtain a treelike head on a lantana, remove all side shoots (as soon as they appear) from the main stem until it reaches a height of 3 ft. or more. When a clean stem of the desired height is attained, nip out the point and pinch all succeeding shoots when they have four to eight leaves. Continue this process until the treelike head is formed. Plants must be carefully staked during this process.

L. camara (kam-*mare*-uh).
RED SAGE.
YELLOW SAGE.
This shrub, which grows 2 to 4 ft. tall, has leaves 2 to 6 in. long, and flower clusters 1 to 2 in. across. The flowers are first yellow, then change to orange and red, often having all three colors at the same time. Charming when used as a bedding plant in borders, or as a pot plant for accent on the terrace, it is hardy outdoors only in Zones 9 and 10. Most cultivated varieties are classified under *L. hybrida*. The dwarf hybrids are only 1 to 3 ft. tall and can be started from seed indoors in early February to flower all summer. A rugged houseplant, it can be forced into bloom almost any time. Full sun or very light shade, and rich garden soil, well turned to a spade's depth, are right for this plant. 'Confetti' has flowers with pink, white, and red colors intermixed. 'Radiation' has tones of orange and red, while 'Pink Caprice' combines pink and yellow in the same flower clusters. There are many other cultivars.

L. montevidensis (mon-tay-vee-*den*-sis).
TRAILING LANTANA.
WEEPING LANTANA.
A pendulous species with lax stems, widely grown in containers and hanging baskets, or in ground plantings where its trailing propensity is desired. Clusters of rosy-lilac flowers are borne in great profusion all summer.

Lathyrus (*lath*-ihr-us).
Pea Family (*Leguminosae*).
Hardy and half-hardy annuals and perennials, widely distributed over almost all parts of the North Temperate Zone, much cultivated and hybridized. With blue-green leaves (alternate), they usually have climbing stems that support themselves by tendrils. Characteristic pealike

Lamium maculatum 'White Nancy'
SPOTTED DEAD NETTLE

Lantana camara 'Radiation'
RED SAGE

flowers, often brilliantly colored and sometimes fragrant, are pretty in the garden and especially lovely in arrangements of cut flowers. All species come easily from seeds sown outdoors in very early spring, but their cultural needs vary from seashore sand to rich, deep loams.

★**L. odoratus** (oh-dor-*ray*-tus).
SWEET PEA.
This fragrant, beautiful annual, in colors ranging from deepest purple to lightest lavender, from darkest ruby-red to palest pink, white and bicolored, is a great favorite of many gardeners. For best results with the largest, most showy ruffled hybrids, provide a cool atmosphere and unfailing moisture in the soil. Start seeds early so that plants will reach their peak bloom before the sultry hot days of summer. The seeds may even be planted in the fall just before frost. In either case, dig a trench 1^1/$_2$ to

Lantana montevidensis
TRAILING LANTANA

Lathyrus

Lathyrus odoratus
SWEET PEA

2¹/₂ ft. deep, mix in compost and peat moss, a complete fertilizer and enough lime to turn the soil slightly alkaline. Sow the seeds about 2 in. deep. If fall-sown, lay sand at the bottom of the trench to allow for the addition of drainage materials and mulch above it to prevent heaving. After seedlings start in the very early spring, water them well, and add more mulch.

Seeds may also be started indoors in individual peat pots. The seed coat is very hard. To speed germination, soak the seeds overnight and sow, pushing them into the standard soil mix about ¹/₃ in. (Those seeds that have not swelled after soaking should have a small chip of the seed coat removed with a sharp knife and soaked overnight again before planting.)

The vines need support as they grow. This may be in the form of wire fencing, a string trellis attached to a wall or twiggy branches set into the soil at planting time. They also need a

Lavatera trimestris 'Mont Blanc'
ROSE MALLOW

Layia elegans
TIDY-TIPS

sunny exposure, but with some protection from midday sun, when the sun is at its hottest. Continually picking faded flowers will prevent the plant from setting its seed, which ends the blooming period.

Varieties range from the late and early Spencers (Giant and Giant Ruffled) to the more recently developed Cuthbertsons (which bloom very early) and Multifloras (with many flowers per stem), to the heat resistant strains, and now the dwarfs, some of which grow only 6 in. tall and spread out to 14 in. (ideal as a ground cover). Other dwarfs form a low bush only 8 in. tall, with large flowers. Make your plantings in the cutting garden, or use them as a light screen. Also good in the cool greenhouse.

Lavatera (lav-at-*teer*-uh).

Mallow Family (*Malvaceae*).

A small genus of annuals, perennials, shrubs and trees. All have angled or lobed, alternate leaves and showy flowers. The most familiar and useful species are described below. Propagate by seeds or cuttings.

L. trimestris (trye-*mest*-riss).

ROSE MALLOW.

A bold, bright hardy annual from the Mediterranean region, of bushy branching habit, 3 to 6 ft. tall. Pale green, rounded leaves and large flowers, 4 in. across, in shades of pink and red. The largest variety is *splendens* (*splen-*denz); *alba* (*al*-buh) has beautiful white flowers. Blooms all summer if given a sunny and sheltered location.

Ordinary garden soil, not too rich and well dug to spade's depth, will nurture this plant. Sow seeds in late April or early May where plants are wanted, and thin to stand 1¹/2 to 2 ft. apart. Effective at the back of the annual border or as a temporary tall screen. Also useful as a cut

flower. Hollyhock rust will sometimes be troublesome. 'Loveliness' grows 3 to 4 ft. and has deep rose flowers. Award-winning 'Mont Blanc' is much shorter, topping out at 2 ft., and bears pure white flowers. 'Silver Cup', at 2 ft., has light pink flowers. It is also an award-winning variety.

Layia (lay-*ee*-uh).

Composite Family (*Compositae*).

Showy annuals native to California and the Southwest. Attractive in the annual border with their yellow or white daisylike blooms. Useful for a quick covering of rocky slopes, the rock garden or the cutting garden. Will bloom all summer. Sow seeds in early April where plants are wanted. Full sun and good drainage are needed. Ordinary soil, well turned to spade's depth, is all that is required.

L. elegans (*ell*-eg-anz).

TIDY-TIPS.

White tips on yellow petals and dark yellow centers add to the appeal of this species, which grows 1 to 1¹/2 ft. tall. Blooms are 2 in. across. Aromatic, gray-green foliage. Thin to stand 9 in. apart. They also make good cut flowers.

Limnanthes (lim-*nanth*-eez).

MARSH FLOWER.

Limnanthes Family (*Limnanthaceae*).

A small genus of native plants. There is only one species in active cultivation—an attractive, low-growing, hardy annual. It must have a constant supply of moisture, and the roots do best when they stay cool. Given these conditions and a sunny exposure, the plant will thrive in almost any soil and self-sow generously. Plant where wanted early in the spring, and thin to stand 4 in. apart. Makes an effective edging for the annual border, and a fine ground cover. It is also attractive in clumps near the front of the border.

L. douglasii (dug-*lass*-ee-eye).
MEADOW FOAM.
A spreading plant 5 to 8 in. tall, with pale green, feathery leaflets on compound, alternate leaves. The fragrant white blossoms, creamy-yellow at the base, are abundant in early summer. Pink and pale yellow varieties are available.

Limonium (lim-*moh*-nee-um).
SEA LAVENDER.
SEAPINK.
STATICE.
Plumbago Family (*Plumbaginaceae*).
Often listed in catalogs as *Statice*. A large genus, mostly from the Mediterranean region. Annuals and perennials, all easily grown and of great value in dried arrangements for their light airiness. Very useful in the rock garden, mixed borders and the cutting garden. They grow well near the sea coast, as their common name implies. The colors range from white and shades of yellow to pink and lavender. Sow seeds indoors in early March and transplant outdoors in May if very early bloom is wanted. Otherwise, sow seeds outdoors in April where plants are wanted for midsummer bloom. Full sun and a deeply dug, well-drained, porous but not too rich soil are required. When the blossoms are wanted for drying, they should be cut as soon as good color shows.

L. suworowii (soo-wor-*roh*-ee-eye).
RATTAIL STATICE.
RUSSIAN STATICE.
Annual, 10 to 20 in. tall, from Turkestan, with large basal leaves and handsome flower spikes of lavender and green flowers. The rounded

spikes of bloom are gracefully curved and therefore much in demand for flower arrangements. Blooms from mid-July until frost. Thin to 10 in. apart. Favorite cultivars include 'Heavenly Blue', with lovely purple blooms. Most other limoniums commonly used in the garden are perennial and used for cut flowers and as everlastings.

Linaria (lynn-*air*-ee-uh).
Figwort Family (*Scrophulariaceae*).
A genus of 150 species of mostly herbaceous annual and perennial plants, most native to the Mediterranean region. Closely related to snapdragons, they differ by having spurs at the base of the flowers instead of pouches.

L. maroccana (mare-oh-*kahn*-a).
ANNUAL TOADFLAX.
As its name indicates, a native of Morocco. It grows 1 to 1¹/₂ ft. tall with narrow leaves and slender flower spikes. Flower color in improved varieties ranges from pink through purple to yellow and white. Many have contrasting white throats. Easily grown from seed. Sown indoors six to eight weeks before plants are wanted for setting out. Give plants a light, well-drained, fertile soil that is well-watered (although plants are quite drought-tolerant), and full sun. These plants prefer cool temperatures (60-65 degrees daytime, cooler at night), and do well as pot plants in cool greenhouses. Selections include 'Fairy Lights Mixed' and 'Northern Lights'.

Linum (*lye*-num).
FLAX.
Flax Family (*Linaceae*).
The genus includes the economically important crop from which the fiber for linen is produced. There are many graceful species, both annual and perennial, with red, blue, yellow or

Limnanthes douglasii

MEADOW FOAM

Linaria maroccana 'Fairy Bouquet'

ANNUAL TOADFLAX

Limonium 'Heavenly Blue'

STATICE

Linum

Linum grandiflorum rubrum
FLOWERING FLAX

Lobelia erinus
EDGING LOBELIA

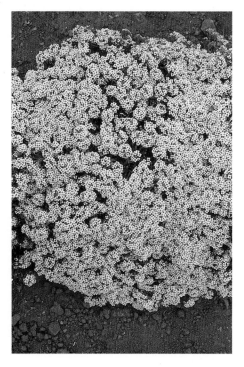

Lobularia maritima 'New Carpet of Snow'

white blossoms and small, narrow, blue-green alternate leaves. (Golden flax has broad leaves.) The blooms last only a day but are followed the next morning by a new crop of flowers. Attractive in the border and, in the case of the smaller species, excellent in the rock garden, where their delicate habit of growth is best displayed. Ordinary garden soil, well turned to a spade's depth, good drainage and full sun required. The annuals are grown from seeds planted outdoors in April, where the plants are wanted.

L. grandiflorum (gran-di-*floh*-rum).
FLOWERING FLAX.

Large flowers, 1¹/₂ in. across, in shades of pink, red and purple. A popular annual from northern Africa, it is 1 to 1¹/₂ ft. tall. The varieties *L. grandiflorum coccineum* (kok-*sin*-ee-um), *L. grandiflorum roseum* (roh-zee-um) and *L. grandiflorum rubrum* (roob-rum) are even showier than the species. All make a good display in the border all summer. The flower stems rise above the foliage with sprays of brightly colored bloom. 'Bright Eyes' is a selection with ivory-white blooms and a chocolate eye.

Lobelia (loh-*beel*-ee-uh).
Bellflower Family (*Campanulaceae*).

Perennials and annuals, all with showy flowers of irregular structure, some suited to the wild garden (especially the native species), others useful in the border or as container plants. Propagate annuals by seeds started indoors in early spring.

L. erinus (er-*rye*-nus).
EDGING LOBELIA.

Half-hardy annual from South Africa, excellent for edgings, the front of borders and window boxes. The type has small blue or lavender flowers, ¹/₂ in. across, with white or yellow throats. Varieties are available in shades of blue, red or white without any markings in the throat. There are two heights: the compact varieties are 4 to 6 in. and the spreading varieties grow 12 to 24 in. long. Seeds should be sown in early March indoors, seedlings hardened off in April and planted out in May, 5 or 6 in. apart. It blooms all summer. Sun or partial shade, plenty of moisture, and light, rich loam, well turned to a spade's depth, are needed. *Lobelia*, particularly trailing kinds, are widely used in containers. They are most satisfactory in cooler summer locations. Compact varieties include: 'Blue Moon', a rich blue; 'Crystal Palace', deep blue with bronze foliage; 'Cambridge Blue', with sky blue flowers; and 'Mrs. Clibran', deep blue with a white eye. Trailing varieties are the Fountain series in blue, lilac and white; and 'Sapphire', blue with a white eye.

Lobularia (lob-yew-*lay*-ree-uh).
SWEET ALYSSUM.

Mustard Family (*Cruciferae*).

There is only one species in cultivation, a valuable little plant from the Mediterranean region. A perennial grown as an annual, it has many uses, but is especially popular as an edging plant. Propagate by seeds sown in spring.

★L. maritima (mar-rit-*im*-uh).

Thrifty, branching and spreading plant ranging in size from 4 in. to 1 ft. Very small, alternate leaves and fragrant flowers, which bloom all summer until frost. There are many fine named varieties in white, lavender and purple shades. Grown easily from seeds, sow indoors in March or outdoors as soon as the ground is warm. Ordinary garden soil and full sun are required. In warm areas, it will self-sow. Thrives in the moist atmosphere of gardens near the sea. Also very attractive when grown in pots indoors or in the greenhouse. Use standard soil mix and keep in a cool, sunny area. Varieties

Lobularia

include: 'Wonderland', in separate shades of deep rose, purple and white; 'New Carpet of Snow', white; 'Oriental Night', dark violet; and 'Rosie O'Day', lavender-rose.

Lonas (*loh*-nuss).

Composite Family (*Compositae*).

There is only one species, an unfamiliar but showy, half-hardy annual from the Mediterranean region. The plant is small, about 1 ft. tall, and needs full sun and a light, rich soil, well turned to a spade's depth. Sow seed outdoors in late April, and thin to stand 10 in. apart.

L. annua (in-oh-*doh*-ruh).

AFRICAN DAISY.

GOLDEN AGERATUM

This plant grows to 1 ft. tall and about 8 in. in width. Its upper leaves are finely divided. The bright yellow, double small flowers in thick clusters bloom all summer and last exceptionally well when cut. Also very attractive when dried for winter arrangements. For this purpose, cut flowers when they have attained a rich color, and hang upside down in small bunches to dry.

Lotus (*loh*-tuss).

LOTUS.

Legume Family (*Leguminosae*).

A genus of about 100 species, only a few of which are used as ornamentals. Entirely different from the lotus of water gardens (*Nelumbo*), they are mostly herbaceous plants. Winged pea (*Lotus tetragonolobus*) is widely used for food, and bird's-foot trefoil (*Lotus corniculatus*) is much grown as an animal forage.

L. berthelotii (birth-eh-*lote*-ee-eye).

LOTUS VINE.

PARROT'S-BEAK.

Although not a vine, this name is derived from its many trailing stems and abundance of fine gray-green leaves. It is most often used as a constituent of container plantings, hanging baskets, window boxes and patio planters combined with other flowers. Although the flowers, borne in June or July, are spectacular (bright red and sharply curved, like a parrot's beak—hence the name), it is the foliage for which it is most valuable through a long season. Usually propagated from cuttings. Give full sun or partial shade, and well-drained soil. Plants will grow to 3 ft. in diameter by the end of summer, and will survive poor soils but benefit from soils with average nutrition levels.

Lunaria (loo-*nay*-ree-uh).

HONESTY.

MOONWORT.

Mustard Family (*Cruciferae*).

One annual or biennial and one perennial, both from Europe and Asia, are the only species. Both are used for winter bouquets, the very flat seedpods having a central, white, satiny wafer section that is revealed when their grayish, parchmentlike covers are peeled off. It is easily grown in ordinary garden soil, well turned to a spade's depth, and does best in full sun. Propagate the annual species by seeds sown in fall or early spring.

L. annua (*an*-yew-uh).

MONEY PLANT.

Annual or biennial, which self-sows once established and provides a continuing supply of lovely white papery disks, $1^1/_2$ to 2 in. across, from its seedpods. The purple flowers are slightly fragrant and bloom in May on a spike.

Lonas annua

AFRICAN DAISY

Lunaria annua

HONESTY

Lotus berthelotii

LOTUS VINE

Lunaria

There are also white- and crimson-colored varieties and a form with variegated leaves called 'Stella'. The seedpods may be gathered from the long stems, 1¹/₂ to 3 ft. tall, in August when they have dried. Zone 4.

Lupinus (loo-*pine*-us).
LUPINE.

Pea Family (*Leguminosae*).

A genus of about 200 species, mostly annuals or herbaceous perennials, but also some shrubby kinds frequently called tree lupines. The best known lupines are selections (known as Russell lupines, or variants thereof) of the short-lived perennial, *L. regalis.* These are splendid perennials for the June garden; their stately spikes resound with color in white, yellow, red, pink and blue, and bicolors that add white. While they are sometimes treated as biennials, they are perennial in a large segment of the country and so are featured in the *Perennials* volume. Seeds of lupines are very hard and should be soaked in water overnight before sowing. The annual species grow well in ordinary garden soil, well turned to a spade in depth, and in full sun.

L. hartwegii (hart-*weg*-ee-eye).

A native of Mexico, this annual grows 2 to 3 ft. high. Flowers are blue with the center petal in rose-pink. A selection from *L. hartwegii* ssp. *cruickshankii* (crook-*shank*-ee-eye) has flowers of blue marked with gold, bronze and white. It is called 'Sunrise'.

L. luteus (*loot*-ee-us).

YELLOW LUPINE.

An annual species much grown for animal feed, but its fragrant, yellow blossoms make it a worthy garden ornamental, too.

L. nanus (*nan*-us).

SKY LUPINE.

This annual, a California native, grows from 6 to 15 in. tall. Flowers are usually blue with a white or yellow spot, but white and yellow forms also occur. 'Pixie Delight' is a selection.

L. texensis (tex-*ens*-is).

TEXAS BLUEBONNET.

Masses of this blue and white lupine grace miles of Texas countryside each spring. Recently, selections in pink and white have been made and are being distributed to gardeners. Grows up to 12 in. Zone 6.

Malcolmia (mal-*koh*-mee-uh).
MALCOLM STOCK.

Mustard Family (*Cruciferae*).

A small genus of annuals and perennials from southern Europe. The species most often found in cultivation is a fast-growing edging plant, useful in rock walls and between stepping stones where traffic is light.

M. maritima (mar-rit-*im*-uh).

VIRGINIA STOCK.

An easily grown, small annual that reaches 6 to 8 in. in height. Prolific and free-flowering, in tones of red, pink, white or lavender. The individual florets, 1 in. across, bloom in June and July. If wanted all summer, successive sowings will give bloom until frost. Sow seed in early spring where plants are wanted and thin to 3 in. apart. Malcolmia self-sows, and there are usually volunteer seedlings once it is established. Likes full sun and a light garden soil, well turned to a spade's depth.

Lupinus texensis
TEXAS BLUEBONNET

Malcolmia maritima
VIRGINIA STOCK

Malope (*mal*-up-pee).

Mallow Family (*Malvaceae*).

A genus of four species from the Mediterranean region, all annuals with mallowlike flowers. Flowers are flared bells with a prominent column in the center, composed of many yellow stamens surrounding the pistil. Grow in full sun.

M. trifida (*tri*-fid-uh).

This is the only species and its selections are commonly grown in the garden. Plants grow to 3 ft. tall bearing numerous 2- to 3-in. flowers. Because they grow best in cool weather, sow seeds outdoors in earliest spring. In areas with cool weather throughout the summer, repeat sowings for a succession of bloom. Blooming is prolonged if spent flowers are removed promptly. They grow well in ordinary garden soil, and need no supplemental water unless

Malope trifida

Malope

Matthiola incana
GILLYFLOWER

there is very dry weather. Flowers on *M. trifida grandiflora* are a rich, royal purple. 'Pink Queen' has flared bells of pink shading to burgundy in the flower centers.

Matricaria parthenium.
See *Chrysanthemum parthenium.*

Matthiola (math-*ee*-oh-luh).
STOCK.
Mustard Family (*Cruciferae*).
Prized and long-familiar annuals and perennials. The following species is one of the few grown for ornamental purposes.

M. incana (in-*kay*-nuh).
GILLYFLOWER.
From southern Europe, a biennial in the wild. The gray-leaved species from which most of the beautiful garden and greenhouse stocks have

Melampodium paludosum 'Medallion'

been developed. Most garden varieties have been developed from *M. incana annua*, (*an-yew-uh*) which is less woody and comes into flower sooner from seed. The true annuals, such as 'Beauty of Nice' and 'Ten-weeks Stock' (blooms ten weeks after seeding), derive from the variety *annua* and grow $1^1/2$ to 2 ft. tall. Sow seed indoors in March; plant out in late May, about 10 in. apart. The heavy flower heads need support; twiggy brush growth is good for this purpose, inserted when the plants are 6 to 8 in. tall. The fragrant, double flowers are available in many colors—every shade from dark purple through lavender, rose and pink to creamy yellow and white.

Useful in borders and in the cool greenhouse. Indoors, maggots and flea beetles may attack the plants. Stocks are best grown to flower in cool weather, in spring or fall or in areas with cool summer climates. It is best to avoid excessive watering; give the plants full sun, rich soil and moderate moisture outdoors. To ensure fully double flowers, transplant only seedlings with a notch in the young leaves. 'Brompton' stock, though a beautiful, true biennial and a variety of incana, is grown as an annual and started early indoors. It is a later bloomer than the others, usually making its best display in August and September. 'Legacy' is a strain with eight colors, earlier than most, and very fragrant.

Melampodium (mell-am-*pode*-ee-um).
Daisy Family (*Compositae*).
A genus of thirty-six species from North and South America. The name comes from the Greek words that mean blackfoot, referring to the black stalks. The species grown in the garden are low, bushy, herbaceous perennials, but treated as annuals for summer garden show. Grow in full sun; plants are tolerant of poor, dry soils.

M. paludosum (pal-you-*dose*-um).
Rough, hairy leaves are surmounted with yellow daisylike flowers. It is easy to grow, either by direct sowing in the garden when the soil and weather are warm, or for earlier flowering, seeding indoors eight weeks prior to outdoor planting. They are tough plants that require no special care and will continue blooming profusely until frost. 'Medallion' grows to 10 in. and has copious 1-in. yellow flowers; 'Showstar' is a compact, bushy plant with flowers of the same size and color.

Mesembryanthemum.
See *Dorotheanthus*.

Mimulus (*mim*-yew-lus).
MONKEY FLOWER.
MUSKFLOWER.
Figwort Family (*Scrophulariaceae*).
Found in many parts of the Western Hemisphere, these attractive and interesting annuals and perennials with odd-shaped five-lobed blooms are beautiful in the wild, and with reasonable care may be grown in cultivated gardens. All the perennials like moisture and either full sun or partial shade. Shady fern gardens, creeks or poolsides, open wet meadows, shady nooks in rock gardens, and moist woodlands all offer good locations. Add leafmold, sphagnum moss or peat moss to the soil if it is not present naturally. The annuals prefer lighter, more porous soil and less moisture.

Seeds may be sown outdoors in early spring and transplanted. Opposite leaves occur in all species. Flowers are yellow, blue, purple and varied shades of white to maroon, and have a long blooming period, into late fall. Sometimes grown in the cool greenhouse. All the species below are worth more attention than they ordinarily get.

Mimulus

Mimulus × *hybridus* 'Malibu Wine'
MONKEY FLOWER

Mirabilis jalapa
FOUR-O'CLOCK

Moluccella laevis
BELLS-OF-IRELAND

M. guttatus (goo-*tay*-tus).

COMMON MONKEY FLOWER.

This native North American is actually a perennial in Zone 9 but can be grown as an annual in the rest of the country. The flowers can be compared to the snapdragon. They are tubular with two lips, yellow with brown spots on the lower lip and throat. These spots sometimes look like a monkey's face, hence the plant's name. The flowers appear through summer and fall, and the plant is somewhat frost-hardy in some locations. It grows to about $1^1/2$ to 2 ft. tall with sessile leaves (no stem) that are ovate, opposite, $1^1/2$ to 2 in. long and sharply toothed. Plant in full sun in a good fertile soil with plenty of organic matter. Start from seed, indoors or out.

M. × hybridus (*high*-brih-dus).

MONKEY FLOWER.

This is the result of a cross between *M. guttatus* and *M. luteus*. It grows to 6 to 8 in. tall and has ovate leaves that are sessile and sharply toothed. The flowers come in yellows and reds and combinations of these colors with brown spots on the two lips and down the throat. It is a trumpet-shaped flower, much like a snapdragon.

Start from seed indoors in early spring and transplant outside after all danger of frost is past. Plant in light to partial shade in moist, well-drained soil that is high in organic matter. It can withstand wet sites and can also be container-grown if regularly watered. Use in an annual bed or in a natural setting near water or in a rock garden. Some good cultivars are: 'Calypso Mixture', a wide range of colors on a compact plant; and Malibu series, taller with yellow and orange flowers.

Mirabilis (mihr-*rab*-il-iss).

Four-o'clock Family (*Nyctaginaceae*).

Natives of the Western Hemisphere, these showy plants with tubular blossoms were familiar in old-fashioned gardens and today add a charming touch to borders and beds. Tender perennials grown as annuals, from seeds either started indoors or, for later bloom, sown outdoors when the ground is warm. Plants are also started from the tubers lifted in early autumn and stored over the winter, like dahlia roots, at a moderate temperature in a dry place. Light, rich soil, well turned to a spade's depth, full sun and shelter from strong winds are desirable.

M. jalapa (juh-*lay*-puh).

FOUR-O'CLOCK.

MARVEL-OF-PERU.

Fast-growing, bushy, sturdy plants, 2 to 3 ft. tall, literally covered with funnel-shaped flowers, 1 to 2 in. long, in colors of red, pink, yellow, white or striped. Opens late in the afternoon on sunny days or all day on cloudy days. Very pleasing in the large border, where colors may be mixed, or for one-color groupings in a bed. Self-sows in warm sections.

Moluccella (mol-yew-*sell*-uh).

Mint Family (*Labiatae*).

There are four species, native to the Old World and either attractive annuals or short-lived perennials, easily grown from seed planted outdoors early in spring. They thrive in light, porous soil in full sun or light shade. This is a free-flowering plant.

M. laevis (*lee*-viss).

BELLS-OF-IRELAND.

SHELLFLOWER.

Grows 2 ft. or more tall. The flowering stalks of this plant are used extensively for indoor decoration, either fresh or dried. The tiny, pink or white, fragrant flowers are relatively inconspicuous, but each is set within a decorative bell-shaped or shell-like calyx. Pale green and delicately veined, these calyxes lend an architectural air to flower arrangements. Grow these plants from seed. For use dried, cut before seed ripens; hang upside down in an airy place.

Myosotis (mye-oh-*soh*-tiss).

FORGET-ME-NOT.

Borage Family (*Boraginaceae*).

Annuals, perennials and biennials native to Europe and America, almost always grown as annuals. One of the most beautiful of the early spring flowers, growing in matlike clusters, the blossoms of sky blue, pink and white are halted only by the heat of summer. Few spring flowers are as valuable or as pretty as edging plants, as underplanting in a bulb garden, in the cutting garden, for naturalizing in the wild garden, in moist woodlands and beside pools and small streams. Also useful in the cool greenhouse. Partial shade and an acid soil give best results, but these flowers are adaptable to many soils and often to full sun. Self-sows abundantly once established. Blooms in January and February on the West Coast and in other warm sections, later in the spring in regions where it is cooler. Sow seeds in fall for earliest spring bloom, but early spring sowing will provide flowers by tulip time on smaller plants.

M. alpestris (al-*pest*-riss).

ALPINE FORGET-ME-NOT.

Smaller flowers and typically smaller growth habit than those below. 'Blue Ball' forms a tidy mound with bright blue flowers; it is ideal for edging. 'Carmine King' has red flowers.

M. sylvatica (sil-*vat*-ik-uh).

Sometimes listed in catalogs as *M. alpina*. Native to England, this is the source of fine garden varieties. A biennial, 1 to 2 ft. tall, it is usually started indoors in March from seed and grown as an annual. Makes bushy, sturdy plants and blooms abundantly. Native to dry woodlands, it grows best in cultivation, in well-drained soil with abundant moisture. There are many varieties listed, including *alba* (*al*-buh), white-flowered; *fischeri* (fish-*err*-eye), pink-flowered; *atrocaerulea* (at-roh-see-*rew*-lee-uh), dark blue-flowered; and *grandiflora* (gran-di-*floh*-ruh), large-flowered.

Nemesia (nem-*meesh*-ee-uh).

Figwort Family (*Scrophulariaceae*).

Herbs and subshrubs from South Africa, with spurred tubular flowers, usually in racemes. They bloom from June to September. Start seeds indoors in early spring, and plant seedlings 6 in. apart. Plants are modest in size, with a rather open habit and lax stems that will spill over the sides if planted in containers, where they excel.

N. strumosa (strew-*moh*-suh).

Annual, to 2 ft. Flowers in white, yellow and various shades of purple appear in racemes 4 in. long. There are several varieties, including *grandiflora* (gran-di-*floh*-ruh), a very large form; *nana compacta* (*nay*-nuh kom-*pak*-tuh), a dwarf; and *suttonii* (sut-*toh*-nee-eye), which has flowers in several colors—white, yellow, rose-pink, orange and scarlet. The upper petals of 'Mello Red and White' are red, lower ones white. 'Carnival Mixed' has a variety of rich colors, while 'Tapestry' has a mixture of pastel tones.

Nemesia strumosa

Nemophila (nee-*moff*-ill-uh).

Waterleaf Family (*Hydrophyllaceae*).

Showy, easily raised annuals, native to California, with lovely, blue or white, saucer-shaped flowers and light green leaves. Partial shade, a light loam with added humus and protection from strong winds constitute ideal conditions, but the plants will do well in almost any soil. Very hot weather shortens the blooming season drastically. Seeds should be sown where plants are wanted, either in the fall in frost-free sections or in early spring where it is cooler. Under favorable conditions, the plants will self-sow. Useful in borders and in the rock garden.

N. maculata (mak-yew-*lay*-tuh).
FIVE-SPOT.

A charming little plant, 4 to 8 in. high, covered with white flowers, 2 in. across, each purple-

Nemophila maculata
FIVE-SPOT

Nicotiana alata
FLOWERING TOBACCO

Nicotiana sylvestris

spotted at the outer edges of the petals. Deeply cut leaves. *N. maculata grandiflora* (gran-di-*floh*-ruh) has flowers considerably larger than the type. There is a white form, *N. maculata albida* (*al*-bid-uh), and a dark purple form, *N. maculata purpurea* (pur-*pew*-ree-uh).

N. menziesii (men-*zee*-zee-eye).
BABY BLUE-EYES.
Low-growing plant, 6 to 8 in. high, decorative in the border and rock garden, with sky blue and white flowers, 1 to 1¹/₂ in. across, tubular in shape. There are many varieties offered by seedsmen—white, blue and purple, with margins and centers of varying tones, and a new variety, 'Pennie Black', of deep purple edged in white. Also attractive in the cool greenhouse.

Nicotiana (nik-oh-shee-*ay*-nuh).
TOBACCO PLANT.
Nightshade Family (*Solanaceae*).
Half-hardy annuals and perennials originally from warm sections of South America, Australia and many of the islands between. Though subtropical in origin, many species do well in temperate climates, and some will self-sow. Tall plants with fragrant tubular flowers, which are white, yellow, crimson or purple. The foliage is large and luxuriant in many of the species. The larger varieties are decorative at the back of borders. Some hybrid varieties, such as those in the Domino series, are quite short.

N. affinis. See *Nicotiana alata*.

★**N. alata** (uh-*lay*-tuh).
FLOWERING TOBACCO.
JASMINE TOBACCO.
ORNAMENTAL TOBACCO.
(Syn. *N. affinis*.) A perennial in its native habitat, this performs well as an annual in colder

climates. A basal clump of ovate 4- to 10-in. leaves covered with sticky hairs gives rise to a short raceme of trumpetlike flowers with a long tube and broad face. There are few of these flowers per raceme, but many racemes are produced, resulting in a dense, rounded clump of 1- to 3-ft. stems. The flowers come in colors ranging from lime-green to white, crimson, lavender, maroon, green, pink and yellow. The species has a corolla that is chalk-white inside and greenish outside. Many of the modern hybrids are believed to be derived from *N. alata* and other species.

Nicotianas flower from early summer to fall and will even tolerate a light frost. Many of the species have flowers that open at night, with sweet fragrance to attract night-flying insects for pollination. However, most modern hybrids open during the day, and their fragrance is greatly diminished. While the straight species can be tall and awkward, the cultivars are lower-branching and more compact. They will survive full sun but prefer partial shade, as flowers may fade in full sun. The soil should be well drained but moist. Provide more water if planted in full sun. They do well in mass plantings or as part of an annual bed or border. They can also be planted in containers. Since this plant is in the same family as the tomato, be sure not to plant the two too closely together, as Nicotiana could attract diseases that will harm tomatoes. Some good cultivars are: Domino series, compact early flowering in a variety of colors; 'Lime Green', 18-in. plant with lime green flowers; Nicki series, wide variety of colors, including a good lime green; 'Sensation Mixed,' 30-in. plants; 'Tinkerbell Mixture,' 10- to 12-in. plants with a variety of colors; 'Dwarf White Bedder,' 12- to 18-in. plants in white.

N. langsdorfii (langs-*dorf*-ee-eye).
This species grows up to 5 ft. tall with branches supporting the greenish-yellow, drooping flowers.

N. sylvestris (sil-*vess*-triss).
Tall perennial, 4 to 5 ft. high, with large leaves and nodding, fragrant, white flowers, 3 to 4 in. long, in thick spikes. Native of Argentina. The flowers open during the day if the sun is not bright. Otherwise it is night-blooming. Likes some shade. Easily grown, and suitable to the large border and the wild garden. *N. sylvestris* 'Daylight' has flowers that usually stay open during the day. Grown in the North as an annual. Start indoors in early March. Set out in May to stand 2 to $2^1/2$ ft. apart.

Nierembergia (nee-rem-*berg*-ee-uh).
CUPFLOWER.
Nightshade Family (*Solanaceae*).
Annuals and perennials native to South America, grown as pot plants, in rock gardens and in borders. The cup-shaped flowers are white, blue or lavender, 1 to 2 in. across. In the North they are grown from seed sown indoors in February and planted out in May. In the South propagate by division, cuttings or layering. These plants need full sun, as well as well-drained, well-watered soil.

N. hippomanica caerulea (hip-poh-*man*-ik-uh see-*rew*-lee-uh).
Annual in the North; perennial in the South. The violet-blue flowers bloom during the summer. 'Purple Robe' is the most widely grown. Flowers are purple with yellow eyes.

N. repens (*ree*-penz).
WHITE CUPFLOWER.
Sometimes called *N. rivularis*. The foliage forms

dense mats and is often used between stepping stones. Grows to 6 in. Flowers are cream-colored, streaked with purple, 1 to 2 in. across. Perennial in warmer climates. Seed is not widely available.

N. rivularis. See *N. repens.*

Nigella (nye-*jell*-uh).
Buttercup Family (*Ranunculaceae*).
Annuals from the Mediterranean region and western Asia. Easily grown, and profuse in bloom. Charming for use as a cut flower, and good in the border. The seedpods are effective in dried arrangements. Sow seeds in early spring where plants are wanted. Successive sowings will give a long season of bloom. It often self-sows. Full sun and ordinary garden soil are ideal.

N. damascena (dam-ass-*see*-nuh).
LOVE-IN-A-MIST.
Feathery leaves, blue or white flowers of spidery structure, 1 to 2 in. across, and a sturdy habit of growth make this species a great favorite for the annual border. Grows $1^1/2$ to 2 ft. tall. 'Miss Jekyll' is sky blue, 'Miss Jekyll Alba' white, both with semidouble flowers. 'Persian Jewels' is a mixture of mauve, purple, rose and white flowers. There are also dwarf forms available—including one selection named 'Dwarf Moody Blue'. Thin to 6 in. apart.

Nolana (noh-*law*-nuh).
CHILEAN BELLFLOWER.
Nolana Family (*Nolanaceae*).
Perennials of sprawling habit from South America, all grown as annuals in North America. Showy, tubular flowers, blue or purple on purplish stems. Spoon-shaped leaves. Pretty for edging borders, for the rock garden

and for hanging baskets. The flowers open in full sun, but remain closed in cloudy weather. Easily grown in any sandy garden soil. Full sun is best. Sow seeds in early spring, where plants are wanted, and thin to stand 5 to 6 in. apart. The seedlings transplant well.

N. paradoxa (pare-a-*dox*-a).
Trailing plant, 4 to 6 in. high, with large, light blue, pale yellow-throated flowers 2 in. across. Plants bloom all summer. Thin to 4 to 6 in. apart. Good in rock gardens and hanging baskets. 'Blue Bird' is most commonly grown. The variety 'Blue Ensign' has darker blue flowers.

Ocimum (*oss*-im-um).
Mint Family (*Labiatae*).
Pungently aromatic leaves and tiny white or purplish florets. Annuals and tender perennials grown as annuals. The annual basil is common in herb and vegetable gardens.

O. basilicum (bas-*sil*-ik-um).
BASIL.
Tender annual, to 2 ft., shorter in the dwarf forms. Slightly crinkled, highly flavored leaves, usually green, but dark purple in some varieties. It has a well-branched habit of growth and is propagated by seed sown directly in the kitchen garden. Sometimes started indoors in flats in late March or April. The seedlings can be set out when all danger of frost is past. It is sometimes grown in rows in the vegetable garden, in beds in the herb garden or—in the case of the dwarf forms—as an edging for the herb border.

Used extensively as a seasoning, particularly for tomato dishes. There is an old-fashioned belief that flies will stay away if a basil plant is kept in the house. Pots of basil cultivated on city terraces and rooftops seem completely

Nierembergia hippomanica caerulea 'Purple Robe'
CUPFLOWER

Nigella damascena
LOVE-IN-A-MIST

Nolana paradoxa 'Blue Bird'
CHILEAN BELLFLOWER

Ocimum

Ocimum basilicum
BASIL

immune to air pollution. 'Dark Opal' and 'Purple Ruffles' are two dark-leaved selections. 'Spicy Globe' forms a mound and bears small leaves.

Onopordum (own-oh-*pord*-um)
SCOTCH THISTLE.
Daisy Family (*Compositae*).
A genus of forty species from Europe, northern Africa and western Asia. They are coarse, branched biennials with spiny-toothed leaves. The flowers are very thistlelike, in purple, rose, blue-violet and sometimes white. These plants prefer sunny, well-drained places in the garden. The Scotch thistle (*O. acanthium*), rarely seen in Scotland and probably an immigrant, is usually the only one grown in gardens.

Onopordum acanthium
SCOTCH THISTLE

Osteospermum ecklonis 'Purple'
STAR OF THE VELDT

O. acanthium (uh-*canth*-ee-um).
SCOTCH THISTLE.
A biennial that in the second year reaches a ghostly 5 to 9 ft. tall, its aspect the result of white, cottony hairs clothing the stems and leaves. Leaves are toothed and prickly. It makes a dramatic statement in the garden as a backdrop for a perennial border. The thistlelike blossoms, usually purple but sometimes white, are very attractive and appealing to birds and bees. Scotch thistle will reseed itself; to prevent an invasion, remove most flower heads immediately after flowers close. Start your own from seed. Sow two months before planting in the garden. The first year's rather insignificant rosette of leaves is climaxed the following year by the stately flowering stalk. Zone 4.

Osteospermum (awst-ee-oh-*sperm*-um).
STAR OF THE VELDT.
Daisy Family (*Compositae*).
A large genus of seventy species that were formerly all clustered under the genus *Dimorphotheca*. They are mostly native to South Africa, although they range as far north as Arabia. Most are herbaceous plants or subshrubs. They bear solitary daisylike flowers with a central eye of tubular disk florets surrounded by petal-like ray florets. Many of them, particularly the ones used most in the garden, flower over a long period. Grow in a warm, sunny garden location, with excellent drainage.

O. ecklonis (ek-*lone*-iss).
A subshrub growing 3 to 4 ft. tall, perennial in frost-free climates, it bears its daisylike flowers over a long blooming period and, as a result, is widely used for summer color in less favored climates. It is especially useful in containers on decks or patios. The white flowers have blue centers, while the undersides of the petals are blue or violet. Most commonly grown from cuttings.

O. hyoseroides (high-oh-sir-*oy*-dees).
(Frequently listed as *Tripteris hyoseroides.*) An annual, growing to 2 ft., that has yellow-orange flowers with violet centers.

Papaver (pap-*pay*-ver).
POPPY.
Poppy Family (*Papaveraceae*).
Some of the loveliest and most exciting perennial, biennial and annual flowers for borders belong to this genus. Native to Europe, Asia and North America, the various species range from 6 in. to 4 ft. tall. The basal leaves of poppies are generally hairy and die down soon after flowering. The flowers have shimmering silky petals in shades of white, cream, pink, yellow, orange and red. (There are blue poppylike flowers, but these belong to the genus *Meconopsis.*) The most popular annual species is the smaller pastel-hued annual Shirley or corn poppies (*P. rhoeas*).

Perennial and annual species have similar cultural requirements. Poppies need well-drained soil, generally on the light and sandy side. Most may be propagated by seed. Seeds sown in the late summer in warmer climates will produce handsome flowers in the spring; in cooler regions they may be planted on the snow or directly in the soil of the border in late winter or early spring. Full sun is required. Seedlings should be transplanted to individual peat pots before the taproot forms for success in later transplanting to the garden. Or seed can be planted where the plants are to flower.

Most poppies make excellent vase flowers. Sear the stem with a lighted match the moment they are cut; this cuts the flow of milky juice from the stem and helps the blossoms last longer in water.

Papaver

Papaver nudicaule 'Oregon Rainbow Giants'
ICELAND POPPY

Papaver rhoeas 'Shirley Varieties'
SHIRLEY POPPY

Papaver somniferum
OPIUM POPPY

P. commutatum. See *P. rhoeas.*

P. nudicaule (nood-i-*call*-ee).

ICELAND POPPY.

Derived from a number of species, all of which are referred to by its species name. Although perennial, they are typically short-lived and most often grown as annuals and allowed to reseed, although some of the desirable characteristics are lost in the progeny. They are available in many colors, including double forms. The shimmering flowers are very beautiful. 'Oregon Rainbows' is a selection with many colors, including bicolors and picotees. 'Wonderland' is a seed selection with large flowers of many colors on short stems.

P. rhoeas (row-*ee*-as).

SHIRLEY POPPY.

(Closely related to *P. commutatum* [com-mew-*tate*-um], which is often called the Flanders poppy.) Most typically these 1- to 1 $^1/_2$-ft. plants have flowers of the bright Flanders poppy red with a black blotch at the base, but variants can be purple or white with shades in between. 'Mother of Pearl' is a unique range of pastel colors. 'Shirley Re-Selected Double Mixture' includes double flowers of pink, white, rose, salmon and crimson.

P. somniferum (sahm-*nyff*-ur-um).

OPIUM POPPY.

This is the species that supplies poppy seeds for cakes and breads, as well as opium and its derivative, heroin. Although it is illegal to cultivate it in the U.S. except under special license, its blooms of pink, purple, lavender and white are very beautiful, and keen gardeners have been known to pass seeds discreetly from one to another.

★★**Pelargonium** (pel-ahr-*goh*-nee-um).

GERANIUM.

STORK'S BILL.

Geranium Family (*Geraniaceae*).

A large group of decorative herbaceous plants with showy leaves and flowers. In their many forms, they are indispensable for the summer garden, both as container plants and for planting beds. There are about 280 species of *Pelargonium,* with more than 200 from South Africa. From several have been derived thousands of hybrids and selections. Although called geraniums, they are distinct from the genus *Geranium,* which is composed of hardy, herbaceous perennials commonly called crane's bill for the shape of the seedpod. The *Pelargonium* pod is even more elongated—thus the common name stork's bill (some botanists but few gardeners use these common names).

Pelargonium 'Catford Belle'

Pelargonium

Pelargonium 'Dolly Varden'
FANCY–LEAFED GERANIUM

For garden purposes, pelargoniums are roughly grouped as follows: zonal geraniums (for the patterned leaves that many exhibit); ivy geraniums, with trailing stems used widely as container plants; regal pelargoniums, with large flower clusters in dramatic colors; and scented species and selections primarily grown for their aromatic foliage. (For a close look at specialty plants and their culture and propagation, see "Garden Geraniums," page 128.)

Zonal Geraniums.

Tender perennials which must be replanted each year, except in frost-free areas along both coasts and in the Deep South. In California, they form large shrubs unless cut back severely. In Florida, they are often most satisfactory in the fall, winter and spring, because the intense heat and humidity of summer adversely affect their growth.

Pelargonium 'Elegante'

Pelargonium peltatum
IVY-LEAVED GERANIUM

Flower colors now are many and varied. Reds come in every variant of hue—scarlet, cerise, orange–red and more. Pinks and roses range from the lightest appleblossom color of spring to intense, electric tones. Some have red or white blotches or both at the bases of petals. In others, lighter–colored petal edges shade to deeper tones at the center. There are vibrant purple varieties, and flowers with red and purple intermixed in a strong but pleasing way. White geraniums are becoming more popular each year. Recently, new varieties, with very deep green foliage that contrasts sharply with flower color, have piqued gardeners' interests.

A few of the many good varieties of geraniums grown from cuttings include: 'Alba', a clear white; 'Blues', cherry-blossom pink with rose and white markings at petal centers; 'Disco', a combination of red and near purple; 'Forever Yours', a vigorous red; 'Schone Helene', two-toned salmon; and 'Tango', a strong orange–red with dark foliage, now the single most popular cultivar.

Seed–grown varieties are usually available in many colors under a series name. Varieties in a series share many similar traits, such as plant size and habit, size of flower head, number of weeks to bloom, and leaf shape and color. Series that are currently popular are: Bandit, Elite, Orbit, Pinto and Ringo. Some novelty colors are available in seed form. 'Picasso' is unique—a vibrant blend of cerise and violet with orange–red markings on two petals in each floret. 'Orange Appeal', a recent introduction, is the first true orange geranium available from seed.

Variegated Zonal Geraniums.

FANCY–LEAFED GERANIUMS.
During the Victorian craze for "bedding out" (filling beds with annuals planted in geometric or fancy designs), scores of varieties with colorfully marked leaves were used. Some of these fancy–leafed geraniums are still available. The most colorful ones are 'Dolly Varden', 'Skies of Italy' and 'Mrs. Cox'. Most fancy–leafed geraniums have relatively small and insignificant flowers, but 'Ben Franklin', 'Mrs. Parker' and 'Wilhelm Languth' bear good–sized blooms in red or pink. These three have similar leaves, rounded and with distinctive white edges.

P. domesticum (doh-*mess*-tee-come).
REGAL PELARGONIUM.
These showy plants are also known as Martha Washington or Lady Washington geraniums. Where nights do not go above 60°F, they will continue setting bud and bloom all summer. Otherwise, they can be enjoyed as a spectacular one–time show lasting approximately six weeks. Not only are individual flowers large, but they are carried in large trusses as well. Flower colors are also amazing, ranging from pure white through reds, lavenders and pinks to burgundy. Many have beautifully contrasting markings within the petals, making the flowers even more colorful.

P. peltatum (pell-*tay*-tum).
IVY–LEAFED GERANIUM.
Ivy geraniums, as they are usually called, are distinguished by the shield–shaped leaves, which strongly resemble English ivy. They also have lax, trailing stems, with a loose cluster of flowers appearing at each node. Individual flowers vary from single to very double, depending on variety.

Flower colors lean toward the pastel and are generally less strident than those of their zonal cousins. Pink, lavender, salmon, white, cherry red and soft red make up the color assortment. Some of the leading varieties are: 'Amethyst',

Pelargonium

GARDEN GERANIUMS

Zonal Geraniums

For many years, bright red zonal geraniums have been the essence of summertime color, resplendently patriotic for the 4th of July and beyond. Zonal geraniums are widely used in window boxes, in hanging baskets and other containers, as well as in beds in the ground. Red is still the most popular geranium color, but that margin is being eaten away year by year as new soft pastels and fluorescent hues have been introduced.

Another change in recent years has been the surge in quality and quantity of geranium varieties that can be grown from seed. Twenty-five years ago, all geraniums were propagated from cuttings. Then varieties that came true to color from seed were developed and for a time, there was a major tussle between the two types for dominance in the garden. Now, it appears there is a major role for both kinds.

The vegetatively propagated varieties are tetraploids (they have twice the number of chromosomes as seed-grown varieties now available), which gives them a huskiness and substance not yet achieved by seed-grown kinds, plus exceedingly large flower heads. Further, most of the vegetatively propagated varieties bear semi-double or double flowers, while seed varieties have single flowers. The vegetatively propagated varieties are also more expensive. Typically, varieties from seed are used in large plantings, while the cutting-grown tetraploids are reserved for special plantings and containers.

Specialty Zonal Geraniums

For the specialist who wants to develop a collection of unusual geraniums, there are hundreds of varieties with great diversity. Rosebud geraniums, which appeared in England as long ago as 1870, have very double flowers. The blossoms never open entirely, giving the flower heads the appearance of a cluster of very small rosebuds. They come in a veriety of colors, including one whose scarlet petals have white reverses.

Tulip-flowered geraniums have blossoms that are tightly incurved so that the flower remains cupped.

Cactus-flowered geraniums have long pointed petals and are available in a wide color range.

Carnation-flowered geraniums bear blossoms with serrated petal edges similar to many single-flowered dianthuses.

Stellar geraniums are distinguished in both flower and foliage. Petals are deeply lobed with serrated edges, and the leaves are deeply incised. Both the blossoms and the leaves can be said to resemble a star; hence the name.

Bird's egg geraniums feature blossoms dappled with light markings of a different color.

Phlox geraniums have broadened petals so that individual flowers look similar to those of phlox.

Growing Zonal Geraniums

Full sun is the key to peak bloom production

with zonal geraniums. They excel in a moderate to rich, moist but well-drained soil. Plant outside after all danger of frost is past and the ground is warm. Space them 12 in. apart. Incorporate a slow-release fertilizer into the soil before planting.

Zonal geraniums can also be grown in tree forms, called standards (as can ivy-leafed and regal pelargoniums, described later). To do this, grow a single stem to the desired height, brushing out all buds which appear along the stem. Then pinch out the top growing tip to allow four to eight branches to grow out into a bushy canopy of leaves and flowers.

Over-wintered in a sunny sindow indoors, zonal geraniums will continue to bloom, although they may grow lanky because of diminished light.

Propagating Geraniums

Propagate zonal geraniums by stem cuttings or by seeds. So far, the widely available semi–double varieties are only available grown from cuttings. Cuttings are easy to root. Approximately eight to ten weeks prior to planting out, take cuttings that are three to four inches long, with short internodes (the spaces between leaf petioles). Remove the leaves from the bottom two inches of the stem and allow the cuttings to rest for several hours to dry the cut portions. Then insert the cut end into a pot or flat of rooting medium; use a sterile mix to prevent disease. (The cut ends can be dipped in a commercial rooting hormone, but it is not necessary for

quick rooting.) Cuttings should root in approximately three weeks. During the first week, cover the cuttings with plastic to reduce moisture loss. After cuttings are well rooted, transplant each one into a four-inch pot.

Geraniums are easy to grow from seed. Because they take their time coming into flower, they must be started early—ten to twelve weeks before outdoor planting for early varieties, even sooner for later types. Gardeners who plan to grow geraniums from seed should place their orders as soon as catalogs arrive.

To speed germination, soak seed overnight in warm tap water, then sow immediately. Sow in Jiffy-7 pellets or in a sterile seed-starting medium in individual cells. Maintain a soil temperature of 70 to 75°F until seeds have germinated, which should occur in five to ten days; a gentle heat source at the bottom of the tray is very helpful. Once germination is complete, a slightly cooler termperature is best. When seed leaves have fully expanded, move seedlings into 4-in. pots. Fertilize weekly with a quarter-strength fertilizer solution. Plant out after ground is warm and frost no longer threatens.

Ivy Geraniums

A group of single-flowered ivy geraniums should be mentioned specifically. Known in Europe for their wide use in balcony window boxes and other containers, they bloom more prolifically than any other ivy geraniums, completely covering the foliage throughout the summer. They perform equally well here

(continued on page 130)

Pelargonium

(continued from page 129)

in North America, and are more heat tolerant than other ivy geraniums. They can even be used as ground covers in full sun in our hot, humid Midwest. Three series are available: Balcon, Cascade and Decora. Each series has varieties with red, pink or lavender-colored blossoms.

Ivy geraniums perform best in cool, coastal or mountain climates with lots of sun. Grown in containers, they thrive in full sun if temperatures are not above 85°F for long periods of time. If this happens, give them northern or eastern exposure, where they are protected from midday to late-afternoon sun. Plant outside only after all danger of frost is past and the weather is reliably warm. Because of their trailing stems, ivy geraniums' primary use is as superb container subjects, either alone or in combination with other plants.

Propagate primarily by cuttings; there is only one seed-grown variety so far, 'Summer Showers Hybrid'. Take cuttings ten to twelve weeks prior to planting out, and treat as for zonals. After cuttings are rooted and growing well, pinch tips once or twice to induce branching.

Species, dwarf and scented geraniums

A number of species pelargoniums have fragrant oils which are released when leaves are stroked or crushed. They are quite popular with gardeners specializing in herbs. The fragrant leaves can be used in sachets as well as in cooking. One specialist firm lists 70 different varieties with fragrance ranging from pine through citrus to nutmeg. Some have attractive foliage but few have flowers of significance. Several favorite species include *Pelargonium tomentosum*, with a strong peppermint fragrance; *P. denticulatum*, with a balsam scent; *P. crispum*, lemon scented; and *P. fragrans*, nutmeg scented.

Other species pelargoniums are also available from specialist suppliers. Some of these are progenitors of the good hybrids most gardeners are growing today. There are also dwarf geraniums whose perfect leaves and flowers are Lilliputian models of larger geraniums.

lavender with silver petal reverses; 'Beauty of Eastbourne', double blossoms of cerise; 'Barock', red semi-double; 'Lulu', fuchsia-colored flowers; 'Salmon Queen', semi-double, light pink flowers; 'Snow Queen', white with red marking at petal throat, double flowers; and 'Mexicana', white petals with red edges.

Perilla (purr-*ill*-uh).
Mint Family (*Labiatae*).

A genus of annuals native to Asia. Grown for their foliage, which resembles coleus, they have square stems, like other members of the mint family. All are herbaceous and grow from 2 to 4 ft. tall.

P. frutescens (froo-*tess*-ens).

The only species commonly grown in American gardens, the purple-leaved form is highly prized in ornamental beds for its metallic sheen. There is also a form with variegated foliage. Plants grow to 3 ft. tall, and if the shoot tips are pinched will become quite bushy. Easily grown from seed, it also roots quickly from cuttings. Perilla is very tender; plant outside after all danger of frost is past. Perilla also has culinary value and is a staple constituent of Asian cookery.

Petroselinum (pet-roh-sel-*lye*-num).

PARSLEY.

Carrot Family (*Umbelliferae*).

This familiar herb from Europe and Asia is cherished for its dark green, curled foliage and its many culinary uses. Only one species is grown, a biennial often grown as an annual, especially in cold climates. Raise from seeds, which are slow to germinate. Soaking in warm water for twenty-four hours before planting speeds germination. Thin seedlings to stand 5 to 6 in. apart. Can be potted up over the winter and grown in a cool, sunny window. Outdoors, likes full sun to partial shade, although shade causes a looser habit and longer stems. Keep well-watered to maintain growth. Gardeners with little space will find it ornamental as well as useful.

P. crispum (*kriss*-pum).

A much branched plant, 1 to 2 ft. high, with finely divided leaves, curled at the edges, and very small, greenish-yellow flowers the second year. Compact and useful for edging or for the herb garden. Tolerates partial shade. The plain-leaved variety, 'Italian Plain Leaf', is commonly called Italian parsley.

The seed may be sown outdoors in late fall

Pelargonium fragrans
SCENTED GERANIUM

Perilla frutescens

Petroselinum

Petroselinum crispum
PARSLEY

Petunia × hybrida 'Red Star'
GRANDIFLORA PETUNIA

Petunia × hybrida 'Double Madness Burgundy'
MULTIFLORA PETUNIA

for an early spring crop. Parsley may also be potted and moved to a cold frame to overwinter. To freeze it for winter use, pinch the foliage off and spread it on a cookie sheet, then quick-freeze and store in an airtight, plastic bag to use a little at a time. For a continuous crop, sow seeds every spring and when, in early summer, last year's parsley plants show signs of going to seed, the new crop will be ready for picking.

Petunia (pet-*tew*-nee-uh).

Petunia.

Nightshade Family (*Solanaceae*).

Annuals and perennials from South America. The multiplicity of today's garden hybrids are derived from crosses between *P. axillaris* (axe-ill-*air*-is) and *P. violacea* (vie-oh-*lace*-ee-uh). Petunias are one of the most popular annuals grown, primarily because of their abundant flowers, which need little care over a long season. The scientific know-how and artist's eye of countless petunia breeders have given birth to dwarf and bedding varieties, giant and balcony types, single, double and ruffled flowers, giant singles and small prolific singles in pink, cream, red, crimson, rose, purple, lavender, blue, white, salmon, copper-rose and yellow. Useful in the annual border, the bulb border for a succession planting to cover the ripening foliage of the bulbs, the rock garden, tops of walls, window boxes and planters, sunny banks and the home greenhouse or sunny window. Full sun, a rich, slightly acid soil, well turned to a spade's depth, and warm summers produce the best flowers.

Start seeds indoors in February in flats filled with moist, milled sphagnum moss. Sow these unbelievably tiny seeds 1/8 in. apart in rows 1 in. apart. Some of the more expensive F1 hybrids are available pelleted with a coating of

inert material so that they are easy to handle. Do not cover the seeds, but tamp them down with a flat board. If more than one kind is planted per flat, label them clearly. Moisten the flat by setting it in a pan of water. Let the excess drain off, then cover the flat with a pane of glass and shade it, being sure not to let the moss dry out. Or seal the flat in a plastic bag.

Petunias should be kept at a temperature of 65° to 75°F until germination, then grown at 60° to 65°F. (The seedlings will actually tolerate as low as 50°F safely.) When a set of true leaves has developed, move them to 2 1/4-in. peat pots. (Do not be scornful of smaller seedlings since some colors in a mixture will be slower to start.) Use unmilled sphagnum moss, or a basic potting mixture with added sand or vermiculite. Petunias do not enjoy being moved, so when transplanting them, try to keep the growing medium around the roots undisturbed. Set the seedlings in full sun and at the cooler temperatures mentioned above.

After danger of frost is past, harden off in a cold frame or a sheltered corner and then transplant them to their final sunny outdoor location. Set bedding varieties 2 ft. apart; dwarfs may be planted 14 in. apart. Handle with care as the stalks are brittle. When the plants are 6 in. tall, begin pinching out the tips to induce compact growth. Mulch to preserve moisture, keep weeds down and prevent rain from spattering the plants. Later in the summer some plants may become leggy; cutting them back will give them a new lease on life.

Used in large plantings, petunias make a strikingly beautiful show. If wanted for winter use in the cool greenhouse or indoors, root cuttings in late summer for winter use. Keep these cuttings in the confines of a shaded cold frame or a cloche to root them quickly. Or plants may be lifted, cut back severely, root-pruned and potted-up.

Petunia

PETUNIAS

For over a century, petunias have been a leading annual in American gardens. Although their exact history is unknown, petunias are believed to have come to North America from their native South America by way of Europe and a French botanist named Petun.

One of the earliest petunia breeders, Mrs. Theodosia Shepherd, started the wave of popularity for this plant with the introduction of her 'California Giants', which were leaders for 50 years. In the early days of petunia growing, these plants were reproduced by cuttings because they would not come true from seed. Modern breeders have been able to develop petunias with increased vigor and flower productivity, improved plant habit and disease resistance, in addition to dependable color.

Garden petunias are divided into two types: multifloras and grandifloras. For a long time, grandifloras got all the attention because their flowers were larger and showier, as one might expect from the name. Although multifloras produced many more flowers, had better disease resistance and were much more weather tolerant, their plant habit was ragged. Now, the distinction has become blurred as breeders have introduced multifloras with larger flowers and better plant habit while retaining the diseases and weather tolerance of their fore-

bears. The result is a dramatic increase in popularity for multiflora petunias, with the prediction by some that they will soon surpass the grandifloras.

The double flowers of both classes are distinctive, with large masses of ruffled petals in many colors. The individual flowers of grandiflora petunias, which can be 3 in. or more in diameter, are especially showy. The tradeoff is that double-flowered petunias have fewer blooms than do singles, and the plant habit is rather straggly. The doubles are particularly good used in containers where their blossoms can be enjoyed close up (and where other plants can disguise the petunia's lackluster figure).

Virtually every flower color is to be found in petunias, including yellow (although no yellow varieties are a match for the vigor of other colors). Distinction can be found in flower character, too, with ruffles, fringed edges, fluting and veining showing up in addition to the classic bell shape of the traditional petunia flower. Diverse color patterns vary from solids to the addition of contrasting netted veins, picotees with white petal edges, star patterns, and bicolors with throats in contrasting colors.

Some popular series of single grandiflora petunias include Falcon, Ultra, Super Cascade, Super Magic, Flash and Dreams. In multiflora singles, choose from the Celebrity, Madness, Prime Time and Carpet series. The most popular multiflora doubles comprise the Tart series. Most double grandifloras are individually named. Particularly good is 'Purple Picotee', whose rich purple blossoms have white petal edges. It is an All America Selections winner.

Growing Petunias

Sow seeds indoors ten to twelve weeks prior to outdoor planting. Use a sterile, moist soil mix. For more even seed distribution, mix the very fine seed with an equal amount of sugar, then broadcast it carefully across the soil surface in a flat or pot. Press into the surface with a flat board but do not cover with soil mix. Cover the container with glass or plastic and germinate in bright light but out of the sun. Seeds sprout in ten to twelve days at 70 to 75°F. Transplant into individual cells when seedlings are easy to handle. Grow on at 60°F, but when plants have covered the top of the container, move to 50°F so they will initiate many branches and stay compact. Petunias may be planted outdoors when it is still too cool for impatiens, begonias and other tender varieties.

Grow in full sun in moderate-to-rich soil. At midseason, if plants have grown lanky, shear them back halfway and in about three weeks blooms will once again return in quantity. An alternative is to pinch petunias back regularly, a few stems every couple of weeks. Petunias are good container plants alone or with other plants but must be mixed with other vigorous species so that the companion plants are not overwhelmed by the petunias.

Chief pests attacking petunias are a form of botrytis (F1 and F2 hybrids are likely to be somewhat resistant) and slugs in regions of moist summers. Avoid growing near tomato, potato and other plants of the Nightshade family.

P. argentea. Name sometimes applied to a form of P. × hybrida.

P. axillaris (ax-il-lay-riss).
A white-flowered species growing to 2 ft. with $2^{1}/_{2}$-in. flowers that are fragrant at night. Probably a parent of P. × hybrida.

★**P. × hybrida** (high-brih-duh).
Technically a perennial, it is grown as an annual and is available in the entire color spectrum with single, double, ruffled, fringed, striped, bicolored, small and large blossoms. There are dwarf varieties under 12 in. high; bedding ones, which are spreading plants growing to 24 in. tall; F1 Grandifloras, which have spectacularly large blooms and can be single or double and fringed; and F1 Multifloras, which are hybrids producing a profusion of blooms and are available in both single and double forms.

Phacelia (fa-*ceel*-ee-uh).
CALIFORNIA BLUEBELL.
Waterleaf Family (*Hydrophyllaceae*).
A genus of 200 species, mostly native to western North America. They are all annuals, biennials or herbaceous perennials. The bell-shaped flowers are in clusters or one-sided racemes. They are blue, white, purple or yellow, and thrive in poor soils and full sun.

P. campanularia. (cam-pan-you-*lare*-ee-uh).
Long, tubular, bell-shaped flowers of gentian-blue crown the l- to 2-ft. plants. There is also a white form.

P. congesta (kahn-*jest*-uh).
BLUE CURLS.
Plants, to 2 ft., are covered with lavender-blue, bell-shaped flowers.

Phaseolus (faze-ee-*oh*-lus).
Pea Family (*Leguminosae*).
This genus includes the great edible beans of the world, such as pole, bush and lima beans. Also included are scarlet runner beans, prized in Europe for their delicious beans as well as for their highly attractive red flowers. These plants need warm, well-drained woil, that is not too rich in nitrogen (or else flowers will drop), and prefer full sun.

P. coccineus (cock-*sin*-ee-us).
SCARLET RUNNER BEAN.
Grown in the United States primarily as an ornamental, there are named varieties, available from mail-order catalogs, selected for their edible qualities as well. A perennial in frost-free climates, it is grown primarily as an annual. Because it is a tall climber, it is useful as a backdrop to the ornamental garden or to cover eyesores. Provide support such as mesh, strings or a teepee of three or four bean poles. The bright scarlet flowers of typical pea shape are in large clusters. Sow seeds in place $1/2$ in. deep after the ground is warm and frost danger is past.

Phlox (flox).
Phlox Family (*Polemoniaceae*).
Annual or perennial herbaceous plants of North America, with lance-shaped leaves, opposite or alternate. The flowers are in loose panicle clusters atop stiff to willowy, erect stems. Each flower has five petals with a long, narrow tube. Colors range from whites to pinks, dark reds and maroons and some lavender-purples. Orange, cream, buff and salmon shades are common in some species and garden strains. Perennial phlox are outstanding for mid- to late-summer bloom in the garden.

P. drummondii (drum-*mon*-dee-eye).
ANNUAL PHLOX.
A popular plant for summer borders. Many hybrids have been developed, so there are named strains ranging from 6 in. to 18 in. high. It is a steady-blooming plant all summer long, with stiff, erect stems and pale green, lance-shaped leaves. Some flowers are star shaped and in mixed colors—mostly shades of white, pink and red.

Easily grown from seed, it needs a sunny open site. Even in hot, sandy soil and considerable drought, this annual phlox goes on blooming; the more it is cut for bouquets, thus preventing seed formation, the more it will bloom. It can also be used for fall and spring color in milder areas.

'Twinkle' is a dwarf star phlox only 12 in. high, but the flowers are as large as an 18-in. type; it provides many colors. The Palona series, with rounded flowers growing to 10 in.,

Petunia × hybrida 'Sky Blue'
GRANDIFLORA PETUNIA

Phaseolus coccineus
SCARLET RUNNER BEAN

Phacelia campanularia
CALIFORNIA BLUEBELL

Phlox drummondii
ANNUAL PHLOX

Phlox

is available in seven separate colors and a mix. And a new award-winning variety is 'Promise Double Pink', with a portion of the flowers semidouble.

Platystemon (plat-iss-*steem*-on).

Poppy Family (*Papaveraceae*).

The one species, an attractive, sturdy annual from California, is effective in the rock garden, at edges of paths or in the front of the border. It grows wild over a large area in its native haunts. Very abundant bloom all summer if given full sun and well-drained, porous soil. Sow seeds outdoors in early spring where plants are wanted.

P. californicus (kal-if-*forn*-ik-us).

CREAMCUPS.

Grows to 1 ft., with slender, gray, lacy leaves and small, yellow and cream-colored flowers that are poppylike in shape.

Polygonum (po-*lig*-oh-num).

Buckwheat Family (*Polygonaceae*).

A genus of about 300 species widely scattered throughout the world. They are mostly annuals and herbaceous perennials.

P. capitatum (cap-i-*tate*-um).

A tender perennial from the Himalayas that makes a good annual ground cover or an attractive plant for hanging baskets or window boxes, where it trails nicely. Narrow green leaves bear a *V*-shaped purple band; flowers are erect pink clusters about 1/2 in. in diameter and borne in profusion. Seed is not widely

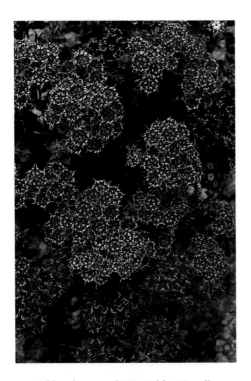

Phlox drummondii 'Twinkle Mixed'
ANNUAL PHLOX

Portulaca grandiflora 'Sundial Pink'
ROSE MOSS

available, so it is normally grown from cuttings. Will grow in partial shade, but full sun will result in thicker growth and better flower production. Use commercial soil mix for planting in containers; apply a balanced slow-release fertilizer when potting in spring.

Portulaca (port-yew-*lack*-uh).
Purslane Family (*Portulacaceae*).
Low, spreading, sun-loving plants, most of them tender perennials from warm, dry sections of South America. All are grown as annuals. The fleshy leaves are cylindrical or spoon-shaped. Bright, abundant blossoms make them very useful for hot, dry slopes, in the rock garden and as a carpeting in any location with full sun and not–too–rich soil. Sow seeds outdoors in spring after danger of frost is past, and thin to stand 6 in. apart. Seeds may also be sown indoors in March and transplanted into the garden. In warm sections they will self-sow, but the offspring will carry less desirable flowers.

P. grandiflora (gran-di-*floh*-ruh).
MOSS ROSE.
ROSE MOSS.
This showy, spreading plant from Brazil has single or double flowers in white, as well as many shades of pink, red and yellow. Sturdy and useful in any location where there is full sun, especially in sandy or impoverished soils. Blooms all summer in the garden. Not useful as a cut flower.

Sundial and Sundance are both hybrid series with large double flowers of pink, salmon, cream, white, orange, yellow, red and fuchsia. 'Cloudbeater' is a mixture of colors in which the flowers stay open all day.

Primula (*prim*-yew-luh).
PRIMROSE.
Primrose Family (*Primulaceae*).
Of the 400 to 500 species of primroses found worldwide, most are from the Northern Hemisphere, with the biggest portion from mountainous regions of Europe and Asia. They are mostly herbaceous perennials, growing with a basal rosette of leaves from which the flower stalks arise. Some bear only one flower; others are surmounted with clusters of bloom. The color range is vast, including white, yellow, apricot, pink, red and blue. Many flowers also have contrasting markings in the throat or as rings in the petals, which adds to the attractiveness. Many species of primroses are grown by plant connoisseurs and specialists in alpine plants, but the varieties from several species can be grown by everyone. In mild winter climates, primroses can be grown as perennials, with bloom starting in late winter and lasting as long as cool weather persists. Elsewhere, they are planted into the garden for spring bloom. In areas where the spring weather fluctuates dramatically from hot to cold, primroses will perform better if slightly shaded. Otherwise, they relish full sun and moist soil. Sow seed in September or October for plants blooming in the spring. The plants are also widely available in spring at garden centers and nurseries.

P. malacoides (mal-uh-*koy*-dees).
FAIRY PRIMROSE.
Grown by many as a winter-flowering annual in mild winter areas, such as coastal California, but too frost-sensitive to grow elsewhere as an outdoor plant. Instead, it is often found at garden centers and florists as a pot plant in spring. The colors are lovely pastels of pink, white, lavender and rose.

Primula

P. × polyantha (pah-lee-*an*-thuh).

POLYANTHUS PRIMROSE.

Not a true species but garden primroses of mixed hybrid origin, probably involving *P. juliae* (*jew*-lee-ay), *P. veris* (*ver*-is) and *P. vulgaris.* The group includes a fine color range—white, yellow, orange, red, blue, brown and bicolored. All are easy to grow, and their early bloom in April and May makes them especially desirable for spring borders and rock gardens. Florets average 1 to 1¹/₂ in. across, on flower stems 6 to 10 in. high.

Long in cultivation, these primroses are familiar in English gardens and are increasing in popularity in the U.S. Hose-in-hose (flower looks as if it has two or more corollas superimposed on each other) and double-flowered forms are prevalent. Some popular hybrids are 'Barnhaven Hybrid', with very large flowers over petite foliage; 'Monarch Strain', with 2-in. flowers in mixed colors or single colors; and 'Pacific Giant', a seed mix of large-flowering plants in shades of blue, yellow, red, pink or white. Zone 4.

P. sieboldii (see-*bold*-ee-eye).

This species forms robust rosettes of leaves with flower stalks 8 to 12 in. high, each topped with a cluster of flowers in cheerful colors, in both bold and pastel hues. Pacific Giant hybrids have flowers over 2 in. in diameter in many colors. Crescendo is another seed strain with many colors.

P. vulgaris (vull-*gair*-iss).

ACAULIS PRIMROSE.

COMMON PRIMROSE.

Native to and widely distributed in Europe. Pale yellow, individual flowers, 1 to 1¹/₂ in. across, are borne on flower stems 6 to 9 in. high, above basal tufts of gray-green, crinkled leaves. Bloom comes early, in mid-April. There are blue and purple varieties, and this is a contributory species to the race of *Polyanthus* primroses. Like the other English primroses, it needs a light mulch for winter protection. The variety *rubra* (*rue*-bruh) has rose-colored flowers.

So much attention has been devoted to developing these springtime beauties that there are many choices, ranging from miniatures like the 'Julianas' to stocky plants with larger flowers timed to start blooming throughout the season. These include the Pageants, Ducats, Saga and Lovely series, all with a wide range of colors. There are also double-flowered varieties available from specialists and mail-order seed firms. Zones 5 to 8.

Reseda (res-*seed*-uh).

MIGNONETTE.

Mignonette Family (*Resedaceae*).

Annuals, biennials and perennials, native to the Mediterranean region. There is one species grown extensively in the flower garden for its delightful fragrance. It is also grown commercially in cool greenhouses for the long-lasting, heavy spikes of tiny flowers. Often, however, the showier greenhouse stalks lack the characteristic perfume. To grow outdoors, sow seeds in early spring where plants are to grow and thin to stand 8 to 10 in. apart. Sow again in June to prolong the blooming season. Likes full sun to very light shade and rich, friable soil, with some added lime, well turned to a spade's depth. Ample moisture is needed.

R. odorata (oh-dor-*ray*-tuh).

A sturdy annual, usually growing about 6 in. high (not more than 1 ft.), with small, white flowers, often tinged greenish-yellow, and small, oval leaves. Grow from seed planted

Primula × *polyantha*
POLYANTHUS PRIMROSE

Reseda odorata
MIGNONETTE

Primula vulgaris 'Pageant Salmon Pink'
ACAULIS PRIMROSE

where plants will grow and thin seedlings to 8 in. apart. Grows in average soils; will tolerate poor, dry flowers. Improved varieties have larger flowers and grow taller than the species, but the fragrance is its primary attraction.

Rhodanthe. See *Helipterum.*

Ricinus (*riss*-in-us).
Spurge Family (*Euphorbiaceae*).
The only species in cultivation is a perennial from Africa, grown as an annual. Plants can grow to 12 ft. or more tall and 9 ft. wide in a single season, from seeds planted in spring. Its striking foliage makes it a bold background plant for large borders and especially for first-year basic plantings, either before permanent shrubs have been planted or while they are still too small to be adequately effective. It has great architectural value in a well-arranged mass planting. Often grown in city rooftop and terrace gardens as a quick screen plant.

In cooler sections start seeds indoors in March to set out after all danger of frost is past. Space plants 3 to 4 ft. apart. The flower spikes, made up of very small individual florets, and the seedpods are useful in arrangements. The seeds themselves are poisonous if eaten, and so should not be allowed to mature. Cut off flower heads after bloom. Plant seeds in full sun and rich, fertile soil, well turned to a spade's depth. May be sown outdoors in warmer sections.

R. communis (kom-*mew*-niss).
CASTOR BEAN.
CASTOR-OIL PLANT.
Very large, 3 ft. across, palmate leaves, which make a handsome if somewhat coarse-textured display. Growing to tree size in the tropics, it reaches 5 to 7 ft. in Zone 4, becoming taller in warmer regions. Interesting varieties are *laciniatus* (las-in-ee-*ay*-tus), with pale green and deeply cleft leaves; *sanguineus* (san-*gwin*-ee-us), with handsome dark red foliage; and *zanzibarensis* (zan-zib-ar-*ren*-siss), with white-veined green leaves. 'Carmencita' has large bronze leaves and bright red flower buds.

Rudbeckia (rud-*bek*-ee-uh).
CONEFLOWER.
Composite Family (*Compositae*).
Annual, biennial and perennial plants, all natives of North America. Though coarse in habit, they are sturdy and especially useful for their August and September bloom. Good in the border, the wild garden or the cutting garden. All the species have raised, conelike, dark centers, and some have two-colored petals. Colors range from pale yellow to orange, with some red tones and some bronze shades. Ordinary garden soil, well turned to a spade's depth, and full sun are the only cultural requirements. Easily grown from seeds or, in the case of the perennials, by root division.

R. hirta (*hert*-uh).
BLACK-EYED SUSAN.
GLORIOSA DAISY.
Familiar wild flower of the Northeast found along roadsides, on hilly slopes and in fields. Biennial grown as an annual. The golden-yellow flowers with red-brown centers make a cheerful show in late July and in August. Should be planted with caution except in the wild garden, for it self-sows abundantly. It is, however, very useful where a sturdy, bright-colored plant is wanted for slopes.

The Gloriosa Daisy strain has 5- to 7-in.-wide single daisies in mahogany, orange, yellow and mixed colors. 'Irish Eyes' is a golden-yellow variety with green centers and 'Goldilocks' is gold. 'Double Gold', growing to 36 in., bears double and semidouble flowers. 'Rustic Dwarfs Mixed' provides a mixture of yellow, gold, mahogany and bronze shades with the contrasting black cone. These are less rampant in growth and can be used freely in the annual border without danger of too much self-sowing. Thin to stand $1^1/2$ ft. apart.

Salpiglossis (sal-pig-*gloss*-iss).

Nightshade Family (*Solanaceae*).

There is only one cultivated species, a charming annual from Chile that deserves to be better known. Good in the cutting garden, the cool greenhouse or the annual border. Needs rich soil, deeply prepared, plenty of water and staking. Seed may be planted indoors in March for late June and July bloom, or outdoors after all danger of frost is past for August to September bloom. Give full sun for good flwer production. For winter greenhouse display, sow seed in September.

S. sinuata (sin-yew-*ay*-tuh).
PAINTED-TONGUE.

Grows 1 to 3 ft. high, with attractive, trumpet-shaped blooms, 2 to 3 in. long, ranging in color from apricot, buff, yellow, bronze, pale and dark brown to dark garnet-red, pale and dark blue and purple. All are velvety in texture and netted with veins in contrasting colors. The blooms last well when cut and are very effective in arrangements. Also attractive as cool greenhouse pot plants in standard soil mix. 'Casino Mixed' is a compact hybrid growing 18 to 24 in., with a wide range of flower colors. 'Kew Blue' is a free-flowering strain with deep blue flowers marked with gold veins.

Ricinus communis 'Carmencita'
CASTOR BEAN

Rudbeckia hirta 'Rustic Shades'
BLACK-EYED SUSAN

Salpiglossis

Salpiglossis sinuata
PAINTED-TONGUE

Salvia argentea
SILVER SAGE

Salvia farinacea 'Victoria'
MEALY-CUP SAGE

Salvia (*sal*-vee-uh).

SAGE.

Mint Family (*Labiatae*).

A large genus, native to many of the world's temperate zones and tropics. Included are annuals, biennials and perennials, as well as shrubs and the kitchen herb sage, *Salvia officinalis*. Almost all have small flowers in showy spikes, and are square-stemmed, as are all mints. Full sun, ample moisture and a fairly rich garden soil, well turned to a spade's depth, are required. They are grown from seed, which is started indoors in February, in late April or early May outdoors. Most sages are grown in borders for their decorative properties, but some are grown commercially and in herb gardens for their pungent leaves, used as seasoning for meats and sausages and for sage tea. Well adapted to the cool greenhouse.

S. argentea (ar-*jen*-tee-uh).

SILVER CLARY.

SILVER SAGE.

Biennial from the Mediterranean area, with lovely foliage, gray-white and hairy. Flower stems 2 to 4 ft. high, with attractive cream, pink or purple flowers. Zone 5, unless started early indoors and planted out in May, when all danger of frost is past. In warmer zones, this species of sage spreads rapidly.

S. farinacea (fare-i-*nace*-ee-uh).

MEALY-CUP SAGE.

A perennial from Texas, it is widely grown as an annual, and increasing in popularity each year because of its gray-green foliage and continous bloom spikes of blue or white (occasionally pink) flowers. Sow the seed in March for plants to set out in May. 'Victoria' is a deep blue and the most popular selection. 'Victoria White' blossoms are white but the calyxes are cream.

S. patens (*pate*-enz).

BLUE SAGE.

GENTIAN SAGE.

Perennial from Mexico, usually grown as an annual because it tends to die in winter. Plant is 1 to 2 ft. tall, with decorative, tapering leaves and spikes of sky-blue or white flowers, 1^1/$_2$ to 2 in. long, in pairs. Good in the border and the cutting garden. There is a dwarf form, and a number of varieties have different shades of color. Start from seed sown indoors in March and plant out in May. Zone 4.

S. sclarea (skla-*ree*-uh).

CLARY.

A sturdy, tall biennial from Europe, 2 to 3 ft. high, with woolly leaves and branched spikes of blue flowers, each with a showy, white or rose-colored bract. Effective in the herb garden or the border. Grow in full sun and ordinary garden soil, well turned to a spade's depth. Sow seeds in early May for bloom the second year. Plant where wanted, and after the first season's flowering there will usually be a number of self-sown plants every year. Seed may be started indoors in early March and plants set out in May, 10 to 12 in. apart. Zone 4.

S. splendens (*splen*-denz).

SCARLET SAGE.

A tender perennial from Brazil, grown as an annual. Spikes of brilliant red flowers. This plant, growing to 3 ft. high, is especially favored in parks and public gardens for bedding out. Also used in rows and clumps as a foundation planting. In fact, it is so omnipresent from coast to coast that the discriminating gardener should use it with discretion. Start seed indoors in late February and set out 12 to 15 in. apart after all danger of frost is past. White, salmon, purple, crimson and bicolored varieties are available, but the bright red is the familiar choice. Both the Laser and Carabiniere series come in separate colors of the above. 'Red Hot Sally' is a very compact and popular red variety, which is early to bloom.

Sanvitalia (san-vi-*tay*-lee-uh).

Composite Family (*Compositae*).

Low-growing annuals from the southern U.S. and Mexico, with small, daisylike, yellow or white flowers. Useful for the front of borders, to edge paths, in the rock garden, along the tops of rock walls or in hanging baskets. Sow seeds in early spring where plants are wanted, and thin to stand 6 in. apart. In warm sections, seeds may be planted in early fall and seedlings thinned the next spring. Zone 7.

S. procumbens (proh-*kumm*-benz).

CREEPING ZINNIA.

A spreading plant, growing 4 to 6 in. high. The flowers, about 1 in. across, are golden-yellow with brownish-purple centers. A double form, *florepleno* (floh-ree-*plee*-noh), is available. 'Gold Braid' has yellow flowers; 'Mandarin Orange' has flowers of the color indicated by its name.

Satureja (sat-yew-*reej*-uh).

SAVORY.

Mint Family (*Labiatae*).

Very aromatic annual and perennial herbs, mostly of Europe. Grown primarily for their leaves, which are valued as seasoning, they are decorative enough to merit a place in the border or rock garden, as well as in the herb garden. Small, compact plants with dark green, glossy foliage and delicate, small pink to white flowers in masses all over the plants. Hardy and easy to grow, they are effective as edgings. They thrive in ordinary garden soil and full sun.

S. hortensis (hor-*ten*-siss).

SUMMER SAVORY.

Shrubby annual to $1\frac{1}{2}$ ft., with small, narrow leaves to 1 in. long and tiny, two-lipped, pink, lavender or white flowers in numerous spikes or clusters. The leaves of this species are frequently used in seasoning. Familiar to all good cooks, summer savory is useful in salads, stuffings and vegetables.

Propagate by seeds, which should be sown in early spring where plants are wanted, and later thin to stand 4 to 6 in. apart. Germination may be slow. If they are available, started plants are better.

Scabiosa (skay-bee-*oh*-suh).

MOURNING BRIDE.

PINCUSHION FLOWER.

SCABIOUS.

Teasel Family (*Dipsacaceae*).

Mostly hardy perennials, but one annual is a great favorite of flower arrangers. Good shades of white, pink, yellow, blue and very dark red and purple. Lasts well when cut, is easily grown in ordinary garden soil, well turned to a spade's depth, and full sun. Good in the border and cutting garden.

S. atropurpurea (at-roh-pur-*pew*-ree-uh).

SWEET SCABIOUS.

Free-flowering annual from the Mediterranean region, dark red in the species, with blossoms 2 in. across on plants 2 to $2\frac{1}{2}$ ft. high. Also white, pink, lavender-blue and red. The pincushion-like bloom and the pale green seedpods are effective for flower arrangements. Sow seed in early spring where plants are wanted and thin to stand 8 to 10 in. apart, or start indoors in early March and set out in May for flowers from July to September. In Zones 8 to 10, sow seed outdoors in fall (where they will

Salvia patens

GENTIAN SAGE

Sanvitalia procumbens

CREEPING ZINNIA

Scabiosa atropurpurea

SWEET SCABIOUS

Scabiosa

Schizanthus pinnatus
BUTTERFLY FLOWER

be slow to establish) for blooms from early spring to midsummer.

Double Mixed is a seed strain that includes long-stemmed, double flowers in purple, crimson, white and pink. 'Dwarf Double Mixed' grows to only l8 in. and is useful in mixed borders.

Schizanthus (skye-*zanth*-us).
BUTTERFLY FLOWER.
POOR-MAN'S ORCHID.
Nightshade Family (*Solanaceae*).
Annuals and biennials from Chile, with feathery, cut foliage and a profusion of delicate flowers in spikes. The flowers are irregular in shape, somewhat resembling oncidium orchids in form, the lower lip usually darker, the upper lip lighter with a yellow spot. An attractive plant when grown outdoors in a protected location receiving part sun and in ordinary

Senecio cineraria 'Silver Dust'
DUSTY MILLER

Tagetes erecta
AMERICAN MARIGOLD

well-drained garden soil. Quite beautiful and showy in a cool greenhouse.

Sow seed indoors in early March for setting out after all danger of frost is past. For greenhouse bloom in winter, sow seeds in July or August. Good winter light is necessary for compact plants. They grow leggy and ugly if winter skies are consistently overcast. Outdoors they need a cool growing season, and will do well in Zone 9, but the season is short where nights remain warm. Generally, they are best suited to areas where primulas and cinerarias thrive. Their only serious drawback is that all the species are subject to blight and wilt, for which there is no dependable control.

S. pinnatus (pin-*nay*-tus).
BUTTERFLY FLOWER.

A fine but variable large-flowered species, 2 to 4 ft. high, with lavender and purple flowers, 1 to 2 in. across, with a purple-marked gold spot on the upper lip. Also white, pink and rose. Quite tender and best handled as a greenhouse plant, except in warm regions. There are many fine varieties available in different colors. 'Disco', 'Angel Wings' and 'Star Parade' are several selections.

Senecio (sen-*nee*-see-oh).
GROUNDSEL.
Composite Family (*Compositae*).

A huge group of mostly herbaceous plants found throughout the world, with a few shrubs or small trees included in the genus. Some species are considered weeds, while others are as intensively cultivated as the florist's cineraria. Many of the perennials are usually grown as tender annuals. Most species of this drought-tolerant genus thrive in well-drained soil and sun. Propagate by seeds, cuttings or division.

S. cineraria (sin-er-*ray*-ree-uh).
DUSTY MILLER.

A perennial, up to $2^1/2$ ft. tall, usually grown as an annual for its decorative foliage. Leaves are 6 to 8 in. long and small, terminal clusters of yellow or cream-colored flowers actually distract from the display. 'Silver Dust', the most widely grown selection has deeply lobed silver leaves. 'Cirrus' has more rounded, shallow-lobed leaves.

Statice. See *Limonium*.

★★Tagetes (tuh-*jeet*-ees).
MARIGOLD.
Composite Family (*Compositae*).

Two of the major classes of these tender plants were long called African and French marigolds, but *Tagetes* are from Mexico and South America, not Africa or France. Extensively hybridized and very popular for their sturdy habit, they have bright blooms in shades from the palest yellow to darkest orange. They are effective in the garden and in containers and as cut flowers. The characteristic musky odor of the finely cut leaves, pungent to all and offensive to some, has been bred out of some of the hybrids. (To remove odor from the skin, wash hands with common salt.) Give full sun and average soil. Sow seeds indoors in March for outdoor planting after the last frost. Or for late bloom, sow in place in any garden soil.

T. erecta (ee-*rek*-tuh).
AMERICAN MARIGOLD.

(Formerly African Marigold but more properly named for its New World origins.) Taller plants, up to 3 ft. high, American marigolds have large showy blooms up to 5 in. in diameter in yellow, gold and orange. Various flower forms have been developed with flat, quilled or

Tagetes

Tagetes patula 'Queen Sophia Mixed'
FRENCH MARIGOLD

Tagetes tenuifolia 'Starfire'

ruffled petals, semidouble or double. Space plants 2 to 3 ft. apart, except for the new dwarf varieties, which should be planted 6 in. apart. 'Inca' and 'Perfection' are most often planted among the taller varieties, while 'Voyager' has highly uniform flowers on somewhat shorter plants, and 'Discovery' bears large, almost identical flowers on dwarf plants (under 12 in.). They are all represented by flowers of yellow, gold and orange. A major search has been under way for many years for a white marigold, and there are several that approach this, although they are still more creamy than white. 'Excel', the first day-neutral American marigold will set buds no matter what the day length, making it possible to get earlier bloom in the garden.

★ **T. patula** (*pat*-yew-luh).
FRENCH MARIGOLD.
A short, bushy plant, 6 to 12 in. high, with abundant, small blooms, yellow or orange with reddish-brown markings. Brilliant, showy edging plant covered with flowers until hard frost.

Space plants 4 to 5 in. apart. Fully double flowers with flat petals include Aurora, Safari, and Queen Sophia series, each with many colors. Fully double-crested flowers are represented by the Boy, Bonanza, Janie and Hero series. Singles include the Disco and Espana series.

T. tenuifolia (ten-yew-i-*fole*-ee-uh).
SIGNET MARIGOLD.
(Syn. *T. signata*.) Very tiny, finely divided leaves and an abundance of small flowers identify these marigolds. 'Lemon Gem', 'Golden Gem', 'Paprika' and 'Starfire' are good examples.

MARIGOLDS

Marigolds, like so many native American plants, went to Europe and came back more civilized. In the last few decades, however, most of the marigold breeding has been done in America. The marigolds we grow today are derived from two species, *Tagetes patula* and *T. erecta*. Those descended from *T. patula* are commonly called French marigolds; those from *T. erecta*, African marigolds. Given the marigold's New World origins, both epithets are misnomers, and some breeders and seed houses are pushing a new label for *T. erecta* types—American marigolds. In fact, the late David Burpee, whose company created so many new marigold varieties a generation ago, lobbied to have Congress name the marigold America's national flower. (The campaign ultimately lost to the rose.)

The color of marigolds ranges from yellow to gold to orange to burgundy, but there has been a search for a white marigold for many years. There are still no pure white marigolds; the ones called "white" are in reality creamy.

Marigolds are so easy to grow that they are often the first garden flower children experiment with. The seeds are large and easy to handle, germination is rapid, and plants grow quickly to blooming size, holding off a child's impatience.

Marigolds are relatively rugged, continuing to bloom in the fall after light frosts have blackened more tender plants. There is only one thing that seems to bother marigolds. When days and nights are hot and humid for weeks on end, most marigolds stall. They stop setting buds so that bloom slowly diminishes. Happily, cooler weather rejuvenates them. Triploid marigolds, derived from crosses between American and French types, are not subject to this problem. Their extra set of chromosomes prevents triploids from setting seed, so they continue blooming no matter what the outdoor conditions.

American marigolds have always been the rangier of the two types, with many varieties growing to 36 in. Recent breeding has brought smaller American marigolds without the typical loose, open habit, and with more copious and higher quality flowers. French marigolds have always been compact plants, but recent breeding has reduced the size still further, so that some gardeners complain about puny plants. No one complains about the quantity of flowers, however. There is also great diversity in flower types. Some are flatheaded, with broad petals overlapping like shingles on a roof; some are crested, with clusters of many narrow, rolled, upright petals in the center; singles, overlooked until recently but now beginning to catch gardeners' fancies, have five petals surrounding a frilly central button.

(continued on page 152)

Tagetes

(continued from page 151)

Because some marigolds bloom in extravagently bright colors, gardeners often combine them with neutral colors, such as blue flowers and gray-leaved foliage plants, creating a lovely combination. Folk wisdom has it that mosquitoes and a number of other bothersome insects and omniverous animals find marigolds particularly unappetizing. For this reason, cheery marigolds are often planted along the borders of garden beds—as a repellent.

Marigolds need full sun and ordinary soil to do their best. Sow seeds where you want the plants to grow, after soil has warmed. Or, for earlier bloom, start seeds indoors, sown in pots or flats five to six weeks before outdoor planting. Marigolds germinate in a week or less. When seedling are 2 in. tall, transplant to individual 4-in. cells or pots. Plant outdoors when frost danger is over; space plants 8 to 15 in. apart, depending on variety.

Tanacetum parthenium. See *Chrysanthemum parthenium*.

Thunbergia (thun-*berj*-ee-uh).
CLOCK VINE.
Acanthus Family (*Acanthaceae*).
Climbing or erect plants from the tropics, with trumpet-shaped flowers in shades of purple, blue, white or yellow. Toothed triangular or oval leaves. They need rich soil, full sun and ample moisture. Propagate by seeds, cuttings or layering. Zones 9 to 10.

T. alata (al-*lay*-tuh).
BLACK-EYED SUSAN VINE.
A vigorous vine that bears yellow, orange or cream-colored flowers with purplish-black centers and heart-shaped leaves. A profuse bloomer and satisfactory greenhouse vine in cold areas, and an excellent annual anywhere. Start seeds indoors in March and set in ground after the last frost. Adapts well to large containers. Needs trellis or support of some kind, no matter where it is grown. 'Susie Mixed' is the most popular.

T. fragrans (*fraig*-rans).
A white-flowered species from India with a somewhat woodier vine than *T. alata,* above, and the flowers average a bit larger. 'Angel Wings' is the most commonly available seed strain.

Thymophylla (tye-moh-*fill*-uh). See *Dyssodia*.

Tithonia (tith-*oh*-nee-uh).
MEXICAN SUNFLOWER.
Composite Family (*Compositae*).
Tall, showy plants with large yellow or red, yellow-centered blossoms. Of tropical origin, from Central America and Mexico. There is only one species in common cultivation, a tender perennial grown as an annual. Start seed indoors in small pots in late February for a minimum of root disturbance when setting out, after all danger of frost is past. Plant 1$^{1}/_{2}$

Thunbergia alata 'Suzie Mixed'
BLACK-EYED SUSAN VINE

Tithonia rotundifolia 'Goldfinger'

to 2 ft. apart in any moderately fertile, well-drained soil. Fine for the back of large borders. Full sun and a warm, sheltered location.

T. rotundifolia (roh-tun-dif-*foh*-lee-uh). Grown as an annual anywhere. To 6 ft., with sunflower-like blossoms, 2¹/₂ to 3 in. across, bright yellow or scarlet all summer. The variety *grandiflora* (gran-di-*floh*-ruh) has larger flowers than the type. 'Goldfinger' has vivid scarlet-orange flowers on plants smaller than the type, only 24 to 30 in. 'Yellow Torch', with chrome-yellow flowers reaches only 4 ft.

Torenia (tor-*reen*-ee-uh). Figwort Family (*Scrophulariaceae*). Varied, lovely shades of blue and purple, as well as white, funnel-shaped, two-lipped flowers make these tender plants from the tropics of Asia and Africa desirable. Useful outdoors anywhere. In colder areas, start seed early indoors, or buy started plants. Good in shade with abundant moisture. Propagate by seeds or cuttings.

T. fournieri (four-nee-*air*-eye). WISHBONE FLOWER. This is the species most commonly grown. Annual of bushy habit, with light green foliage on plants 1 ft. high. Bicolored blossoms, the upper lip a soft, light blue, the lower a rich, dark purple with a yellow throat. There are other color combinations as well. A profuse bloomer from late spring to frost. There are varieties with larger flowers than the type, as well as white-flowered varieties. An additional feature is the warm, reddish-purple color of the foliage in early fall. Start seed indoors in late February for planting out 6 to 8 in. apart after all danger of frost is past. Often self-sows, even in cooler sections. In Zone 10, plant at

any time for year-round bloom. Makes a good show at the front of borders, in the rock garden and in window boxes. A great pot plant for portable color in the shaded summer outdoor living area. 'Clown Mix' is a recently developed and award-winning seed strain, with not only the typical colors but rose and red as well.

Trachymene (trak-*kim*-en-ee). Carrot Family (*Umbelliferae*). A small genus, Australian in origin, of which one species is now popular in flower gardens and greenhouses. Though a tender perennial, it can be treated as an annual. Sow seed outdoors after all danger of frost is past, in the locations where plants are wanted. Give it full sun and ordinary garden soil. Often grown in the cool greenhouse for winter bloom. Seeds sown in September will bloom in midwinter. Plants taken from the garden before frost will bloom in the greenhouse during the winter. Indoors or out, plants should stand close together so the flower heads may support each other and thus avoid elaborate staking. A superb and choice cut flower.

T. caerulea (see-*rew*-lee-uh). BLUE LACEFLOWER. Blue, lacy flower heads, 2 to 3 in. across, on stems 1¹/₂ to 2¹/₂ ft. high, above deeply divided foliage.

Tripteris hyoseroides. See *Osteospermum hyoseroides*.

★★**Tropaeolum** (trop-*pee*-ol-um). NASTURTIUM. Nasturtium Family (*Tropaeolaceae*). Showy, fragrant annuals and perennials from the American tropics, a great favorite in old-

Torenia fournieri
WISHBONE FLOWER

Trachymene caerulea
BLUE LACEFLOWER

fashioned as well as modern gardens. They grow best in full sun and poor, dry soil. If planted in rich soil, an abundance of lush green foliage and few flowers result. In poor soil the funnel-shaped, spurred flowers, in every shade from cream through yellow to orange and red, flaunt their brightness all summer. When ground is warm, sow seeds where plants are wanted. Useful in beds by themselves, especially in front of stone walls, in the annual border, in the rock garden, in window boxes and in the cutting garden. Since the green leaves are good in salads and the unripe, green seeds are sometimes pickled as a substitute for capers (*Capparis spinosa*), nasturtiums may be appropriately included in the herb garden also. Even the bright flowers are edible. Attractive to bees and hummingbirds. Propagate either by seed or —for some of the double forms—by cuttings.

★ **T. majus** (*may*-jus).

GARDEN NASTURTIUM.

A rapid-growing annual. There are many varieties, including dwarf and climbing kinds, in colors ranging from yellow through various shades of orange to a brilliant red. The climbing kinds attach themselves by twisting leaf stems rather than by twining plant stems. The Gleam varieties with their short, bushy habit are excellent, and include the popular 'Golden Gleam' and 'Scarlet Gleam'. Doubles are also found, 'Dwarf Cherry Rose' being one example. A much publicized novelty, 'Alaska', has leaves splashed and blotched with cream markings. Sow seed outdoors in place, or start indoors in peat or paper pots that can be planted later. Seedlings do not withstand transplanting very well. Nasturtium (*Tropaeolum majus*) stems, leaves, and seeds are used at the gourmet's table. Nicknamed "Indian cress," the

Tropaeolum

Tropaeolum majus
GARDEN NASTURTIUM

Tropaeolum peregrinum
CANARY CREEPER

tender leaves are reminiscent of the peppery flavor of watercress, and are delightful in salads or used sparingly in cocktail dips. The blossoms also are used in salads, sandwich spreads and as garnishes for hors d'oeuvres.

T. peregrinum (per-eg-*grye*-num).
CANARY CREEPER.
A climbing nasturtium, with deeply lobed leaves and light yellow flowers 1 in. across. Long green spurs. This is fast-growing, reaching 8 or 10 ft. and forming an excellent screen.

T. speciosum (spee-see-*ose*-um).
FLAME FLOWER.
A choice climbing species that is a perennial in frost-free areas but is often planted for seasonal screening and brilliant flowers elsewhere. It grows from fleshy, perennial roots. Flowers are vermilion-red, about 1 1/2 in. long.

Ursinia (err-*sin*-ee-uh).

Daisy Family (*Compositae*).

A genus of about forty species mostly from South Africa. They are all annuals, perennials or sub-shrubs. They have finely divided leaves and daisy-like flowers of yellow, orange or red. Plants need average, well-drained soil and full sun, and bloom in summer from seed sown in the garden.

U. anthemoides (an-the-*moi*-dees).

This species grows to about 1 ft. tall, with finely divided leaves and many flowers 1 to 1½ in. in diameter, yellow to yellow-orange color accented by a purple eye.

Venidium (ven-*id*-ee-um).

Monarch of the Veldt.

Daisy Family (*Compositae*).

A genus of over twenty species, all native to South Africa. Most are tender perennials, grown as annuals for summer color. They bear daisylike flowers, which are often marked with bands of contrasting color across the petals. Only one species is commonly grown.

V. fastuosum (fast-you-*ose*-um).

Quick-growing and many-branched bushy annuals, they have large daisylike flowers. The flowers, typically yellow and orange with black centers, are unusual in that each petal is marked near the base with a purple blotch. 'Zulu Prince' is a selection with creamy-white flowers. Sow seeds indoors in March for transplanting outdoors after the danger of frost is past.

Verbascum (ver-*bask*-um).

Mullein.

Figwort Family (*Scrophulariaceae*).

A hardy genus, native to Europe and Asia, but naturalized in the U.S. Biennials of tall, erect habit, with straight, rigid, dense spikes of white, yellow, orange, red or purple bloom. Many species have felty, gray-green foliage and stems. Handsome and imposing in the large border and the wild garden. The straight spikes of seedpods when dried and the small basal rosettes of thick, gray leaves of young plants are effective in dried arrangements. Of easy culture in ordinary garden soil, with good drainage and in full sun. Propagate by seeds or root cuttings. Often self-sows, blooming freely the next year. Zone 4.

V. bombyciferum (bomb-bi-*siff*-ur-um).

A species with very hairy foliage and stems giving it a silky gray appearance. A biennial, it develops a basal rosette of leaves the first year, followed the next summer by a tall (4-to-6 ft.) spire with sulfur yellow blooms. Certainly one of the most handsome species. Reseeds vigorously. To curtail this, cut off flower heads after bloom.

V. olympicum (ol-*limp*-ik-um).

Olympian Mullein.

Very tall, 6 to 8 ft., with branched spires of densely packed, large bright yellow flowers, blooming in July and early August. Native to Greece. This is the most handsome and showiest species. Makes a stately background for the summer border. Bold, felty white foliage, in a fountainlike habit of growth below the heavy flower sprays.

★★Verbena (ver-*bee*-nuh).

Vervain.

Verbena Family (*Verbenaceae*).

A large genus of annuals and perennials, almost all native to the U.S. Attractive, rounded clusters of small, tubular flowers in a large color range from white through every shade of red and blue make the hardy species excellent garden plants, and the tender species useful cool-greenhouse plants. These plants are often fragrant

Verbena

Verbena × hybrida 'Silver Anne'
GARDEN VERBENA

Viola tricolor
JOHNNY-JUMP-UP

and are in bloom all summer. Fine for the border, the rock garden, as edgings, as ground cover in bulb beds and for cutting. Full sun and rich garden soil are required. Propagate by seeds started indoors in late March.

V. hortensis. See *V. × hybrida.*

V. × hybrida (*high*-brih-duh).
GARDEN VERBENA.
Often listed in catalogs as *V. hortensis.* Hybrid of several species, with many beautiful and very useful varieties developed for the fine color range, large size of florets and clusters and strong habit.

A number of forms have been selected for containers: they trail over the edges. These include 'Sissinghurst', a robust pink, and 'Silver Anne', a glowing pale pink. Bedding varieties are available in a mounding habit: 'Trinidad' and the Novalis series, many colors; and new variety called 'Peaches 'n' Cream', several shades of colors within each cluster. Another, trailing type, which reaches up to a 18 in. diameter by summer's end but only 6 in. in height includes the Romance, Amour, Showtime and Springtime series. Sow seed 12 to 14 weeks prior to planting out in the garden. Chill the seeds in the refrigerator before sowing. Wet seed flats 24 hours before sowing, sow the seed and cover it with a soil mix (do not water it). Cover with black plastic until germination, and transplant when the first true leaves appear. Plant out when the ground and air temperatures are warm.

Vinca rosea. See *Catharanthus roseus.*

Viola (*vie*-oh-luh).
VIOLET.
Violet Family (*Violaceae*).
A large genus of annuals and perennials found in temperate zones throughout the world. Most are

low-growing plants, with shield-shaped leaves and five-petaled flowers with a spur on the lowest petal. They bloom in spring, some continuing throughout summer. New, more cold-tolerant varieties make it possible to plant in the fall in milder regions for bloom all winter, or when the weather warms enough for growth to resume. Almost all thrive in moist, shady areas, although they will tolerate almost any kind of garden soil and situation. Violets are easy to propagate by seed and by division.

V. tricolor (*try*-kol-or).

JOHNNY-JUMP-UP.

This is a short-lived European perennial with overlapping petals in blue, white or yellow. Naturalized in eastern U.S. In the baby violas, 'Princess Blue', 'Princess Cream' and 'Princess Purple with Face' provide floods of color over a long season. See *V.* × *wittrockiana* for growing tips.

V. × wittrockiana (wit-roh-kee-*ay*-nuh).

PANSY.

There are many different varieties, in a mixture of colors and sizes. They prefer some shade, and, if the spent blossoms are kept cut, will continue to bloom all summer. Flowers range up to 4 in. in diameter, and 'Majestic Giants' have long been favorites, with their large ruffled blossoms. 'Crystal Bowl', 'Crown' and 'Maxim' pansies deliver medium-sized flowers in a wide range of colors. Also popular are mixes of closely related hues, such as 'Imperial Pink Shades' and 'Shades of Blue'. There is even a 'Black' pansy, so saturated with color that it reads as black.

Seeds germinate best under 65°F. Sow eight to ten weeks prior to planting in the garden. When first true leaves appear, transplant into separate cells and grow at 60°F until well established. Then reduce temperatures to 50°F nights and protect from frost until planting in the garden. For fall planting and wintering over, plant young plants into the garden eight weeks prior to the first expected hard freeze. In cool climates they will perform acceptably all summer long if plants are sheared back by half when they become untidy. In hot climates, replant with something else when protracted hot weather sets in.

Xeranthemum (zeer-*anth*-em-mum).

IMMORTELLE.

Composite Family (*Compositae*).

Long-lasting, attractive annual from the Mediterranean. Showy and unfading in the border, and useful dried for winter arrangements.

X. annuum (*an*-yew-um).

COMMON IMMORTELLE.

Grayish leaves and stems, with white, purple or rose-pink flowers, single or double, 1 to $1^1/2$ in. across. Plants grow 2 to 3 ft. high. Some of the doubles have rounded, zinnialike heads. Easily grown from seed in light soil and full sun. Sow outdoors in April, and thin plants to stand 6 in. apart. For use in winter arrangements, cut flowers at their peak, tie in bunches and hang in a dark, airy place.

Zinnia (*zinn*-ee-uh).

Composite Family (*Compositae*).

The zinnia is a garden favorite. Breeders have produced a tremendous range of size, color and type of bloom. Native to North and South America, especially Mexico, zinnias offer everything, from hedgelike plants 4 ft. high, to tiny-flowered edging plants of grace and charm. Many flower forms are available, and all bloom abundantly the entire summer, transplant easily, last very well when cut and make a splash of riotous color. Full sun, plenty of heat and moderately rich, friable soil are needed. Sow seed outdoors when the ground is warm. Thin according to the size of the plant, 3 in. apart for the smallest to 1 ft. or more for the largest.

Zinnia

Z. angustifolia (an-gus-tif-*oh*-lee-uh).

MEXICAN ZINNIA.

A narrow-leaved plant, 1 to 2¹/₂ ft. tall, with orange flowers, 1¹/₂ in. across. The variety *haageana* (hah-jee-*ay*-nuh) has yellow, red-tipped blossoms. There are many hybrids of varied colors and patterns. All are fine for edging and bedding plants.

Z. elegans (*ell*-eg-anz).

GARDEN ZINNIA.

Modest, purple or lilac-colored parent of the numerous varieties, which have showy, brilliant or pastel colors, every size and shape of blossom and plants ranging in size from 6 in. to 4 ft. high. The tall dahlia-flowered 'Zenith' strains have flowers 5 in. across; the 'Jumbo' series has even larger blooms, as well as quilted and ruffled petals in soft pastels and bolder colors. Cactus-flowered types have narrow, twisted petals in soft colors. Those of medium height, derived from the variety *pumila*

(pew-*mil*-uh), are about 2 ft. high and have smaller, less spectacular blossoms. These are listed in catalogs as 'Border Beauty', 'Cut-and-Come-Again' and many other group names. A race of large flowered zinnias appear on dwarf plants: 'Peter Pan' and 'Dasher'. 'Thumbelina', which comes in all colors, grows to only 6 in., with copious 1¹/₄ in. flowers.

Z. linearis (lin-ee-*ay*-riss).

Tidy species to 9 in. tall, with a small, single bloom in two shades of golden-yellow. Comes into abundant bloom very early and makes a fine display all summer. Good for the front of borders, as a path edging and as a cut flower.

Zinnia angustifolia 'Golden Orange'
MEXICAN ZINNIA

Zinnia elegans 'Border Beauty'
GARDEN ZINNIA

UNDERSTANDING THE ZONE MAP

REGIONAL GARDENING

Hardiness is the ability of a plant to survive winter cold temperatures in a given region. The country has been divided into "hardiness zones," determined by winter minimum temperatures. Hardiness zones are very important to biennials, which only bloom during their second year.

Zone hardiness ratings are not relevant when discussing true annuals, however, because these plants are only grown for a single season, then replaced. True annuals are not expected to survive winters (except as seeds, of course)—that is what defines them as annuals. Much more important to true annuals than zone hardiness is whether they will bloom in shade or full sun.

However, hardiness zone and climate remain significant factors when planting annuals. Some annuals wither and die away in the extremely hot, humid conditions to be found in a Florida or Gulf Coast summer. A wider spectrum of typical annuals thrives in the dry heat of California, while cool-loving plants are at their best in places like coastal California, which is tempered by the ocean and summer fog. (The Lompoc Valley of California has such a temperate climate that most of the world's supply of sweet pea seed, a cool-loving plant, is produced there, yet Santa Barbara, only 45 miles away, enjoys subtropical weather.) Tropical foliage plants, such as Joseph's-coat (*Alternanthera* spp.), make

superb showings in summer plantings in winter-glacial Minneapolis or Chicago.

Climatic conditions may determine when or where plants can be used for seasonal color. Many annuals that are enjoyed in the summer in the North are grown for fall, winter and spring in Florida, because the hot, humid conditions of the summers there are too inhospitable.

On the other hand, in areas with short growing seasons, plants can be brought to large, blooming sizes indoors in sunrooms or greenhouses for instant displays when the weather warms sufficiently for good outdoor growth. For instance, in the Rocky Mountains, where the frost–free season can be less than two months long, warm–season annuals such as geraniums, begonias and dahlias cannot be set out safely until late June or early July. (If they are not already full of bloom, there is not time for them to produce much of a show before frost blackens them in late August or early September.) Also, fuchsia baskets by the thousands are grown by gardeners in Anchorage, Alaska. The plants are cut back in fall, then stored by commercial greenhouses for unveiling again in spring.

A discussion of regional differences must be very general, for climatic variations make an important difference in the success of seasonal plantings, and there is not sufficient room to discuss the many details here.

(continued on page 164)

HARDINESS

Hardiness, commonly accepted as the ability of a plant to withstand low temperatures, should rather be considered a plant's ability to grow well in the presence of a complex variety of physical conditions, of which temperature may be only one factor. Other factors are high temperatures, drought and humidity (rainfall), altitude, soil characteristics, orientation and exposure (sun, shade, available light, prevailing winds), day length (latitude), air quality and ground drainage.

PLANT HARDINESS

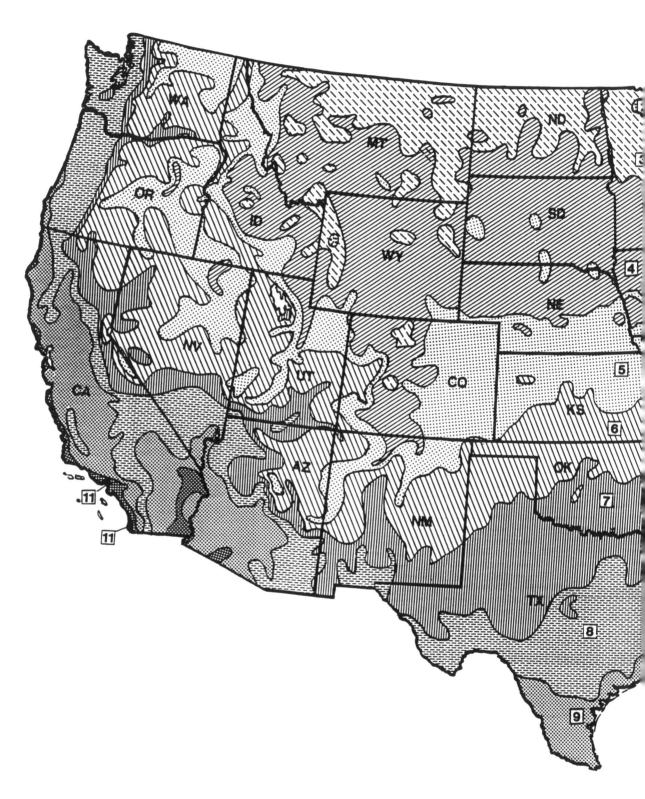

Z O N E   M A P

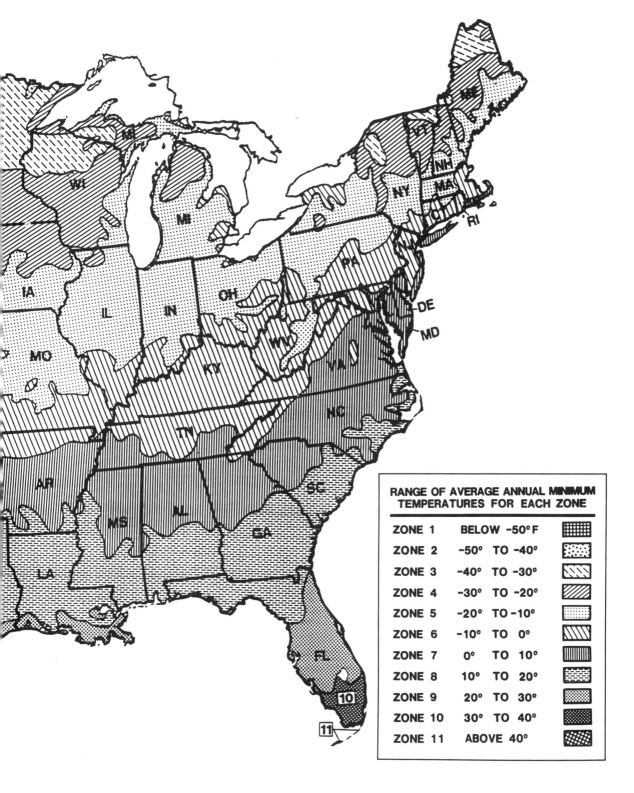

RANGE OF AVERAGE ANNUAL MINIMUM TEMPERATURES FOR EACH ZONE	
ZONE 1	BELOW -50°F
ZONE 2	-50° TO -40°
ZONE 3	-40° TO -30°
ZONE 4	-30° TO -20°
ZONE 5	-20° TO -10°
ZONE 6	-10° TO 0°
ZONE 7	0° TO 10°
ZONE 8	10° TO 20°
ZONE 9	20° TO 30°
ZONE 10	30° TO 40°
ZONE 11	ABOVE 40°

(continued from page 161)

Such elements as rainfall, percentage of cloud cover, elevation, differential between day and night temperatures, and humidity can all play a big part in what grows well and what does not. Also, no matter where they live, gardeners typically challenge the rules of thumb by trying new plants in unusual situations.

Northeast. Generally characterized by hot, humid summers, but coastal areas have modified temperatures that provide longer springs and more protracted falls, allowing the use of cool season annuals such as pansies to stretch the season on both ends.

Midwest. Continental winters are frigid, while summers are hot and humid, causing warm-loving annuals to develop fast once the ground has warmed. Plants preferring cool weather, such as fuchsias, will perform acceptably if the surrounding conditions are modified somewhat, such as by dappled shade.

Mid-south. Spring comes early with hot, humid summers, lengthy autumns and short, mild winters. Pansies, petunias and snapdragons can be planted early for spring bloom and repeated in the fall when weather moderates, even living through the winter in some years. Heavy clay soils are the rule; amending with organic matter improves soil structure, allowing for better root systems and plant performance.

Gulf Coast and Florida. Because of its mildness, winter is an ideal time to grow many annuals reserved for summer up North. Conversely, the hot, humid conditions of midsummer find tropicals such as *Catharanthus* (vinca) and *Lantana* popular when other plants languish. The best garden months are from September to May. The lack of winter frosts makes weed, insect and disease control of major importance.

Mountain. Many gardens are affected by elevation, resulting in short growing seasons, frequently with cool nights, and with short springs and autumns. (The rule of thumb is that every thousand feet of additional elevation is equivalent to moving 300 miles north). Most gardeners in the mountains can enjoy only one season of annuals. Very alkaline soils, low in organic matter, are commonplace in these areas. Many gardeners amend soils heavily with manure, peat or other organic matter to improve their structure and then treat them chemically to make them less alkaline.

Coastal California. A true Mediterranean climate with hot, dry summers and mild, rainy winters. Cool season annuals thrive here in winter, while others perform well the balance of the year so long as they are well watered. Summer fog and onshore breezes moderate many gardens near the water. Chronic water shortages are leading gardeners to shift more to drought-tolerant plants such as senecio and salvia. Weed, insect and disease problems are more severe where the lack of killing frosts in winter means no interruption of life cycles.

Pacific Northwest. Most of the population lives in a modified Mediterranean climate with mild, rainy winters and cool, dry summers. Long, cool springs (often beginning in February) merge into cool, sunny summers and lengthy falls. Gardeners can plant for each season, with some species such as primroses and pansies overwintering for a repeated long blooming season when the weather warms in the spring. Cool nights, even in midsummer, slow the growth of warm-loving plants, but fuchsias, lobelia, ivy geraniums and other plants that prefer moderate temperatures are at their best here.

COMMON NAME INDEX

ACAULIS PRIMROSE. See *Primula vulgaris.*

AFRICAN DAISY. See *Arctotis breviscapa, A. stoechadifolia; Dimorphotheca sinuata; Lonas inodora.*

AGERATUM, GOLDEN. See *Lonas inodora.*

ALKANET. See *Anchusa.*

ALPINE FORGET-ME-NOT. See *Myosotis alpestris.*

ALYSSUM. See *Lobularia.*

AMARANTH. See *Amaranthus.*

AMARANTH, GLOBE. See *Gomphrena globosa.*

AMERICAN MARIGOLD. See *Tagetes erecta.*

ANNUAL DELPHINIUM. See *Consolida ambigua.*

ANNUAL GAILLARDIA. See *Gaillardia pulchella.*

ANNUAL PHLOX. See *Phlox drummondii.*

ANNUAL TOADFLAX. See *Linaria maroccana.*

ARTICHOKE. See *Cynara scolymus.*

ASTER, CHINA. See *Callistephus.*

BABY BLUE-EYES. See *Nemophila menziesii.*

BABY'S-BREATH. See *Gypsophila.*

BACHELOR'S BUTTON. See *Centaurea cyanus*

BALSAM, GARDEN. See *Impatiens balsamina.*

BARBERTON DAISY. See *Gerbera jamesonii.*

BASIL. See *Ocimum basilicum.*

BEGONIA, TUBEROUS. See *Begonia × tuberhybrida.*

BEGONIAS, FIBROUS-ROOTED. See *Begonia semperflorens.*

BEGONIAS, WAX. See *Begonia semperflorens.*

BELLFLOWER. See *Campanula.*

BELLFLOWER, Chilean. See *Nolana.*

BELLS, CANTERBURY. See *Campanula medium.*

BELLS, CATHEDRAL. See *Cobaea scandens.*

BELLS-OF-IRELAND. See *Moluccella laevis.*

BELVEDERE. See *Kochia scoparia.*

BLACK-EYED SUSAN. See *Rudbeckia hirta.*

BLACK-EYED SUSAN VINE. See *Thunbergia alata.*

BLANKET FLOWER. See *Gaillardia.*

BLOOD LEAF. See *Iresine.*

BLUEBELL, CALIFORNIA. See *Phacelia.*

BLUEBONNET, TEXAS. See *Lupinus texensis.*

BLUE CURLS. See *Phacelia congesta.*

BLUE DAISY. See *Felicia amelloides.*

BLUE-EYES, BABY. See *Nemophila menziesii.*

BLUE FELICIA. See *Felicia amelloides.*

BLUE LACEFLOWER. See *Trachymene caerulea.*

BLUE SAGE. See *Salvia patens.*

BORAGE. See *Borago.*

BORAGE, COMMON. See *Borago officinalis.*

BUGLOSS. See *Anchusa.*

BURNING BUSH. See *Kochia scoparia.*

BUSY LIZZIE. See *Impatiens.*

BUTTERFLY FLOWER. See *Schizanthus; Schizanthus pinnatus.*

BUTTON, BACHELOR'S. See *Centaurea cyanus.*

CABBAGE. See *Brassica oleracea,* Acephala Group.

CABBAGE, ORNAMENTAL. See *Brassica oleracea,* Acephala Group.

CALIFORNIA BLUEBELL. See *Phacelia.*

CALIFORNIA POPPY. See *Eschscholzia californica.*

CANARY CREEPER. See *Tropaeolum peregrinum.*

CANDYTUFT. See *Iberis.*

CANTERBURY BELLS. See
Campanula medium.

CAPE MARIGOLD. See
Dimorphotheca;
Dimorphotheca sinuata.

CAPE MARIGOLD, WINTER.
See *Dimorphotheca sinuata.*

CARDOON. See *Cynara*
cardunculus.

CASTOR BEAN. See *Ricinus*
communis.

CASTOR-OIL PLANT. See
Ricinus communis.

CATHEDRAL BELLS. See *Cobaea*
scandens.

CHAMOMILE, FALSE. See
Chrysanthemum parthenium.

CHERRY PIE. See *Heliotropium*
arborescens.

CHILEAN BELLFLOWER. See
Nolana.

CHINA ASTER. See *Callistephus.*

CHINA PINK. See *Dianthus*
chinensis.

CHINESE FORGET-ME-NOT. See
Cynoglossum amabile.

CIGAR FLOWER. See *Cuphea*
ignea.

CIGAR PLANT, MEXICAN. See
Cuphea ignea.

CILANTRO. See *Coriandrum*
sativum.

CLARY. See *Salvia sclarea.*

CLARY, SILVER. See *Salvia*
argentea.

CLEOME. See *Cleome*
hasslerana.

CLOCK VINE. See *Thunbergia.*

COCKLE, CORN. See
Agrostemma.

COCKSCOMB. See *Celosia*
arguta cristata.

COLEUS. See *Coleus × hybridus.*

COMMON BORAGE. See *Borago*
officinalis.

COMMON FENNEL. See
Foeniculum vulgare.

COMMON FOXGLOVE. See
Digitalis purpurea.

COMMON IMMORTELLE. See
Xeranthemum annuum.

COMMON MONKEY FLOWER.
See *Mimulus guttatus.*

COMMON SUNFLOWER. See
Helianthus annuus.

CONEFLOWER. See *Rudbeckia.*

COPPERLEAF. See
Alternanthera.

CORIANDER. See *Coriandrum*
sativum.

CORN COCKLE. See
Agrostemma.

CORNFLOWER. See *Centaurea,*
C. cyanus.

COSMOS, YELLOW. See *Cosmos*
sulphureus.

CREAMCUPS. See *Platystemon*
californicus.

CREEPER, CANARY. See
Tropaeolum peregrinum.

CREEPING ZINNIA. See
Sanvitalia procumbens.

CUCUMBER-LEAF SUNFLOWER.
See *Helianthus debilis.*

CUP-AND-SAUCER VINE. See
Cobaea scandens.

CUPFLOWER. See *Nierembergia.*

CUPFLOWER, WHITE. See
Nierembergia repens.

CURLS, BLUE. See *Phacelia*
congesta.

CYPRESS, SUMMER. See
Kochia scoparia.

CYPRESS VINE. See *Ipomoea*
quamoclit.

DAHLBERG DAISY. See
Dyssodia tenuiloba.

DAISY, AFRICAN. See *Arctotis*
stoechadifolia; Dimorphotheca
sinuata; Lonas inodora.

DAISY, BARBERTON. See
Gerbera jamesonii.

DAISY, BLUE. See *Felicia*
amelloides.

DAISY, DAHLBERG. See
Dyssodia tenuiloba.

DAISY, ENGLISH. See *Bellis*
perennis.

DAISY, GLORIOSA. See
Rudbeckia hirta.

DAISY, KINGFISHER. See *Felicia*
bergerana.

DAISY, LIVINGSTONE. See
Dorotheanthus bellidiformis.

DAISY, PARIS. See
Chrysanthemum frutescens.

DAISY, SWAN RIVER. See
Brachycome iberidifolia.

DAISY, TRANSVAAL. See
Gerbera jamesonii.

DAME'S ROCKET. See *Hesperis*
matronalis.

DAME'S VIOLET. See *Hesperis*
matronalis.

DEAD NETTLE. See *Lamium.*

DEAD NETTLE, SPOTTED. See
Lamium maculatum.

DELPHINIUM, ANNUAL. See
Consolida ambigua.

DUSTY MILLER. See *Centaurea*
cineraria; Senecio cineraria.

EDGING LOBELIA. See *Lobelia erinus.*

EMERALD FERN. See *Asparagus densiflorus* 'Sprengeri'.

ENGLISH DAISY. See *Bellis perennis.*

EVERLASTING. See *Helichrysum; Helipterum.*

EVERLASTING, SWAN RIVER. See *Helipterum manglesii.*

FAIRY PRIMROSE. See *Primula malacoides.*

FALSE CHAMOMILE. See *Chrysanthemum parthenium.*

FAREWELL-TO-SPRING. See *Clarkia amoena.*

FELICIA, BLUE. See *Felicia amelloides.*

FENNEL. See *Foeniculum.*

FENNEL, COMMON. See *Foeniculum vulgare.*

FEVERFEW. See *Chrysanthemum parthenium.*

FIBROUS-ROOTED BEGONIAS. See *Begonia semperflorens.*

FIRECRACKER PLANT. See *Cuphea ignea.*

FIVE-SPOT. See *Nemophila maculata.*

FLAME FLOWER. See *Tropaeolum speciosum.*

FLAX. See *Linum.*

FLAX, FLOWERING. See *Linum grandiflorum.*

FLOSS FLOWER. See *Ageratum houstonianum.*

FLOWERING FLAX. See *Linum grandiflorum.*

FLOWERING KALE. See *Brassica oleracea,* Capitata Group.

FLOWERING MAPLE. See *Abutilon.*

FLOWERING TOBACCO. See *Nicotiana alata.*

FOAM, MEADOW. See *Limnanthes douglasii.*

FOLIAGE PLANT. See *Coleus.*

FORGET-ME-NOT. See *Myosotis.*

FORGET-ME-NOT, ALPINE. See *Myosotis alpestris.*

FORGET-ME-NOT, CHINESE. See *Cynoglossum amabile.*

FOUR-O'CLOCK. See *Mirabilis jalapa.*

FOXGLOVE. See *Digitalis.*

FOXGLOVE, COMMON. See *Digitalis purpurea.*

FOXGLOVE, PERENNIAL. See *Digitalis lutea.*

FOXGLOVE, YELLOW. See *Digitalis grandiflora.*

FRENCH MARIGOLD. See *Tagetes patula.*

GAILLARDIA, ANNUAL. See *Gaillardia pulchella.*

GARDEN BALSAM. See *Impatiens balsamina.*

GARDEN HOLLYHOCK. See *Alcea rosea.*

GARDEN NASTURTIUM. See *Tropaeolum majus.*

GARDEN VERBENA. See *Verbena* × *hybrida.*

GARDEN ZINNIA. See *Zinnia elegans.*

GAZANIA. See *Gazania* × *hybrida; Gazania rigens.*

GENTIAN, PRAIRIE. See *Eustoma grandiflorum.*

GENTIAN SAGE. See *Salvia patens.*

GERANIUM. See *Pelargonium.*

GILLYFLOWER. See *Matthiola incana.*

GLOBE AMARANTH. See *Gomphrena globosa.*

GLORIOSA DAISY. See *Rudbeckia hirta.*

GODETIA. See *Clarkia.*

GOLDEN AGERATUM. See *Lonas inodora.*

GOLDEN-CUP, MEXICAN. See *Hunnemannia.*

GOLDEN-FLEECE. See *Dyssodia tenuiloba.*

GROUNDSEL. See *Senecio.*

HAWKWEED. See *Crepis.*

HEATHER, MEXICAN. See *Cuphea hyssopifolia.*

HELIOTROPE. See *Heliotropium; Heliotropium arborescens.*

HOLLYHOCK. See *Alcea.*

HOLLYHOCK, GARDEN. See *Alcea rosea.*

HOLY GHOST. See *Angelica archangelica.*

HONESTY. See *Lunaria.*

HOPS. See *Humulus.*

HOUND'S-TONGUE. See *Cynoglossum.*

HYACINTH, SUMMER. See *Galtonia.*

HYACINTH BEAN. See *Dolichos lablab.*

ICELAND POPPY. See *Papaver nudicaule.*

IMMORTELLE. See *Helipterum; Xeranthemum.*

IMMORTELLE, COMMON. See *Xeranthemum annuum.*

JASMINE TOBACCO. See *Nicotiana alata.*

JOSEPH'S-COAT. See *Amaranthus tricolor.*

KALE. See *Brassica oleracea,* Capitata Group.

KALE, FLOWERING. See *Brassica oleracea,* Capitata Group.

KALE, ORNAMENTAL. See *Brassica oleracea,* Capitata Group.

KINGFISHER DAISY. See *Felicia bergerana.*

LACEFLOWER, BLUE. See *Trachymene caerulea.*

LANTANA, TRAILING. See *Lantana montevidensis.*

LANTANA, WEEPING. See *Lantana montevidensis.*

LARKSPUR. See *Consolida.*

LARKSPUR, ROCKET. See *Consolida ambigua.*

LAVENDER, SEA. See *Limonium.*

LISIANTHUS. See *Eustoma grandiflorum.*

LIVINGSTONE DAISY. See *Dorotheanthus bellidiformis.*

LOBELIA, EDGING. See *Lobelia erinus.*

LOTUS. See *Lotus.*

LOTUS VINE. See *Lotus berthelotii.*

LOVE-IN-A-MIST. See *Nigella damascena.*

LOVE-LIES-BLEEDING. See *Amaranthus caudatus.*

LUPINE. See *Lupinus.*

LUPINE, SKY. See *Lupinus nanus.*

LUPINE, YELLOW. See *Lupinus luteus.*

MADAGASCAR PERIWINKLE. See *Catharanthus.*

MALCOLM STOCK. See *Malcolmia.*

MALLOW, ROSE. See *Lavatera trimestris.*

MAPLE, FLOWERING. See *Abutilon.*

MARGUERITE. See *Chrysanthemum frutescens.*

MARIGOLD. See *Tagetes.*

MARIGOLD, AMERICAN. See *Tagetes erecta.*

MARIGOLD, CAPE. See *Dimorphotheca; D. sinuata.*

MARIGOLD, FRENCH. See *Tagetes patula.*

MARIGOLD, POT. See *Calendula officinalis.*

MARIGOLD, SIGNET. See *Tagetes tenuifolia.*

MARIGOLD, WINTER CAPE. See *Dimorphotheca sinuata.*

MARSH FLOWER. See *Limnanthes.*

MARVEL-OF-PERU. See *Mirabilis jalapa.*

MEADOW FOAM. See *Limnanthes douglasii.*

MEALY-CUP SAGE. See *Salvia farinacea.*

MEXICAN CIGAR PLANT. See *Cuphea ignea.*

MEXICAN GOLDEN-CUP. See *Hunnemannia.*

MEXICAN HEATHER. See *Cuphea hyssopifolia.*

MEXICAN SUNFLOWER. See *Tithonia.*

MEXICAN TULIP POPPY. See *Hunnemannia.*

MEXICAN ZINNIA. See *Zinnia angustifolia.*

MIGNONETTE. See *Reseda.*

MONARCH OF THE VELDT. See *Venidium.*

MONEY PLANT. See *Lunaria annua.*

MONKEY FLOWER. See *Mimulus; Mimulus × hybridus.*

MONKEY FLOWER, COMMON. See *Mimulus guttatus.*

MOONFLOWER. See *Ipomoea alba.*

MOONWORT. See *Lunaria.*

MORNING-GLORY. See *Ipomoea.; I. purpurea.*

MOSS ROSE. See *Portulaca grandiflora.*

MOURNING BRIDE. See *Scabiosa.*

MULLEIN. See *Verbascum.*

MULLEIN, OLYMPIAN. See
  Verbascum olympicum.
MUSKFLOWER. See *Mimulus.*

NASTURTIUM. See *Tropaeolum.*
NASTURTIUM, GARDEN. See
  Tropaeolum majus.
NICOTIANA. See *Nicotiana alata.*

OLYMPIAN MULLEIN. See
  Verbascum olympicum.
OPIUM POPPY. See *Papaver
  somniferum.*
ORCHID, POOR-MAN'S. See
  Schizanthus.
ORNAMENTAL CABBAGE. See
  Brassica oleracea, Acephala
  Group.
ORNAMENTAL KALE. See
  Brassica oleracea, Capitata
  Group.
ORNAMENTAL PEPPER. See
  Capsicum annuum.
ORNAMENTAL TOBACCO. See
  Nicotiana alata.

PAINTED-TONGUE. See
  Salpiglossis sinuata.
PARIS DAISY. See
  Chrysanthemum frutescens.
PARROT'S-BEAK. See *Lotus
  berthelotii.*
PARSLEY. See *Petroselinum.*
PATIENCE PLANT. See
  Impatiens.
PEA, SWEET. See *Lathyrus
  odoratus.*

PEA, WINGED. See *Lotus
  tetragonolobus.*
PEPPER, ORNAMENTAL. See
  Capsicum annuum.
PEPPER, RED. See *Capsicum.*
PERENNIAL FOXGLOVE. See
  Digitalis lutea.
PERIWINKLE, MADIGASCAR.
  See *Catharanthus.*
PERIWINKLE, ROSE. See
  Catharanthus.
PETUNIA. See *Petunia.*
PHLOX, ANNUAL. See *Phlox
  drummondii.*
PIMPERNEL. See *Anagallis
  monellii.*
PINCUSHION FLOWER. See
  Scabiosa.
PINK, CHINA. See *Dianthus
  chinensis.*
PLUMED CELOSIA. See *Celosia
  arguta plumosa.*
POCKETBOOK PLANT. See
  Calceolaria.
POLYANTHUS PRIMROSE. See
  Primula × polyantha.
POOR-MAN'S ORCHID. See
  Schizanthus.
POPPY. See *Papaver.*
POPPY, CALIFORNIA. See
  Eschscholzia californica.
POPPY, ICELAND. See *Papaver
  nudicaule.*
POPPY, MEXICAN TULIP. See
  Hunnemannia.
POPPY, OPIUM. See *Papaver
  somniferum.*
POPPY, PRICKLY. See
  Argemone.
POPPY, SHIRLEY. See *Papaver
  rhoeas.*

POT MARIGOLD. See *Calendula
  officinalis.*
PRAIRIE GENTTIAN. See
  Eustoma grandiflorum.
PRICKLY POPPY. See *Argemone.*
PRIMROSE. See *Primula.*
PRIMROSE, ACAULIS. See
  Primula vulgaris.
PRIMROSE, FAIRY. See *Primula
  malacoides.*
PRIMROSE, POLYANTHUS. See
  Primula × polyantha.

RATTAIL STATICE. See
  Limonium suworowii.
RED PEPPER. See *Capsicum.*
RED SAGE. See *Lantana
  camara.*
ROCKET LARKSPUR. See
  Consolida ambigua.
ROCKET. See *Hesperis.*
ROCKET, DAME'S. See *Hesperis
  matronalis.*
ROCKET, SWEET. See *Hesperis
  matronalis.*
ROSE MALLOW. See *Lavatera
  trimestris.*
ROSE MOSS. See *Portulaca
  grandiflora.*
ROSE PERIWINKLE. See
  Catharanthus.
ROTHSCHILD GLORIOSA LILY.
  See *Gloriosa rothschildiana.*
RUSSIAN STATICE. See
  Limonium suworowii.

SAGE. See *Salvia.*
SAGE, BLUE. See *Salvia patens.*

SAGE, GENTIAN. See *Salvia patens.*

SAGE, MEALY-CUP. See *Salvia farinacea.*

SAGE, RED. See *Lantana camara.*

SAGE, SCARLET. See *Salvia splendens.*

SAGE, SILVER. See *Salvia argentea.*

SAGE, YELLOW. See *Lantana camara.*

SATIN FLOWER. See *Clarkia concinna.*

SAVORY. See *Satureja.*

SAVORY, SUMMER. See *Satureja hortensis.*

SCABIOUS. See *Scabiosa.*

SCABIOUS, SWEET. See *Scabiosa atropurpurea.*

SCARLET RUNNER BEAN. See *Phaseolus.*

SCARLET SAGE. See *Salvia splendens.*

SCOTCH THISTLE. See *Onopordum; Onopordum acanthium.*

SEA LAVENDER. See *Limonium.*

SEAPINK. See *Limonium.*

SHELLFLOWER. See *Moluccella laevis.*

SHIRLEY POPPY. See *Papaver rhoeas.*

SIGNET MARIGOLD. See *Tagetes tenuifolia.*

SILVER CLARY. See *Salvia argentea.*

SILVER SAGE. See *Salvia argentea.*

SILVER-LEAF SUNFLOWER. See *Helianthus argophyllus.*

SKY LUPINE. See *Lupinus nanus.*

SLIPPERWORT. See *Calceolaria.*

SNAPDRAGON. See *Antirrhinum.*

SNOW-ON-THE-MOUNTAIN. See *Euphorbia marginata.*

SPIDER PLANT. See *Cleome hasslerana.*

SPOTTED DEAD NETTLE. See *Lamium maculatum.*

SPURGE. See *Euphorbia.*

STAR OF THE VELDT. See *Osteospermum.*

STATICE. See *Limonium.*

STATICE, RATTAIL. See *Limonium suworowii.*

STATICE, RUSSIAN. See *Limonium suworowii.*

STOCK. See *Matthiola.*

STOCK, MALCOLM. See *Malcolmia.*

STOCK, VIRGINIA. See *Malcolmia maritima.*

STORK'S BILL. See *Pelargonium.*

STRAWFLOWER. See *Helichrysum bracteatum.*

SULTAN, SWEET. See *Centaurea moschata.*

SULTANA. See *Impatiens.*

SUMMER CYPRESS. See *Kochia scoparia.*

SUMMER HYACINTH. See *Galtonia.*

SUMMER SAVORY. See *Satureja hortensis.*

SUNFLOWER. See *Helianthus.*

SUNFLOWER, COMMON. See *Helianthus annuus.*

SUNFLOWER, CUCUMBER-LEAF. See *Helianthus debilis.*

SUNFLOWER, MEXICAN. See *Tithonia.*

SUNFLOWER, SILVER-LEAF. See *Helianthus argophyllus.*

SWAN RIVER DAISY. See *Brachycome iberidifolia.*

SWAN RIVER EVERLASTING. See *Helipterum manglesii.*

SWEET ALYSSUM. See *Lobularia.*

SWEET PEA. See *Lathyrus odoratus.*

SWEET ROCKET. See *Hesperis matronalis.*

SWEET SCABIOUS. See *Scabiosa atropurpurea.*

SWEET SULTAN. See *Centaurea moschata.*

SWEET WILLIAM. See *Dianthus barbatus.*

TASSEL FLOWER. See *Amaranthus caudata.*

TEASEL. See *Dipsacus sylvestris.*

TEXAS BLUEBONNET. See *Lupinus texensis.*

THISTLE, SCOTCH. See *Onopordum; Onopordum acanthium.*

THOROUGH WAX. See *Bupleurum rotundifolium.*

THROW WAX. See *Bupleurum rotundifolium.*

TIDY-TIPS. See *Layia elegans.*

TOADFLAX, ANNUAL. See *Linaria maroccana.*

TOBACCO, FLOWERING. See *Nicotiana alata.*

TOBACCO, JASMINE. See
  Nicotiana alata.
TOBACCO, ORNAMENTAL. See
  Nicotiana alata
TOBACCO PLANT. See
  ·Nicotiana.
TOUCH-ME-NOT. See *Impatiens.*
TRAILING ASPARAGUS. See
  Asparagus desnsiflorus
  'Sprengeri'.
TRAILING LANTANA. See
  Lantana montevidensis.
TRANSVAAL DAISY. See *Gerbera
  jamesonii.*
TREASURE FLOWER. See
  Gazania × hybrida.
TUBEROSE. See *Polianthes;
  Polianthes tuberosa.*
TUBEROUS BEGONIA. See
  Begonia × tuberhybrida.
TULIP POPPY, MEXICAN. See
  Hunnemannia.

WAX BEGONIAS. See *Begonia
  semperflorens.*
WEEPING LANTANA. See
  Lantana montevidensis.
WHITE CUPFLOWER. See
  Nierembergia repens.
WINGED PEA. See *Lotus
  tetragonolobus.*
WINTER CAPE MARIGOLD. See
  Dimorphotheca.
WISHBONE FLOWER. See
  Torenia fournieri.

YELLOW COSMOS. See *Cosmos
  sulphureus.*
YELLOW FOXGLOVE. See
  Digitalis grandiflora.
YELLOW LUPINE. See *Lupinus
  luteus.*
YELLOW SAGE. See *Lantana
  camara.*

VERBENA, GARDEN. See
  Verbena × hybrida.
VERVAIN. See *Verbena.*
VINCA. See *Catharanthus.*
VIOLET. See *Viola.*
VIOLET, DAME'S. See *Hesperis
  matronalis.*
VIRGINIA STOCK. See
  Malcolmia maritima.

ZINNIA, Creeping. See
  Sanvitalia procumbens.
ZINNIA, GARDEN. See *Zinnia
  elegans.*
ZINNIA, MEXICAN. See *Zinnia
  angustifolia.*

WALLFLOWER. See *Cheiranthus
  cheiri.*
WAX, THOROUGH. See
  Bupleurum rotundifolium.
WAX, THROW. See *Bupleurum
  rotundifolium.*

GLOSSARY

achene. A single-seeded, dry fruit that does not split open when ripe. The seeds of *Fragaria* (strawberry) are achenes, as are *Helianthus* (sunflower) seeds.

alternate. Referring to the way twigs, branches or, especially, leaves have their point of attachment or emergence at different levels, not opposite one another, on stem or trunk. Technically, one leaf at each node (joint) of a stem. Compare OPPPOSITE and WHORL.

annual. A plant that completes its lifecycle, from germination to seed formation, in one year. Contrast BIENNIAL, PERENNIAL.

anther. The part of a stamen in which pollen is produced by a seed plant. The anther opens when the pollen is ripe.

apetalous. Without petals. Compare GAMOPETALOUS.

apomixis. Nonsexual reproduction, in which contact between male and female gametes is not necessary, as in *Hosta ventricosa* (blue hosta). Often, the development of unfertilized egg cells or non-egg cells. The new plants are called apomicts, and have the same genetic make-up as the parent plant.

aril. An outer covering or appendage on some seeds. It is often colored, as in *Celastrus* (bittersweet).

awn. A bristly appendage on some anthers and on the fruits of some plants, notably on grains such as wheat and oats.

axil. The angle formed where a leaf, stalk or branch diverges from the main stem.

axillary. Forming part of an axil. For example, the flowers of *Clematis heracleifolia* (tube clematis) grow in axillary clusters; the clusters grow out of the axil—the angle between the main stem and leaf stalks.

basal. At the base of the plant.

beard. The fringelike, often bristly growth on a petal, as on many irises.

berry. A thin-skinned, fleshy or pulpy stoneless fruit, with small, soft or tough seeds, that develops from a single ovary. Typical true berries are the blueberry, grape, tomato and eggplant. The word is incorrectly applied to many true fruits, notably *Fragaria* (strawberry), blackberry, mulberry.

biennial. A plant that requires two years to complete its life cycle. In the first year, it makes only vegetative growth (although some biennials will flower if started early in the year). In the second year, it flowers and produces seed, then dies. Contrast ANNUAL, PERENNIAL.

bigeneric. Involving two genera. Commonly referring to a hybrid produced by crossing plants of different genera.

bipinnate. Twice pinnate; with leaves arranged in double-feather fashion.

bisexual. Term commonly applied to a flower having both stamens and pistils.

blade. Strictly, the more or less flat, expanded part of any leaf (not to be confused with the leafstalk or petiole). Loosely, blade is a common term for any long, narrow, pointed leaf, as in grass.

bolt. To set seed suddenly, rapidly and prematurely.

botrytis. Also known as gray mold, this common fungal problem thrives on fruits and flowers in moist conditions, usually infecting dead tissue first. Some plants, such as *Paeonia* (peony), are particularly susceptible. Treat by removing the blighted plant parts, and prune plants back to encourage better air circulation.

bract. One of the small, scalelike leaves that emerge from a flower stalk and enclose a flower bud. Although usually green, bracts may be beautifully colored. The "flowers" of *Cornus* (dogwood) and *Euphorbia* (poinsettia), for example, are really bracts.

bulb. Loosely, any globular or markedly swollen underground stem that produces top growth and basal roots. Strictly, a true bulb is a modified plant bud enclosed in thick, fleshy scales held together by a fibrous base that sends forth roots. Examples: daffodil, hyacinth, lily, onion, tulip. Crocus, dahlia, gladiolus, iris are produced from related rootstocks classed as corms, rhizomes or tubers.

callus. The repair tissue that forms over a stem or root that has been cut. In the rooting of most forms of cuttings, it is from the callus tissue that new roots emerge.

calyx. The small, petal-like parts, called sepals, that surround the true petals of a flower. The calyx is commonly green, but in some flowers, such as the lily and *Anemone*, it assumes the flower's color.

capitate. Formed in a head (a compact, dense cluster).

carpel. A pistil or one of the units of a pistil; a simple pistil is made up of one carpel, and a compound pistil is made up of a number of carpels.

chlorosis. The state of a plant abnormally characterized by the loss of green coloring matter in leaves and stems.

clasping. Surrounding the stem, either partially or completely. Refers to the growth of some leaves.

clone. A group of identical plants, all descended by vegetative or asexual reproduction by cuttings, division, layering, from a single plant produced from seed. Examples: 'Baldwin' apple, 'Concord' grape and named varieties of many common garden plants.

cold frame. An outdoor, boxlike construction, without a bottom and usually covered in glass or clear plastic on top, used to control weather conditions; in particular, often used to germinate seeds and force bulbs.

compound. Composite; composed of two or more similar parts in one organ, usually in a flower or leaf. A compound leaf, for example, has two or more leaflets.

cordate. Describing a leaf that is ovate in form, and that has lobes at its base on either side of the point where the leaf and the leaf stalk meet, resulting in a heart-like shape.

corm. A swollen but flattish underground stem that resembles a bulb but is more solid and lacks the typical thick scale leaves of a bulb. Gladiolus and crocus are cormous plants.

cormel. A small corm produced at the base of a corm.

corolla. Usually, the showy parts of a flower, consisting of petals.

corona. The circular crown—which may be cup-shaped or tube-shaped—immediately surrounding the stamen of a flower. For example, the cup of a daffodil.

corymb. A flower cluster that is flat on top because of the elongation of the side stems to match the height of the central stem. The flowers bloom from the edges inward. Contrast CYME.

cotyledon. The first seed leaf (or one of the first pairs or whorl) to develop within a seed.

crested. Having an elevated, sometimes toothed, ridge. The fasciated inflorescence of cockscomb is described as crested. Some irises show a raised ridge, called a crest, on the surface of the petals (where the beard is in common garden irises).

crown. The upper part of the rootstock from which shoots grow, as in *Lupinus*, *Paeonia*, *Delphinium* and *Chrysanthemum × superba* (Shasta daisy). Also, the entire foliage of a tree and the corona or corolla of a flower, which is usually the part between petals and stamens.

cultivar. Abbreviation: cv. A new plant developed in cultivation through a breeding program. By contrast, a VARIETY occurs spontaneously, either in the wild or in cultivation, and is simply selected, propagated and named by the grower.

cutting. A rootless piece of plant used to produce a new plant.

cyme. A large, broad, sometimes flat flower cluster that blooms from the center outward—always with a flower at the end of the main or central stalk. Example: *Phlox*. Contrast CORYMB.

deciduous. A plant that drops its leaves every year and always before new leaves come. Contrast EVERGREEN.

decumbent. Growing close to the ground, but with ascending tips; *Campanula poscharskyana* (Serbian bellflower), for example.

dicotyledon. Sometimes shortened to dicot. A plant with two seed leaves (two leaflike structures on the embryo plant within a seed). Contrast MONOCOTYLEDON.

dioecious. With staminate and pistillate flowers on separate plants. Contrast MONOECIOUS.

disbud. To remove certain buds in order to produce better flowers from remaining buds or to induce stronger growth or a more symmetrical shape.

disk. The central portion of the flower head of plants of the *Compositae* (Daisy Family). Also, the part of the inflorescence producing the tubular central flowers.

diurnal. Flowers that open only during daylight hours, as in *Hemerocallis*.

divide. To cut, pull apart or otherwise separate the roots or crowns of a plant or clump in order to produce additional plants. See DIVISION, PROPAGATION.

division. A method of propagating multicrowned plants (usually herbaceous ones) by separating the roots into smaller portions capable of independent growth.

dorsal. The back or underside of a plant part. In a leaf, the dorsal side is the surface turned away from the main stem, hence the underside.

double. Flower form that has a greater than normal number of petals.

down. Soft hairs that cover a plant surface, usually the leaves.

drill. A small furrow in the ground in which to sow seeds. Also, to sow or plant in a drill.

elliptic. Widest at the middle, narrower at the ends. Usually referring to leaf shape.

embryo. The microscopic plant inside a seed. When the seed is ripe, the embryo comprises root, stem and leaf cells—all arranged in a way characteristic of the mature plant into which it will develop.

encurved. Curved upward or inward. Contrast REFLEXED.

endemic. Referring to a plant native to, and found wild only in, a particular region.

endosperm. The tissue inside a seed that contains nourishment for the embryo.

entire. Referring to a leaf with smooth, continuous edges. For example, a rhododendron leaf. An elm or beech leaf is not entire, because its edges are toothed.

epicotyl. The stem tip (above the cotyledons or seed leaves) of an embryo plant. From it develop the true leaves, stems, flowers and fruits of the full-grown plant. See HYPOCOTYL.

epidermis. The "skin" of a leaf.

equitant. Overlapping; said of leaves whose bases overlap the leaves within or above them, as in many irises.

escape. Colloquially, a cultivated plant that has gone wild and perpetuates itself without further care. Also, the naturalization of such a plant. *Convallaria* (lily-of-the-valley) and *Hemerocallis* (daylily) frequently escape from the strictly cultivated state.

evergreen. A plant that does not lose all its foliage in the autumn, hence appears to retain its leaves the year round. Contrast DECIDUOUS.

everlasting. A plant that retains its form and color when dried.

exotic. A plant being grown in a region to which it is not indigenous. Contrast NATIVE.

exserted. By derivation, extended or protruding. In application, relating especially to staminate or pistillate flower parts that project beyond the corolla. Contrast INCLUDED.

eye. The growth bud on a tuber or on the stem of a plant. Also, the distinctive center of a flower, as in some members of the *Compositae* (Daisy) Family.

fall. In iris, one of the flower's three outer, reflexed segments. The three inner parts are called STANDARDS.

fasciation. An unusual widening and flattening of a plant stem, as in cockscomb.

female. Referring to pistillate flowers or flower parts. Also, colloquially, a plant having pistillate flowers.

fertile. Referring to a plant able to produce fruit (seeds); to a flower possessing the organs of reproduction; to a soil abundantly supplied with the ingredients necessary to plant growth and in a condition appropriate to the support of that growth.

fibrous-rooted. Plants with finely divided, fiberlike roots, as opposed, for example, to fleshy, tuberous or bulbous roots.

filament. The slender stalk that supports the anther and, with it, constitutes the stamen of a flower.

floret. One of the flowers in a composite cluster; loosely, any single flower, usually small, in any multiple inflorescence.

flower. The popular term for the combination of sexual structures having to do with complex plants. The concept usually includes color and a definite organization. If plants did not have flowers, they could not produce seed with which to reproduce their kind.

follicle. A dry, one-celled fruit that bursts open along a single seam. For example, seed pods or fruits of *Delphinium*, *Asclepias* (milkweed), *Paeonia* (peony).

friable. Crumbly; easily crushed.

frond. The leaf of a fern (the word is sometimes applied to palm leaves).

fruit. Botanically, a fruit is the mature seed-bearing ovary of any plant. It may or may not be edible or ornamental, large or small, borne singly or in clusters—on trees, bushes or herbaceous plants.

funnelform. The shape of certain flowers, in which the tube gradually widens upward and outward like a trumpet.

gamopetalous. A flower whose petals are completely or almost completely fused. For example, *Campanula* (bellflower). Compare APETALOUS.

genus. Plural, genera. A quite closely related and definable group of plants that includes one or more species. The genus name is the first half of the horticultural name of a species.

glabrous. Smooth; lacking hairs. Contrast PUBESCENT.

glaucous. Covered with a waxy bloom that is powdery and bluish-white to bluish-gray . Generally a reference to foliage.

glomerate. Clustered, often referring to dense, globular flower heads.

glume. A chaffy bract, especially one of the two bracts at the base of the spikelet in many grasses.

hair. Fine filaments growing from a plant surface.

half-hardy. A half-hardy perennial is one used outdoors in summer and taken indoors or to the greenhouse during the winter. Half-hardy annuals cannot stand frost, so are bedded out or seeded when danger of frost is past.

hardiness zone. The region in which a plant can overwinter outdoors, and in which summers are not too hot for the plant.

head. A dense flower or leaf cluster that more or less resembles a head. Commonly, anything from a composite flowerhead (daisies) to a head of lettuce.

heart-shaped. Usually applied to leaves that are ovate (egg-shaped) and bear two rounded basal lobes; see CORDATE.

heaving. Swelling or bulging (as in a plant bed). Changing temperatures cause freezing, defrosting and refreezing of soil water, causing it to expand and contract, damaging plants.

herb. By definition, a seed plant having soft, fleshy tissue rather than the persistently woody tissue associated with trees and shrubs. Such plants are generally termed herbaceous. Commonly, "herb" refers to plants used for medicinal or culinary purposes.

herbaceous. Plants that have soft, fleshy tissues; not WOODY.

hip. The enlarged, fleshy, berrylike, often quite handsome fruit of the rose.

humus. Decomposed plant and animal matter used as a soil ingredient. Humus provides nutrients, natural drainage and the ideal pH.

hybrid. The progeny resulting from the cross-fertilization of one genus, species or variety of plant with another, different plant. Hybrids occur naturally in nature; they are also the preoccupation of many plant breeders.

hypocotyl. In a newly germinated seedling, the stem below the cotyledons and above the root. (The stem above the cotyledons is part of the EPICOTYL.)

imperfect. A flower that produces male or female reproductive organs (stamens or pistils) but not both. Contrast PERFECT.

included. Referring to stamens or pistils that do not protrude beyond a flower's corolla. Contrast EXSERTED.

incurved. Referring to flowers having parts curved toward the center; also to the parts themselves, such as an incurved ray petal. Contrast RECURVED.

indeterminate. Plants in which the vegetative growth does not terminate in flower or fruit clusters. Such plants continue to extend shoot growth indefinitely, at the same time producing flowers and fruit until frost.

inferior. A plant ovary that develops beneath a flower calyx. The rose has an inferior ovary, familiarly known as the rose hip. Contrast SEMNIFEROUS, SUPERIOR.

inflorescence. The general and total flowering arrangement of a plant; also, the way individual florets are arranged in a cluster.

inserted. Attached by natural growth (as with certain flower parts).

internode. The part of a plant stem between nodes.

involucre. A whorl of bracts or small, often scalelike leaves around the base of a flower or fruit (conspicuously on *Centaurea*, zinnia and many other members of the *Compositae* Family).

irregular. An unsymmetrical flower, in which various parts differ in size or shape from the other parts in the same flower group. For example, all orchid flowers are irregular.

jointed. With nodes (joints)—places at which a leaf or bud is attached to the stem. Separation is natural at these nodes. Bamboo stems are jointed.

keel. A ridge on the back of a leaf or petal, somewhat resembling a boat keel and V-shaped in section.

lanceolate. Of a much greater length than width, tapering at the ends (lance-shaped), and having convex sides; generally refering to leaf shape. Compare OBLANCEOLATE.

lateral. A branch, shoot or bud borne at the side of a plant. Contrast TERMINAL.

lax. Loosely or widely spaced.

leaf. Basically, a leaf consists of a more or less flat, wide part, known as the BLADE, and a stalk, known as the PETIOLE. Some leaves also have two small bracts, called STIPULES, at the base of the petiole, where it joins the stem. Though variously shaped, most leaves have a one-piece blade and are therefore called SIMPLE leaves. But in some leaves, such as in the rose, the blade is divided into several leaflets. Such leaves are called COMPOUND.

leaflet. One part of a compound leaf's whole blade.

leafmold. A layer of soil made up mainly of decayed vegetable matter.

linear. Long and uniformly narrow, as are many leaves.

lip. The protruding, sometimes pendulous, lip-like part of an irregular corolla, as in the orchid, snapdragon and violet.

lobe. A significant segment of a plant organ, usually a leaf, formed by a division up to halfway to the organ's middle.

male. Referring loosely to a plant bearing only STAMINATE (pollen-producing) flowers.

marginal. Partial. For instance, a marginal water plant, such as *Asclepias* (milkweed), is one that grows either partially submerged in shallow water or in the moist soil alongside a body of water.

midrib. The principal, usually central, vein or rib of a leaf. The exposed midrib of a pinnately compound leaf is a RACHIS.

mildew. A fungus-caused plant disease characterized by a usually-white, cottony coating on surfaces of affected parts of the plant.

monocarp. A plant that flowers and sets seeds once, then dies. All annuals and biennials are monocarps.

monocotyledon. Sometimes called monocot. A flowering plant with only one seedleaf (a single leaflike structure on the embryo). Its flowers have three (or a multiple of three) petals, sepals and stamens; its leaves are parallel-veined. Among the monocotyledons are amaryllis, irises, lilies, orchids and the grasses. Contrast DICOTYLEDON.

monoecious. A plant with separate male and female flowers, but with both kinds on the same plant. For example, cucumber, oak and walnut. Contrast DIOECIOUS.

monotypic. Referring to a genus having only one species.

mulch. An insulating layer, made of peat, compost, dried leaves, straw or other material, used to cover a planting. Spread around plant bases, it serves to protect against frost, conserve water and fight weed growth.

multifid. Divided into many parts, referring especially to leaves; compare PINNATIFID.

mutant. A SPORT resulting from a mutation, due to genetic changes in a particular plant or part of a plant.

mutation. A natural, spontaneous change in a plant gene that results in the development of a new variety. Also, the result of such a change.

native. A plant indigenous to a particular region. Contrast EXOTIC.

neck. The stemlike extension at the top of many bulbs.

nectar. A dilute sugar solution formed by many flowers. By attracting insects and birds, it aids in pollination.

nectary. A flower part, usually a gland near the base of petal or stamen, that exudes nectar.

nematode. Microscopic, threadlike worm, also known as an eelworm. Although there are many types, both beneficial and parasitic, gardeners are generally only concerned with the parasitic nematodes, which can be very destructive.

node. The joint at which a leaf, bud or branch meets the stem; hence, often, a joint, sometimes quite conspicuous. The space between two nodes is an INTERNODE.

nodule. A tubercle or small outgrowth on the root of a legume; *Lupinus* (lupines), for instance, have nodules. These nodules take nitrogen from the air and put it in the soil.

oblanceolate. Refers to leaf shape; widest toward the leaf edge and tapering to the base; inversely LANCEOLATE.

obovate. Egg-shaped, with the wide part upward; commonly referring to the shape of a leaf. Contrast OVATE.

offset. A short shoot that runs laterally from the base of a plant, producing leaves and usually roots at the end, thus forming a new plant. For example, a strawberry runner. Also, a small bulb that forms at the base of a mature bulb.

opposite. Referring to two leaves or branches attached to a stem directly across from each other, so they seem like pairs. Whether a plant has opposite or alternate leaves is one of the chief and obvious determinants of plant identification. Contrast ALTERNATE and WHORL.

orbicular. Round or almost round.

ovary. In the flowers of angiosperms, the enlarged organ at the base of the pistil that holds one or more ovules. After pollination, the ovules develop into seeds. The ovary, containing the seeds, develops into a fruit.

ovate. Egg-shaped, with the wide end downward; commonly referring to the shape of a leaf. Contrast OBOVATE.

ovule. One of the globular bodies within an ovary that develop into seeds after fertilization.

palmate. A leaf with lobes or veins that radiate from a common point at the base, finger-fashion. Typical palmate leaves with palmate veining are those of English ivy, maple.

panicle. A loose flower cluster with the earliest-blooming florets at the bottom. The flower stem does not have a terminal floret bloom. *Yucca* produces a typical panicle, as do *Phlox paniculata* (garden phlox) and many grasses.

parasite. A plant (often a fungus) that lives on, and at the expense of, another living plant, called the host plant. Examples: mistletoe, corn smut.

parted. Leaves, or sometimes petals, divided almost to the base.

pedicel. The stalk of any floret in a flower cluster; a division of a PEDUNCLE.

peduncle. The stalk of a single or solitary flower when branched. The branches are PEDICELS.

peltate. A leaf with its stem attached at or near the center, not at the margin. Examples: nasturtium, lotus.

perennial. A plant that lives from year to year. All trees, shrubs and many flowering bulbs are perennial; but the word is applied most commonly to herbaceous plants, especially the better-known border flowers. Contrast ANNUAL, BIENNIAL.

perfect. A bloom that contains both male and female reproductive organs (STAMENS and PISTILS). Contrast IMPERFECT.

perianth. Technically, all the floral leaves of a blossom. The word is used especially where the calyx is almost indistinguishable from the corolla. Among gardeners, perianth most commonly designates the petals from which the cup or crown of a narcissus rises.

persistent. Leaves, fruits or seed pods that remain or hang on, even if withered.

petal. Strictly, the leaf of a corolla. Colloquially, the leaf or segment blossom, which is usually showy.

petaloid. Sepals or stamens that have the form, appearance or texture of a petal.

petiole. The stalk of a leaf.

petiolule. Strictly, the petiole of the leaflet in a compound leaf.

picotee. A type of carnation (*Dianthus*) whose flower has an outer margin of another color, usually red.

pinnate. A compound leaf of which the leaflets or leaf parts are similarly arranged on either side of a principal stem, feather-fashion. Also, a single leaf of which the principal veins branch off at a number of points along a midrib.

pinnatifid. Divided or parted in a pinnate manner. Contrast MULTIFID.

pinnule. The smallest and ultimate division of a compound leaf.

pip. Commonly, the individual root-stock (a single stem bud with roots) of *Convallaria* (lily-of-the-valley); occasionally also *Anemone* and some others. Colloquially, a seed of an apple, orange or pear.

pistil. The female reproductive organ of a flower. It consists of three parts: The swollen, bulbous base—the OVARY—contains the ovules that develop into seeds. Leading from it is a fleshy, tubelike stalk called the STYLE (not always definable). The enlarged tip of the style is the STIGMA, with a sticky surface on which pollen adheres and is conveyed through the style to the ovary.

pistillate. Having only a pistil (no stamens); female.

pod. Strictly, a dry, dehiscent fruit, such as a peapod. Loosely, any dry fruit or podlike organ that contains seeds.

pollen. The microscopic grains, usually resembling yellow dust, produced on the anther of a stamen. When ripe, dry pollen becomes windborne; sticky pollen is picked up by insects and birds. After pollen is deposited on the stigma of a pistil, it will produce the sperm cells that may fertilize ovules.

polycotyledon. A plant with more than two cotyledons or seed leaves, as the pine and other conifers.

polygamous. A plant with both perfect and imperfect flowers.

propagation. Plant reproduction, which can occur by a variety of means, including seeds, division of the CROWN, bulblets produced by mature bulbs, and shoots emerging from roots or stolons.

pubescent. Covered with soft, fine hairs. Contrast GLABROUS.

pyrethrum. One of several kinds of *Chrysanthemum*, such as *C. coccineum*, used as a source of insecticides; an insecticide made from a pyrethrum *Chrysanthemum*.

raceme. A long flower cluster with only one main stem, from which the stems of individual florets branch. The cluster blooms from the bottom upward. There is no flower at the end of the main stem. (A compound raceme is produced when the main stem is branched.) Examples: honey locust (*Gleditsia triacanthos*), *Convallaria* (lily-of-the-valley).

rachis. The main stalk of a flower cluster; the main leaf stem or PETIOLE of a compound leaf.

radical. Pertaining to or proceeding from the root.

radicle. The root portion of an embryo. Also, the first root developed by a germinating seed.

ray. Strictly, a flattened corolla radiating from the central disk of a composite flower head, as in *Aster* and *Helianthus* (sunflower). Loosely, any flat, straplike petal in the outer part of a flower.

receptacle. The part of the stem on which the flowers are borne. A rose hip is an enlarged receptacle. So is *Fragaria* (strawberry).

recurved. Backward- or downward-curving, usually in reference to petals. Contrast INCURVED.

reflexed. Curved sharply backward or downward, usually in reference to petals. Contrast ENCURVED.

regular. A flower that is basically symmetrical in the arrrangement of its parts, such as petals, sepals, and so forth; *Chrysanthemum* (daisy) is an example. Most flowers are regular.

remontant. A plant that blooms twice in the same season; some roses, for example.

revolute. Leaves or petals with margins or tips rolled backward or downward.

rhizomatous. Having or producing rhizomes, such as *Anemone*.

rhizome. The fleshy, somewhat elongated rootstock (underground stem) of some herbaceous perennials. It has stem buds on the upper side and small roots on the lower side.

root cutting. A piece of root or rootstock used for propagation.

root hair. One of the countless delicate hairs somewhat above the tips of the smallest roots. The hairs are the actual food- and water-gatherers.

root-hardy. Referring to perennial plants whose roots survive even though above ground parts may die because of climatic extremes.

rootstock. A fleshy, underground stem with eyes and roots, as herbaceous *Paeonia* (peony) or *Rheum* (rhubarb). It differs from the actual root in that it stores food but does not gather it. Also, colloquially, the root or rooted understock upon which a scion or bud is grafted.

rust. Any of a number of specific plant diseases, usually requiring two different hosts during their lifecycle and manifesting in reddening or browning of twigs and needles and the release of rust-colored spores. To control, either pull up all diseased plants and replace with resistent species, or prune and space plants to encourage air circulation. Burn infected plants in the fall.

salver-form. A flower with a slender tube topped by an expanded, flat circle of petals; a *Phlox* blossom, for example.

scale. One of the scalelike leaves protecting a bud before it opens. Also, a small, thin, often dry bract. Also, short for scale insect.

scalloped. Having a pattern of bulging extensions at the edges.

scape. A single leafless, branchless stem rising from the ground and topped by a flower or an inflorescence, as in *Amaryllis* spp., *Sanguinaria canadensis* (bloodroot), *Hemerocallis* (daylily), *Narcissus* spp. (daffodil).

scion. Shoot or other part of a woody plant that, when detached, contains one or more buds from which a duplicate plant may be developed by grafting.

seed. The fertilized and ripened ovule of a flowering plant that contains an embryo plant capable of germination and growth.

segment. A division of a leaf or petals. Leaflets are often called segments.

self-sow. Referring to plants that seed themselves and produce new plants without human assistance.

self-sterile. A plant that cannot be fertilized by itself or by another plant of the same variety is self-sterile. This is true of many species of *Dianthus* (carnations) and *Papaver* (poppies).

semidouble. Flower form that has an incomplete extra floral envelope, for example *Anemone × hybrida*.

semniferous. Usually a plant ovary surrounded by a cup formed by the perianth and stamens, which are fused together. Compare INFERIOR, SUPERIOR.

sepal. One of the outermost, usually green, scales of a flower bud. First leaflike, later often petal-like, the sepals make up the CALYX.

septum. A dividing wall or partition within an organ; usually applied to fruit, as in *Lunaria annua* (honesty).

serrate. Having a pattern of pointed extensions at the edges; saw-toothed.

sessile. Lacking a stalk.

set. A part of a plant used for propagation, as an onion set. Also refers to the potential conversion of flowers into fruit; example: "The tomato plant sets many fruits."

sheath. The plant part that encases the lower end of a stalk in many plants, notably the grasses. Also refers to the envelope that protects buds of cattleya orchids until they are ready to open.

shoot. A young branch that may produce flowers or leaves or both.

simple. A single flower or a leaf with a single whole blade. Also, but rarely, a medicinal herb.

single. Flower head made up of only one floral envelope.

sinus. The cleft or open space between the lobes, or points, of a leaf —notably, in many oaks.

spadix. The thick flower spike (with fleshy, cylindrical center) characteristic of plants in the *Aracae* (Arum Family) and some others. The spadix is usually enclosed in a SPATHE, which is often the showy part of the flower. The most familiar example is *Arisaema triphyllum* (Jack-in-the-pulpit), in which the club-shaped spadix (Jack) is surrounded by the arching green-and-purple spathe (pulpit).

spathe. The leaflike bract or pair of bracts sheathing an inflorescence (often a SPADIX), as in calla lily and *Arisaema triphyllum* (Jack-in-the-pulpit).

spatulate. Oblong, with a narrow base and a pointed tip; spatula-shaped.

species. A group of plants within a genus. Species of the same genus are all different but contain one or more common characteristics. Species may reproduce themselves from seeds and may often be interbred, sometimes in nature.

spike. An elongated flower cluster in which each individual blossom is connected without a stalk to the main stem. Example, mignonette.

spikelet. A small spike, as the inflorescence of grasses.

spore. The microscopic, unicellular reproductive body of fungi, algae, ferns, mosses and lichens.

sport. A mutant plant, with different characteristics than the parent plant. Sports occur naturally or can be induced by gardeners.

spray. A single, fragile shoot, stem or branch, along with its leaves, flowers, and any other growth.

sprig. A young shoot. Also, the act of planting stolons of some turf species, such as the bents, to make a lawn.

sprout. Referring to the development of new growth.

spur. A long, hollow appendage of the corolla or calyx of plants such as *Aquilegia* (columbine) and *Delphinium* (larkspur). Also, a short flower- or fruit-bearing shoot on a tree (called a fruit spur) and a comparable shoot producing foliage (leaf spur).

stalk. The stem or main axis of a plant. The word also has such specialized meanings as leaf-stalk (PETIOLE), flower stalk (PEDUNCLE), a slender stalk (PEDICEL), the stalk of an anther (FILAMENT).

stamen. The male reproductive organ of a flower. It comprises a slender stalk (the FILAMENT) and a swollen tip (the ANTHER). The latter produces pollen.

staminate. Having stamens; male.

staminode. A stamenlike organ that does not produce pollen.

standard. A tree or shrub with a single straight stem topped by a compact head of foliage. Examples: weeping mulberry, tree rose, catalpa. Also, the erect, upper petal of a pea flower. Also, one of the three erect petals of an iris bloom (as contrasted with the drooping petals or FALLS).

stem. A confusing term with several meanings: Most commonly, it refers to the main axis of a plant, as the trunk of a tree or the stalk of a zinnia. A rootstock or rhizome is an underground stem. Broadly, any leaf- or flower-bearing stalk is also a stem.

sterility. A plant's inability to reproduce. Some plants are absolutely sterile; others are sterile only under certain circumstances.

stigma. In pistillate flowers, that part of the style, usually the expanded tip, that receives the pollen from the anthers of staminate flowers. A stigma is said to be receptive when its surface becomes sticky, so that it holds the pollen for the initiation of the fertilization process.

stipule. One of the small, leaflike appendages at the base of many petioles.

stock. The rooted plant to which a scion is grafted.

stolon. A shoot that runs along the ground and takes root, and from which new plants sprout.

stoloniferous. Having or producing stolons, for example *Coreopsis auriculata* (mouse-eared coreopsis).

stoma. Plural, stomata. An infinitesimal pore in the epidermis of a leaf that opens during the day to admit essential carbon dioxide and permits water vapor to escape, closes at night when carbon dioxide cannot be used.

strain. A group of plants of the same variety that have a distinct common characteristic, such as greater vigor, longer stems, better flowers than the type.

style. The stalklike or tubelike growth that connects the ovary to the terminal stigma of a pistil.

subshrub. A small, generally herbaceous plant that has woody and shrubby stems, as *Chrysanthemum* and *Pachysandra*.

subspecies. A subdivision of a species, ranking between species and variety.

succulent. A fleshy plant, such as a cactus, that stores water in stems or leaves in order to survive in hot, dry, desert regions (the native habitat of the majority of succulents).

superior. Usually a plant ovary borne above rather than below the calyx, as in lilies. Compare INFERIOR, SEMNIFEROUS.

suture. Botanically, the line or seam between parts of a fruit; also, where the mature fruit normally splits, as a peapod.

syncarp. An aggregate or collective fruit, usually fleshy.

systemic. A pesticide applied to the roots of a plant and absorbed through the plant's system.

taproot. The large, central root of many plants. It usually goes straight down to considerable depth.

teeth. Repeated projections at the edge of a leaf.

temperate. Neither excessively cold nor excessively hot. In the Northern Hemisphere, the Temperate Zone lies between the Tropic of Cancer and the Arctic Circle.

tender. Plants that cannot survive winter in the regions where frost is common.

tendril. A slender, springy, coiling part of climbing plants. Usually an extension of a stalk or leaf, it wraps around any available means of support. Plants with tendrils include the grape, pea, glory-lily.

terete. Cylindrical (with a circular cross-section); said of plant stems or leaves, as of some orchids.

terminal. Buds or flowers at the tip of a stem. Contrast LATERAL.

ternate. In threes, as in compound leaves, or divided into three parts or lobes.

throat. The opening of the tubular part of many flowers.

tomentose. Having a covering layer of short, dense, matted woolly hairs.

trichome. A hair or hair-like bristle.

truss. Colloquially, any flower cluster at the end of a stalk, such as lilac.

tube. The cylindrical or funnel-shaped basal portion of a united calyx or corolla.

tuber. A fleshy, swollen stem, usually underground, having lateral as well as terminal growth buds or "eyes" and producing roots along its length or at the distal end.

tubercle. A nodule on the root of a legume. Also, the characteristic growth or knob on many cacti.

tuberous. Having or producing tubers. Also, tuber-like.

umbel. A flat-topped or dome-shaped flower cluster, as in the *Umbelliferae* (Carrot Family) and *Allium*. All the flower stems rise from a common point on the main stalk.

understock. Another name for the stock on which a scion is grafted.

union. The point at which stock and scion join in grafting or budding.

unisexual. Flowers having stamens or pistils but not both. Also, loosely, plants having such flowers on separate plants.

utricle. A small fruit that does not split; it may contain one to four seeds.

variegation. Variation in appearance or color; patches of different colors, as in leaves.

variety. The lowest, or final, natural classification of plants. Not all species have natural varieties, but most species have several. Each variety retains the species' basic character, but has one or more distinctive characteristics of its own.

vegetative. Reproducing asexually.

vein. Strand or bundle of vascular tissue forming the frame or skeleton of a leaf.

venation. The arrangement of veins in a leaf.

ventral. The inner surface of a plant part, as the surface of a petal facing toward the center of the flower.

vernalization. Exposing seeds or plants to low temperature to induce flowering. Literally, the approximation of the effects of spring.

vernation. The arrangement of leaves within a bud.

viviparous. Plants that produce organs of reproduction or living sprouts while attached to the parent plant. Examples: the sprouting leaf edges of kalachoes; bulbils of the multiplier onion.

voles. Mouse- or rat-like rodents that are a plant pest.

whorl. A circle of three or more petals, leaves, twigs or flowers, all from the same point on a stalk.

wing. A membranous or woody appendage on the seed or stalk of many plants. For example, the seed-bearing wings of the maple.

woody. Plants whose stems are made of hard, tough fibers that do not die back (i.e. are PERSISTENT). Contrast HERBACEOUS.

xerophyte. A plant adapted by nature to withstand drought, by storing water or by resisting waterless conditions for long periods.

zygomorphic. An irregular flower that can be divided into two similar parts on one plane. Snapdragons and all orchids are examples.

ACKNOWLEDGMENTS

The text for *The Hearst Garden Guides* is based on *The Good Housekeeping Illustrated Encyclopedia of Gardening*, a sixteen-volume set originally compiled under the auspices of the Editors of *Good Housekeeping* and published in 1972. The project began as the work of Ralph Sargent Bailey, garden editor for more than a quarter of a century at *House Beautiful* and *House and Garden* (now *HG*); unfinished at the time of Mr. Bailey's death, the work was completed by then Garden Editor at *House Beautiful*, Elvin McDonald.

Mr. McDonald assembled some of the finest garden writers of the day to work on different sections of the encyclopedia. In addition to Messrs. Bailey and McDonald, we would like in particular to acknowledge Dr. John Philip Baumgardt, horticultural consultant to the *Encyclopedia*, former editor of *American Horticultural Society Magazine* and author of *How to Prune Almost Everything*, and George Taloumis, former editor of *Horticulture* and author of *The Moveable Garden*, for theirfine essays on annuals, which were the basis for the essays herein.

For this edition, Sue Baldwin-Way and her husband Robert G. Way did a great deal of work on organizing the manuscript. We would like also to thank Ruth Lively for her suggestions based on her impressive horticultural knowledge, Tom Starace for his computer expertise and Durrae Johanek for thoroughly copyediting the text.

Andrew Lawson shot the glorious specimen and general garden photographs. The illustrations by Lisa Zador and Wendy Frost lend beauty as well as crisp visual reference to the book.

PHOTOGRAPHY CREDITS

Andrew Lawson provided the photography for this book, except for the following:

p. 35, Ted Marston;

p. 36 (top), Jerry Pavia;

p. 38 (bottom left), Ted Marston;

p. 38 (top right), Elvin McDonald;

p. 41 (left), Elvin McDonald;

p. 45 (top left), Elvin McDonald;

p. 45 (bottom left), Jerry Pavia;

p. 45 (top right), Ted Marston;

p. 45 (bottom right), Ted Marston;

p. 46 (left), Ted Marston;

p. 50 (top), Ted Marston;

p. 53 (top), Ted Marston;

p. 53 (bottom), Pamela Harper;

p. 54 (left), Elvin McDonald;

p. 57 (top left), Elvin McDonald;

p. 57 (bottom), Elvin McDonald;

p. 58 (top), Elvin McDonald;

p. 60 (top left), Ted Marston;

p. 60 (bottom), Elvin McDonald;

p. 63 (top), Elvin McDonald;

p. 65 (top), Ted Marston;

p. 65 (bottom), Ted Marston;

p. 66 (top right), Joanne Pavia;

p. 68 (top left), Ted Marston;

p. 68 (bottom), Elvin McDonald;

p. 75 (top left), Elvin McDonald;

p. 76 (bottom left), Elvin McDonald;

p. 76 (top right), Elvin McDonald;

p. 76 (bottom right), Ted Marston;

p. 79 (top right), Elvin McDonald;

p. 79 (bottom right), Elvin McDonald;

p. 81 (top left), Elvin McDonald;

p. 82 (top left), Jerry Pavia;

p. 82 (bottom left), Ted Marston;

p. 82 (top right), Joanne Pavia;

p. 85 (left), Ted Marston;

p. 86 (top), Ted Marston;

p. 86 (bottom left), Jerry Pavia;

p. 86 (bottom right), Joanne Pavia;

p. 88, Elvin McDonald;

p. 92 (top left), Elvin McDonald;

p. 92 (bottom left), Joanne Pavia;

p. 92 (top right), Ted Marston;

p. 92 (bottom right), Jerry Pavia;

p. 97 (top), Ted Marston;

p. 97 (bottom), Ted Marston;

p. 98 (bottom left), Ted Marston;

p. 101 (top left), Jerry Pavia;

p. 101 (top right), Ted Marston;

p. 105 (top right), Ted Marston;

p. 105 (bottom), Elvin McDonald;

p. 109 (bottom), Elvin McDonald;

p. 111 (top left), Elvin McDonald;

p. 111 (bottom), Elvin McDonald;

p. 112 (bottom), Elvin McDonald;

p. 114 (top left), Ted Marston;

p. 114 (bottom), Elvin McDonald;

p. 117 (top), Ted Marston;

p. 121 (top), Elvin McDonald;

p. 122 (bottom right), Elvin McDonald;

p. 124 (top), Ted Marston;

p. 124 (bottom left), Joanne Pavia;